Contents

Foreword 9
Introduction 13

I Connaught Place and the Cinematic Circle 27

1 Regal, Connaught Place 29
2 Rivoli, Connaught Place 34
3 Odeon, Connaught Place 38
4 Plaza, Connaught Place 43
5 Shiela, Paharganj 47
6 Imperial, Paharganj 52
7 Khanna, Paharganj 56

II Celluloid Charms Shahjahanabad 61

8 Delite, Asaf Ali Road 63
9 Golcha, Netaji Subhash Marg 67
10 Jagat, Jama Masjid 71
11 New Amar, Hauz Qazi 76
12 Excelsior, Lal Kuan 80
13 Moti, Chandni Chowk 85
14 Kumar, Chandni Chowk 91

15 Majestic, Fawwara, Chandni Chowk 94
16 Jubilee, Old Delhi Railway Station 98
17 Novelty, Old Delhi Railway Station 103
18 Westend, Sadar Bazar 106
19 Minerva, Mori Gate 110
20 Ritz, Kashmere Gate 114
21 Delite Diamond, Asaf Ali Road 119

III Talking Films Up North 121

22 Palace, Roshanara Road 123
23 Amba, Clock Tower 127
24 Robin Talkies, Old Subzi Mandi 131
25 Alpna, Model Town 135
26 Hans, Azadpur 140
27 Aakash, Azadpur 144
28 Samrat, Britannia Chowk, Shakurpur 147
29 Batra, Mukherjee Nagar 150
30 Deep, Ashok Vihar 150
31 Kala Mandir, Mangolpuri 151
32 Kushal, Jahangirpuri 151

IV Cameras Rolling Westward 153

33 Suraj, Najafgarh 155
34 Ajanta, Najafgarh Road 158
35 Raaj, Tilak Nagar 159
36 Vishal, Rajouri Garden 163
37 Janak, Janakpuri 166
38 Lokesh, Nangloi 166
39 Milan, Karampura 167

Delhi: 4 Shows

Talkies of Yesteryear

Ziya Us Salam

Foreword
Sharmila Tagore

OM
Om Books International

First published in 2015 by

OM

Om Books International

Corporate & Editorial Office
A-12, Sector 64, Noida 201 301
Uttar Pradesh, India
Phone: +91 120 477 4100
Email: editorial@ombooks.com
Website: www.ombooksinternational.com

Sales Office
107, Darya Ganj, New Delhi 110 002, India
Phone: +91 11 4000 9000, 2326 3363, 2326 5303
Fax: +91 11 2327 8091
Email: sales@ombooks.com
Website: www.ombooks.com

ISBN: 978-93-80070-26-1

Printed in India

10 9 8 7 6 5 4 3 2 1

For
The one and only Chhoti Maa
(the world calls her Natasha Raina Kanwar)

40 Natraj, Moti Nagar 168
41 Payal, Naraina 168
42 Rachna, Rajendra Place 169
43 Satyam, Patel Nagar 170
44 Shobha, Sultanpur Road 170
45 Sonia, Vikaspuri 171
46 Vivek, Patel Nagar 172
47 Liberty, New Rohtak Road 175

V Halls in Between 179

48 Naaz, Cycle Market, Jhandewalan 181
49 Filmistan, Rani Jhansi Road 185

VI Cinemascape South 189

50 Chanakya, Chanakyapuri 191
51 Archana, Greater Kailash I 196
52 Sudershan, Gautam Nagar 200
53 Uphaar, Green Park 204
54 Sapna, East of Kailash 208
55 Paras, Nehru Place 212
56 Chanderlok, Chittaranjan Park 215
57 Anupam, Saket 219
58 Seble, Badarpur 222
59 Shalimar, Ashram, Mathura Road 225
60 Race Course-Stadium-Palam, Race Course, National Stadium, Palam 228
61 Alankar, Lajpat Nagar 230
62 Defence, Delhi Cantonment 231
63 Eros, Jangpura 232

64 Grandlay, New Friends Colony 232
65 Kamal, Green Park 233
66 Priya, Vasant Vihar 234
67 Sangam, RK Puram 234
68 Savitri, Greater Kailash II 235
69 Virat, Deoli 236

VII Movie Waves Along the Yamuna 237

70 Swarn Cinema, Vishwas Nagar 239
71 Gagan, Nand Nagri 243
72 Radhu, Shahdara 246
73 Gianand, Shahdara 250
74 Chand, Trilokpuri 254
75 Radhu Palace, Laxmi Nagar 256
76 Kisan, Kalyan, Laxmi, Mandawali, Seelampur and Gandhinagar 257

VIII Ghaziabad, Noida and Faridabad Go Housefull 261

Delhi's Cinema Culture: An Essay 269
Glossary 277

Foreword

India has just celebrated a hundred years of cinema. I have been asked many times to comment on the changes I have seen over the years. True, cinema has changed and so has the audience, and with it the entire movie-going experience. So much so that for today's generation, which has grown up in the time of multiplexes, Ziya Us Salam's *Delhi: 4 Shows—Talkies of Yesteryear* a narrative of the single-screen cinema halls of Delhi might well belong to a mythical Neverland.

For people of my generation and those that followed up till the 1980s, the film-going experience often began with the pleasant anticipation of scanning the newspapers for exciting film ads—'2nd Housefull Week', '50 Glorious Days', 'Showing to Great Rush'—as Ziya fondly recalls. These ads used to be a big attraction for all film lovers, with many of us actually opening the newspapers and going straight to these. Today's youngsters might well marvel at the thought that tickets had to be actually booked days in advance. The 'one-line advisory' that these ads wisely proclaimed—'Book your seat in advance to avoid disappointment!'—filled us with a sense of urgency and everyone made haste to do exactly that.

Delhi: 4 Shows is a revealing account of the evolution of cinema halls in Delhi, from the silent era to the advent of the talkies. That was when mere Motis and Kumars theatres became Moti 'Talkies' and Kumar 'Talkies'. The trend began in the old Delhi areas of Chandni Chowk and Jama Masjid and slowly spread towards Connaught Place. These theatres enjoyed loyal patronage. The Muslim gentry favoured Jagat near Jama Masjid while the Hindus gave their custom to Moti. Ritz and Minerva actually boasted of private boxes for women where large numbers of burqa-clad Muslim women experienced the magic of cinema away from the public gaze.

And what were the marketing strategies the halls employed to bring in the audience? Huge hoardings in English, Urdu and Hindi adorned the street corners. One remembers how MF Husain began his journey in the world of art with these hoardings. Decorative carts and cycle rickshaws with tarpaulin covers, painted over with film posters, were used. In Connaught Place, it was not uncommon to see *ekka*s plying from near Plaza and Odeon. Later, *phut-phut* rickshaws started plying from Odeon to Majestic cinema in Chandni Chowk.

Back in the '50s, horse-drawn carriages and mule-drawn carts would circle Connaught Place, displaying posters of the films then showing at Rivoli or Odeon. At Filmistan, a Ford used to be parked with a couple of posters and banners of the film playing at the hall. Back then, a Ford in Delhi was a rarity, so using a Ford in such an innovative manner caught instant attention and the film garnered easy recall value. In other parts of Delhi, even tempos were used for a similar purpose.

Some cinemas had rickshaw-pullers attached to them for ferrying viewers to and from the theatre. This helped to get more women viewers as most women in those days did not drive and preferred to watch films not too far from their home. You might think this is too primitive by today's high-tech media campaigns, but it worked and the films ran to full houses. Remember, those days literacy rates were not high and many people identified a film by its stars. Incidentally, cinema houses as well as local exhibitors often devised ingenious ways of attracting people to films. I distinctly remember, when AVM's *Do Kaliyan* was being screened at Minerva, there would be cash contests for viewers at the cinema hall where they would be asked questions around the movie. In other cases, merchandise would be handed out to viewers for the right answers.

Most halls had a 35 mm screen, and those that had a 70 mm screen took pride in inviting viewers to its 'cinemascope screen'. Kamal cinema in south Delhi advertised itself as a 'cinema on stilts'. Then we used to have Defence cinemas maintained by the Canteen Store Department where tickets were first given to our defence personnel, reinforcing the belief that cinema provided a rare mode of entertainment for our *jawan*s. Such cinemas in Delhi Cantt and Anand Parbat shut down a little more than 30 years ago. But they served their purpose.

The stories of Shiela, Chanakya, Imperial and other cinemas are equally fascinating—how Chanakya was initially called 'Chanakyarama' and prided itself as a '70 mm cinema with stereophonic sound'; how Shiela narrowly missed the honour of being Asia's first 70 mm cinema thanks to the bureaucratic red-tape of the electricity board; how it was a place frequented by Pandit Jawaharlal Nehru and Indira Gandhi. These theatres were as assuredly a part of Delhi's cultural and historical heritage, as her many architectural monuments. And it is with a sense of resignation that one accepts that many of these landmarks that were once so alive have either ceased to be or are in a state of total disrepair. And yet, they remain a part of the Delhiite's everyday discourse since localities continue to be identified by their proximity to these landmarks. Paras Cinema in Nehru Place has closed down, but the area continues to be called Paras Mode. The same holds true for Chanakya, Uphaar or Savitri cinemas.

Evolution and change are the only certainties of life. As Indians, we remain passionately loyal to our cinema but our movie-going experience has changed irrevocably since the heyday of single-screen cinema halls. That is why it is imperative to record and document the way things were. By taking this loving, nostalgic look at Delhi's cinema halls, that is exactly what this book does—preserves the past. It is an ode as much to these landmark structures as to a way of life; an elegy to a world now lost forever.

Sharmila Tagore

Introduction

As a child, I used to get a rupee as pocket money every Sunday. Of this, 40 paise were lavished on the weekend edition of *Patriot.* Over time, the price for the weekend edition went up to 60 paise before peaking at one rupee. Fortunately by then, my weekly entitlement had been hiked to two rupees!

Films were strictly forbidden at home, with the exception of the Sunday feature film in the heyday of Doordarshan. So I satiated my appetite for films by looking at insertions in *Patriot.* For years on end, I would sit with the pages, skimming over news, and scanning advertisements instead. On festive occasions, *Patriot* used to have three, even five pages devoted to film advertisements. Most of them were two column-wide and 10 cm-long insertions. I would carefully read and memorise the names of films, the cast, the directors and the banners. At the bottom of each advertisement would be the name of the distributor.

Thanks to the now defunct *Patriot,* names like Bobby Art International, Moti Talkies and Distributors, Rajshri Release and so on, became an integral part of my life. All the advertisements seemed to follow a pattern. The list of cinemas invariably first gave the name of the hall in Connaught Place showing the film, followed by an Old Delhi talkies, and thereafter by halls of North, West, South and East Delhi. At the end of the listing, would come the halls on the Delhi-Uttar Pradesh border, concluding with the name of a Ghaziabad cinema showing the film. For instance, the advertisements of *Sholay* (1975) used to mention Plaza first, followed by Jagat, Filmistan, Amba and so on. Or take *Muqaddar ka Sikandar* (1978) that opened, we were told by newspaper insertions, at 'Plaza, Jagat, Filmistan, Amba, Vivek, Vishal, Alankar, Eros, Radhu, Vasant (G'bad)'. The advertisement gave a fair idea of every star's box-office appeal. Hence, Amitabh Bachchan lorded over the visuals, leaving only a little space for co-stars Vinod Khanna, Rekha and Rakhee, and none for villains and character actors like Amjad Khan, Ranjeet and Nirupa Roy. *Hero* (1983), according to advertisement insertions, graced 'Shiela, Jagat, West End, Vivek, Rachna, Uphaar, Alankar, Radhu, Chaudhary (G'Bad)'. Though projecting Jackie Shroff and Meenakshi Seshadri, the film's lead pair through big visuals, the text informed cinegoers that 'Pakistan's noted artist, Reshma' had sung for the film. The reference was to the popular song, 'Lambi Judaai'.

Thanks to them, I came to know that films like *Jugnu* (1973), *Chambal ki Kasam* (1980), *Samadhi* (1972), *Mela* (1971), *Azaad* (both 1955 and 1978), *Khoon Kharaba* (1980), *Gupt Gyan* (1974), *Raftaaar* (1975), *Sky High* (1985), *The Body* (1974) and earlier *Prem Pujari* (1970), *Do Badan* (1966), *Dil Ne Phir Yaad Kiya* (1966) collected decent numbers on the morning show circuit.

Every ad began with the grand announcement '2nd Housefull Week', if the film was in its second week. If the film was in its third week, it had to be '3rd Grand Week'. When the film was in its fourth week, there was a one-liner—'Defying all opposition, marching ahead…' By the 50th day or as it was better known then, the '8th Glorious Week', the film was declared a smash hit! By the 15th week—many films showed that long in those days—advertisers announced in bold letters 'Super Hit'. Hindi and Urdu newspapers, on the other hand, informed their readers about the films showing in halls with simple expressions like *'Doosra shandaar hafta'* (Second Glorious Week) or *'Bhaari rush le raha hai'* (Drawing huge crowds).

Silver jubilees were announced in bigger adverts with elaborate floral patterns, and pictures of bells and earthen lamps, and an accompanying advisory: 'Book your seat in advance to avoid disappointment.' Since plans—the term used in film circles for advance booking—for Hindi films opened on Mondays, it effectively meant that the weekend was sold out before the film's release! For Hollywood films, though, bookings for an upcoming Friday started on a Sunday.

Though I was well into my teens when I watched my first film in a cinema hall, I felt as though I had 'seen' and 'lived' all the movies, thanks to those insertions I habitually pored over in *Patriot* and occasionally in *The National Herald*.

In the early years after Independence, cinema-viewing in Delhi was unassuming, and had the simplicity of street plays: no state-of-the-art technology, no lofty banners, no grand premieres. There were two kinds of viewing arenas: temporary, mobile cinema houses, and theatres. Before showing a film, often a play was staged in many halls, hence the suffix 'theatre' attached to many cinemas. Parsi theatre reigned supreme in those times.

Theatres like Imperial screened silent films too. In the 1920s, like its counterpart in Bombay which used to host orchestra soirées, Imperial in Delhi—similar in architecture and design to the one in Bombay—used to organise dancing as well as orchestra soirées. Only after the screening of *Alam Ara*,

India's first talkie, starring Master Vithal and Zubeidaa, in 1931, did most cinema halls acquire a different identity.

As the silent era gave way to the age of black-and-white films with songs and dialogues, most theatres started screening films regularly, with some even specialising in select Hollywood shows. The newly proliferating halls were called 'talkies', and many halls added the term as a suffix to their names—Moti Talkies, Kumar Talkies, Robin Talkies. Being a 'talkies' was fashionable, a sign of modernisation.

The culture of 'talkies' subsisted for more than half a century after *Alam Ara*. Of course, the front-benchers also referred to them as '*mandva*'.

Cinema halls in Chandni Chowk were the oldest, most dating back to the early 1930s or even the late '20s, followed by the ones in Connaught Place. Between Chandni Chowk and Connaught Place stood two landmark halls of Paharganj—Imperial and Khanna, the former built even before the 'talkies' of Old Delhi. These were permanent theatres with their next release and premiere guaranteed, unlike temporary theatres in other parts of the city. Each permanent hall had dedicated banners that offered it their films. Each hall had its loyal patrons—the Muslim gentry preferred Jagat, which was near Jama Masjid; Hindus took the narrow alleys of Chandni Chowk to Moti. To avoid being easily recognised at Jagat, a few old *nawabi* families too went to Moti. For the burqa-clad Muslim ladies, being seen at a cinema hall in and around Jama Masjid would invite opprobrium. So they chose Ritz and Minerva near Kashmere Gate to satiate their thirst for movies. Ritz, in particular, with its private box, was an ideal place. Women would gather at Purdah Bagh—a women's-only park near Netaji Subhash Marg—then take a cycle-rickshaw or tonga to the theatres at Kashmere Gate.

Getting the audience to the halls was no mean task. Illiteracy among the masses was a prime concern. But more importantly, some cinegoers could read only Urdu, while others could read only Hindi. Exhibitors and distributors had to cover all bases, and hoardings would have the names of films written in three languages—English, Urdu and Hindi. This was true not just of films like *Anarkali* (1953) and *Mughal-e-Azam* (1960) which had very obvious Muslim subjects, but also of movies like *Hanuman* (1960) and *Jai Santoshi Maa* (1975). It was a comment on the times when Urdu was not regarded as the language of any one community.

In the 1970s, major cinema halls started putting up film posters at strategic points in the city, with a little slip at the bottom giving the name of the nearest hall showing it. The slip merely informed people that the film would be shown in 'daily four shows' without specifying the time. It was understood that meant noon, matinee, evening and night. Posters were put up on Thursday nights and scrupulously avoided any place of worship. Faith and fun were not to be mixed. Besides, on Thursday nights, the set-up in the halls changed with each new film to be screened.

A hall like Shiela, which played Hollywood films till the Emergency, used to book major traffic intersections up to a radius of about eight kilometres, its presumed catchment area for target viewers. Others enlisted the help of local distributors. Spectacularly huge hoardings with visages or portraits of the lead cast in garish colours, and, at times, scenes from the movies, were an integral part of the Delhi skyline. Distributors or proprietors of cinema halls supplied billboard painters with material for them to capture the lead cast's likeness. A few hoardings had cut-outs too. Both portraits and cut-outs were in demand till the late '80s.

Though the local newspapers, notably, *Partap*, *Punjab Kesari* and *Veer Arjun*, carried much information about films showing in the city, *Patriot* was miles ahead. In the late 1970s and early '80s, *The National Herald* joined in, and the two newspapers found their readership in the cinephiles of Delhi.

In the 1940s, '50s and even the late '60s, films were promoted in Old Delhi and pockets of west, east and central Delhi by people on moving carts and cycle rickshaws. The practice still continues on a much smaller scale in Azadpur, Najafgarh, and some pockets of east Delhi. Usually, proprietors of cinema halls kept cycle rickshaws ready for the task—a fresh coat of paint would be applied to them, then these would be covered with tarpaulin and on all four sides, a film's posters would be pasted. A man with a loudspeaker would sit inside and, at a traffic intersection or in a lane, he would repeatedly announce the name of the film playing at the hall. Occasionally, the more enterprising ones would reel out the names of the cast and even play snatches of the film's songs. This was to draw in those who could not read the posters.

Some cinema halls went a step further. Besides having a loudspeaker in the rickshaw, they employed at least half a dozen local artistes. One of them walked ahead, beating a drum suspended from his neck. In front of him would be two boys dressed up as girls, doing a little jig every now and then. They would also sing a few lines from the movie's songs.

Towards the end of the 1960s, when north and south Delhi had a considerable number of movie halls, their owners took unusual steps to draw the crowd. For instance, special buses were arranged to and from Alpna to ferry viewers. The hall, located in Model Town, was not easily accessible, so buses were parked at Kashmere Gate and other vantage points to transport viewers to and from the hall. Deep Cinema too employed special buses from Subzi Mandi, while tempos plied for Suraj in Najafgarh.

Most halls would announce the forthcoming films, and design boards and sections of the lounge to publicise them. During the interval, a trailer from a forthcoming film would be played. In addition, every hall played the national anthem at the end of the film, unlike Bombay, where it was played at the beginning.

Till the mid-'70s, cinegoers were mainly men. However, devotionals or family dramas saw women queue up in large numbers as well at the ticket counter. The booking clerk was a much sought-after man; even when he was off duty, people would strike up a conversation with him to ensure they were in his good books. But once the counter opened, there would be mayhem, requiring the intervention of security personnel. Often, cops had to resort to a mild *lathi*-charge to restore order. Part of the chaos would be caused by black-marketeers who booked a bunch of tickets in advance and sold them many times over the market price minutes before the show. Many were in league with the local *paanwala,* the hugely popular *chaiwala* and the ushers and guards, who would happily keep tickets with them. That way, a black-marketeer would be let off after a reprimand as the cops couldn't recover any extra tickets from him. Of course, the cops themselves were not always above board.

Speaking of the good old *paanwala,* he did brisk business in the days of yore. Many balcony patrons were habitual consumers of betel nuts, and the *paanwala* provided them several other alternatives. Aware of such habits, the cinema management placed spittoons on the staircase and in the lounge. This did not necessarily mean that the walls were free of stains.

The men who queued up for tickets were chivalrous. The moment a lady arrived at a ticket counter, they would tell the clerk, *'Pehle ladies ko de do'* (First, give the ticket to the ladies). The word 'ladies' was always used in plural, even if it referred to a single lady. The management too was mindful of their concern for security and privacy. Many halls had a specially designated box attached to the balcony where ladies could watch films without the fear of any intrusive male gaze. The boxes were used by families too. Some cinemas like Liberty, which did not have a box, seated women in groups in the balcony and the stalls, out of concern for their security. In later years, a thousand love stories must have bloomed in the boxes of Ritz, Jagat, Regal, and the dress circle of Shiela. And of course, there were stray instances of indiscreet couples being bundled out of the hall too.

Back then, nearly every hall had a different audience profile for each show, and a different crowd for each section of the hall. Working-class men preferred night shows while families would stream in to catch the evening show. Matinee shows were frequented more by women while noon shows often had sex workers, nautch girls and undergraduate students. Poorer audiences went for the more affordable stalls, while the middle or upper middle class opted for the expensive balcony and box. This was not the case in the morning shows when balconies were seldom full, and most viewers opted for the stalls.

Parallel cinema offerings, few and far between, had more discerning viewers while dubbed versions of South Indian and Hollywood films were preferred by men looking for 'scenes'. In fact, a hall or two had their permits cancelled for inserting objectionable scenes in routine movies!

From the 1930s to the year 2000 and beyond, tickets were slips made of recycled paper. Usually garish pink, but occasionally light green or blue, they were of such poor quality that if you kept a ticket in your shirt pocket on a hot summer afternoon, chances were you would end up with a stain.

Separate boxes, cooled and air-conditioned comfort, and big screens were a part of the permanent cinema halls in Delhi. While Old Delhi and Connaught Place had a well-established cinema culture in the '50s, cinema became an entertainment in south and west Delhi in the '70s, with most of its leading halls coming up then. Eros was, for a long time, the premier hall in south Delhi.

And until 1971, there was no hall in Rajouri Garden. The closest was Amba in Shakti Nagar, some 15 kilometres away. That year, Vishal came up in Rajouri Garden, filling a vacuum.

Temporary halls came up on barren stretches of land for a period of two to six months at a time. Makeshift tin-and-tarpaulin structures with foldable chairs, they would show films thrice a day. A white sheet with 'maskings' acted as the screen. Mobile toilets used to accompany every such 'hall'. Areas like Model Town, Zakhira, Subhash Nagar, Shakarpur, Rajouri Garden and even RK Puram used to have naturally air-cooled temporary cinemas. They showed leading films of the time such as *Aan* (1952), *Nagin* (1954), *Naya Daur* (1957), *Har Har Mahadev* (1950). Later, some temporary permit holders were granted permanent licences, and over time, most areas of Delhi had at least one hall in the vicinity—Suraj in Najafgarh, Lokesh in Nangloi, Samrat in Shakurpur, Raj in Tilak Nagar, Seble in Badarpur and Gagan in Nand Nagari. People beyond the geographical proximity seldom frequented these areas, yet permanent halls here enjoyed a fine run. Each had a spin-off effect: the neighbourhood bioscope-man who showed snatches of songs, the local music bands that hung around the hall for possible business before or after the show and signboard artists who sought work from hall managers. A hall was a hub of social interaction.

Film-viewing was not just an escape from the humdrum of everyday life, it was a passion and an art in itself. Little wonder then that cinemas were named with style and care, the idea being to cultivate a bond with viewers that went beyond a show.

Nearly all cinemas had their unique ways of wooing cinegoers. While Alpna was named following newspaper advertisements asking readers to suggest a possible name for a new cinema, most others had lofty, pretentious names. Coming up soon after Independence, before the nation could wean itself away from its colonial past, or from the reign of the local '*rajas*' in certain pockets, cinema halls had names that directly or indirectly alluded to royalty. Hence, there was Regal in Connaught Place, Imperial in Paharganj, Majestic in Chandni Chowk and Palace on Old Roshanara Road. Later, there was Samrat in Shakur Basti. Similarly, in Bombay, halls had impressive and aristocratic names like Royal, Edward and, well, Regal. Bombay's Regal came up soon after the one in Delhi.

Only one hall's name reflected that India was an independent nation—Liberty, established in the mid-'50s. Some halls were also named after parts of the universe—Lokesh (firmament) in Nangloi, Suraj (sun) in Najafgarh, Jagat (the world) near Jama Masjid, Gagan (sky) in Nand Nagri, Chand (moon) in Trilokpuri, Chanderlok (realm of the moon; heaven) in Chittaranjan Park and Aakash (sky) in Adarsh Nagar.

Other halls had equally impressive but clearly British or European names—Plaza, Ritz, Odeon, Rivoli and Delite. Only a handful had names spelling out their direct relationship with films—Jubilee in Chandni Chowk, Filmistan on Rani Jhansi Road and Sapna in East of Kailash, alluding to the dream world of movies.

Watching films might not be the same today. Multiplexes lack the familiarity and warmth of single-screen halls. Till the mid-'80s, Delhi was different from other metropolises. Bombay had style and fanfare; Calcutta was either too cerebral or too low key but Delhi celebrated cinema. Some movies came to Delhi much after their release in Bombay; others came to Delhi before being released in Calcutta. Halls in Delhi like Minerva and Liberty did not share the distinguished history of their counterparts elsewhere, yet they were all special. Some brought the joy of watching films in 'Bharat' to India's capital; others had you believe that you were in Los Angeles, with Hollywood stars attending premieres in movie halls in Connaught Place!

In present times, many single-screen halls like Imperial, Hans and Moti in Delhi are just about eking out a living, like Royal, Alfred, Nishat, their counterparts in Bombay that have had to battle all odds for their survival. Yet, they play a role in giving Hindi cinema an eclectic audience. Today, when we hardly find a hall in Delhi that has tickets priced in single digits, Gulshan in Bombay continues to fulfil the needs of an audience who cannot afford to pay much. Ticket prices for a film at these halls are less than the price of a cup of tea at a multiplex. In that model lies their sustenance. In history lies their relevance. From *Raja Harishchandra* (1913) to *Bombay Talkies* (2013), they have seen, and shown, them all.

Delhi: 4 Shows, a culmination of my passion for cinema, would not have been possible without the Sunday editions of *Patriot.*

SK Pankaj often accompanied me as I tried to find my way through the bylanes of Chandni Chowk, and Delhi's famed film distribution circles where history is buried under layers of dust.

Veteran RS Seble was happy to share his priceless photographs and anecdotes over many, many meetings.

Shyam Sahni, Uday Kaushish and Rajan Gupta never lacked in warmth or time; meeting them brought back the old days once more.

Sri Ram Talwar, who saw Alpna, Batra and Vishal scale new heights, was generous enough to provide access to sepia-tinted photographs from his personal collection.

The venerable GK Sharma was full of laughs and stories over morning cups of tea and *'biscut'* at Amba.

Of course, Sanjay Mehta allowed me to string together stories that he had recounted over several years of our association.

Atul Mital trudged along on chilly mornings, hot afternoons and late evenings to capture halls in their present state. He clicked photographs with the passion of a schoolboy, helping to give a more rounded perspective of our cinemas. Aslam Khan helped me restore some images which seemed irretrievable and kept me in good spirits during the long hours of waiting to see the finished product. Aftab Alam helped too with his polite nudges, and regularly keeping in touch with the developments.

My wonderful colleagues Vijay Lokapally and Anuj Kumar, my co-authors in *Housefull: The Golden Age of Hindi Cinema,* a book that I edited, shared their insights as they read *Delhi: 4 Shows*. The book is as much theirs as it is mine.

Anjana Rajan and Sangeeta Barooah Pisharoty provided useful inputs at various stages of the book. As did S Ravi.

Ajay Mago lent his enthusiasm and support.

Dipa Chaudhuri ensured that *Delhi: 4 Shows* could finally be a reader's delight.

My lovely wife, Uzma, was my anchor when I hit the writer's block, and with a quiet nod, she assured me she was there. As did my lovely daughters, Maryam and Aliza, and my sisters, Muslima and Sajida.

Thanks to them all, *Delhi: 4 Shows* is here!

Ziya Us Salam

I

Connaught Place and the Cinematic Circle

1 REGAL, Connaught Place

'In the 1950s, whenever Raj Kapoor and Nargis visited the theatre, they sat here,' says Amar Singh Verma, pointing to the settee in front of his table. Verma, an eminently likeable 73-year-old manager of Regal, has been at the cinema for more than 35 years. He has seen the ownership of the hall transfer from the family of Wazir Dayal to the Mahajans from Jammu. The property where Regal was built initially belonged to Sir Sobha Singh and was transferred to the Dayals in 1938 when Wazir Dayal, after whom the Wazirabad bridge in north Delhi is named, was a chief executive engineer with CPWD. In pre-Independence India, Regal was easily the most illustrious hall in central Delhi. For the first three decades since then, it was like a conductor of an orchestra of halls in Connaught Place.

Like its counterparts in the Walled City, it too began as a theatre in 1932. To this day, it has a stage where Prithviraj Kapoor's plays like *Pathan* were once presented. The age-old green room is still there, bringing back a taste of the days when the cognoscenti preferred to watch plays over movies. In the early years as a theatre, it staged The London Review Company and The Russian Ballet Troupe shows for British diplomats and Indian royals. It even had a bar inside. Despite being designed by English architect Walter Sykes George, the hall had many Mughal influences. There were frescoes, floral motifs, and the front portion employed the half-dome technique. Unlike other cinemas, Regal never stood alone; it was located in a building which had high-end shops and popular restaurants.

The who's who of politics, including Pandit Jawaharlal Nehru, Dr Rajendra Prasad and Lord Mountbatten, were among the visitors. In fact, Nehru often referred to it as 'New Delhi's premier theatre'. The men and women who mattered in films and theatre chose it above all else. Much before it became Raj Kapoor's preferred hall in Connaught Place, Regal was favoured by Prithviraj Kapoor. Then Dilip Kumar, Sanjeev Kumar, Shashi Kapoor, Hema Malini joined the list. The patronage was well deserved: it was, after all, the cinema that hosted the India premiere of *Gone With the Wind* (1939). Once, Nehru himself brought a film, *Chalo Dilli* (1956), to Regal while on his way back from Rangoon. It was about Netaji Subhash Chandra Bose's fight for Independence and was screened at Regal for Congress party members. The film created a bit of a controversy since it was an uncensored version but the timely intervention of Nehru solved that problem. When the 20th Century Fox film, *The Robe* (1953), was screened here, Regal notched up another milestone by installing cinemascope. Nehru was present for the first show.

Regal, for a long time, had no competition. In an era when even Odeon did not have a balcony for the more discerning of audiences, Regal provided separate boxes, six in all. Called family boxes, they could seat upto 40 guests. Back then, they were preferred by joint families but are now called 'couple's boxes', favoured by lovebirds in search of privacy.

Old-timers still recall how, despite changing over the decades, Regal has essentially remained the same. In the 1950s, Davicos stood adjacent to Regal. Then came Standard

Restaurant. The queues in front of the advance-booking counter used to go right up to the eateries near the cinema. It was said that *'Jo bhi* film *kahin nahin chalti thi, woh yahan chalti thi'* (A film which did not run elsewhere did well here).

That was true. Raj Kapoor's *Satyam Shivam Sundaram* (1978) failed to find a cinema in the Walled City—even Moti was 'bold' enough to show the film only after 35 years of its release, that too for four shows only—but it completed a silver jubilee at Regal, a feat in which relatively nondescript halls like Apsara and Chaudhary in Ghaziabad joined it, in the 25th week. The film, often criticised for its bold scenes, was shown here after a *havan* at the hall. Shashi Kapoor and Zeenat Aman, the film's lead pair, arrived amid showers of marigold.

Satyam Shivam Sundaram was not the only film to do a jubilee run in the '70s. Before it, was *Bobby* in 1973, which was such a hit that students would skip school to watch the film. Dating couples would have a wonderful time at the hall, take in the movie in the privacy of their box, go down to Standard or Wengers for a bite and walk down the Circus. A little after that there was the ever-so-gentle, soothing *Rajnigandha* (1974). *Mili* (1975), Jaya Bhaduri's cute little film, ran for weeks on end. At around the same time, Shyam Benegal's *Nishant* (1975) and *Ankur* (1977) found a consistent audience here, with the former celebrating a 50-day run.

The 1970s was a phenomenal decade for Regal, and its movies did excellent business. Most films shown here were gentle, with barely a flash of violence. If *Rajnigandha* was a middle-of-the-road film for young urban Indians, *Mili* appealed to their sensitive side. Young couples with individual ambitions could identify with *Abhimaan* (1973), Amitabh Bachchan and Jaya Bhaduri's much talked about super-hit that drew such a rush at Regal that the film's original run of four weeks had to be extended. It had space for Asit Sen's *Safar* (1970), as also Academy award winner *Cactus Flower* (1969) in the same week.

The success of the '70s spilled over into the '80s when films like *Pratighaat* (1987) and *Pataal Bhairavi* (1985) notched up the numbers, the latter's four daily shows were almost always booked completely in advance. For both, it was very difficult to buy a ticket as the booking counters opened for a short while and queues were far from orderly. It was marginally easier to get a ticket for *Woh Saat Din* (1983), the Anil Kapoor-Naseeruddin Shah film for which both actors came to Regal. The film completed a 100-day run after which the staff got a bonus, the equivalent of a 15-day salary, from the distributors. Later, K Viswanath's *Sur Sangam* (1985) had a limited run in daily four shows but picked up in the morning slot soon after. The film, with its ragas and dances, did well enough to remind the knowledgeable of its original Telugu version, *Shankarabharnam* (1979). Then in the '90s came films like *Saajan* (1991), *Dil Aashna Hai* (1992) and *Maachis (1996)*, all good enough to keep the hall buzzing. But these impressive tales paled in comparison to the intoxicating joys of the '50s, and much of the '60s, for the 658-seater hall. At that time, watching a film, irrespective of how it eventually panned out, was an experience in itself. Some pulled up in tongas, others in chauffeur-driven cars which stopped right at the portico. Palm trees lined the entrance and from there, VIPs were escorted inside by the staff. With many taking their eatables inside, watching a film here was a real pleasure.

With films like V Shantaram's *Do Aankhen Barah Haath* (1958) and *Dahej* (1950), Guru Dutt's *Pyaasa* (1957) and *Kaagaz Ke Phool* (1959), Mehboob Khan's *Andaaz* (1949) and *Mother India* (1957), and Sohrab Modi's *Sheesh Mahal* (1958) playing here, no competitor could hold its own in front of Regal. It was well and truly regal. That was until it slipped badly with films like Aziz Sejawal's *Chhupa Rustam* (2001), Onir's *Bas...Ek Pal* (2006), Ramgopal Varma's *Aag* (2007) (the film was initially called *Sholay* before being renamed *Ramgopal Varma ki Aag*). Even Goutam Ghose's controversial *Yatra* (2006) failed to restore Regal's lost sheen.

2 RIVOLI, Connaught Place

It did the simple little things well. It accomplished great deeds. Good old Rivoli could have been your neighbourhood theatre, identifiable, personable. It went much beyond that, turning into a cinema that for decades knew no lean days. It attracted fans from far and near. Big budget blockbusters, art-house offerings, the best of Hollywood, Rivoli treated them all alike—with a lot of care, love and good humour.

Films were a relationship here; as new ones were built, the old ones were not jettisoned. Many films came back to have a longer run in the second stint after a limited first run. As a theatre of choice for English cinema since 1941, it had few peers during much of the 1950s and '60s. Along with Odeon, it presented an unbeatable combination for distributors—a film given away for a stipulated period to the Sahnis, the brains behind the two cinemas, alternated between the two halls, now soaking up the rush at Odeon, now taking in the niche crowd at Rivoli. Incidentally, the property belonged to Sir Sobha Singh, and the Sahnis took the cinema on lease before buying it in the early '50s.

Rivoli did not change for more than 50 years. Air-cooled and comfortable rather than plush, with about 440 seats and simple utilitarian architecture, with an interplay of black and white, it was far from being a big hall. It made the most of its limited resources. During its heyday, it provided healthy competition to the best in the business and, at times, the management out-thought and out-manoeuvred rival cinemas. Alfred Hitchcock's *Psycho* (1960) opened here and not at any of the halls with better facilities. Hitchcock came to the hall himself, and as a consequence, the film ran for several weeks to housefull shows. Rivoli had acquired a rare share of stardust.

Despite such occurrences, Rivoli often had to appeal for attention, and gain dignity with its shows. That it managed to do so without much ado meant that it found a way to operate within its limitations. Pleasing connoisseurs, catering to critics and appealing to the general public, the queues at the turnstiles were long and the tickets limited. Black-marketeers often made a killing at Rivoli that was forced to function on the 'first-come, first-served' principle due to the sheer demand.

As far as Hollywood was concerned, Rivoli proved extremely proactive. *Dial M for Murder* (1954), *Story of a Woman* (1970), *An Affair to Remember* (1957) and more, found a screening here. Many of them did so more than once. But with Hindi films, it was always reactive. When it played Dev Anand's *Love Marriage* as a one-off in 1959, it opened a little window of hope to other distributors. Then it played Shakti Samanta's *Aradhana* (1969) on Rajesh Khanna's request, and that changed the way Rivoli showed films for good. *Aradhana* did a 100-day run in 1969, opening the floodgates for other Hindi film biggies. The charisma of Rajesh Khanna, the dimpled charm of Sharmila Tagore and the film's heady music meant not a show was less than housefull for the first month. The viewers were happy because it meant watching a top-banner film in a centrally located hall, with easy accessibility on *phut-phut* rickshaws from Palika Bazar, buses from Shivaji

Stadium and the shared tongas that plied from Chandni Chowk to Connaught Place. With Indian Coffee House next door and Delhi Coffee Home close by, taking in movies at Rivoli was a pleasure.

Soon after *Aradhana*'s screening, Rivoli started playing Hindi movies for three shows a day, reserving only one show or sometimes two, for Hollywood. It was among a handful of halls to play the highly controversial *Aandhi*, the Sanjeev Kumar-Suchitra Sen starrer, for a long stretch of time and promoted the film as 'the story of a great woman political leader in post-Independence India' in April 1975.

Julie (1975) completed a silver jubilee at Rivoli in the mid-'70s. *Safed Haathi* (1977) too notched up the numbers, as did *Haathi Mere Saathi* (1971). This was all mainstream fare, lapped up by an easy-to-please audience. For the discerning, Rivoli made a special slot to play films like *Yeh Nazdeekiyan* (1982), *Kamla* (1984) and *Mandi* (1983). In doing so, it took a cue from the neighbouring Regal which did a good job of showing parallel cinema.

The 1980s, probably the most creatively challenged of decades, threw up many action flicks, and Rivoli played countless potboilers starring Jeetendra, Dharmendra, Jaya Prada, Sridevi and Vijayshanti. However, for every *Insaaf Kaun Karega* (1987), *Tejasvini* (1994) or *Thanedaar* (1990), it played a *Sapnon ka Mandir* (1991) or a *Shaheed-e-Azam* (2002) too. They all worked at the box office. The success of *Shaheed-e-Azam*, starring Sonu Sood, was particularly laudable as the film, which related the story of revolutionary freedom fighter Bhagat Singh, was pitted opposite two more big banner-big star films on Bhagat Singh: Bobby Deol's *Shaheed* (2002), directed by Guddu Dhanoa and Ajay Devgn's *The Legend of Bhagat Singh* (2002), directed by Raj Kumar Santoshi.

It was good as long as it lasted. Over the years, the competition grew considerably. Plenty of halls had central air-conditioning and almost as many offered a 70 mm screen. Rivoli, despite an occasional *Men in Black-II* (2002), was found sluggish, and investment in the hall was all but absent. It slowly stepped down from the A-grade stakes and began screening skin flicks instead. While Jagmohun Mundra's films and others like *Bedroom Eyes* (1984), *Her Nights* (2002), *Garam* (2005) and *Taak Jhaank* (2006) collected the moolah, Rivoli paid with the loss of its image. As the past moved further away, even the Sahnis stepped back. In February 2006, Rivoli made a comeback in a new avatar as PVR Rivoli under the PVR Heritage Cinema category. It is a decision that does not sit easy with the Sahnis.

3 ODEON, Connaught Place

After running 20-odd cinemas in Rawalpindi, Peshawar and Murree, the Sahnis headed to relatively unexplored Delhi. In the late '30s, Isherdas Sahni, the patriarch of the Sahni clan, took Odeon, now a grand old cinema, on lease. Lacking neither in self-belief nor in enterprise, his endeavour did not go unrewarded. Predictably, Odeon paved the way for many other cinemas in the city and beyond. In isolation, Odeon, which the Sahnis bought in the early '50s, could have cut a forlorn figure. Despite being in Connaught Place, the neighbouring area had few residents and only elementary means of public transport. Yet, it looked splendid, eventually attracting cinegoers from beyond the immediate circle. Over a period of time, Odeon did enough to not just stay in business but also to mount a serious challenge to the hegemony of Regal and the aspirations of Plaza. In the years just before Independence and those following immediately after, Odeon was on the cusp of great things and gradually came to be taken seriously in film circles. Big banners, seasoned directors and ace heroes, all wanted to have a piece of its pie.

Hindi film merchants were not alone in aspiring for a slot at Odeon. Hollywood biggies and popular distributors like United Artistes, Paramount, 20th Century Fox and Warner were interested in getting a long billing at the hall in the 1950s and much of the '60s. James Bond films packed in the crowd while *The Sound of Music* (1965) was heard and seen by many. Odeon's Victorian architecture, uniquely oval-shaped auditorium and welcoming atmosphere helped it to carve out a niche. Some English films ran for a weekend, others for four days, beginning Monday. A few bucked the trend and stayed long enough to have a repeat audience.

Odeon was destined to get even better. In late 1961, the cinema closed down for about nine months. During this period, Kothari and Associates gave the hall a new look, and a balcony with about 340 seats was added. It reopened with *Come September* (initially released in 1961) on a windswept afternoon in 1962. Among the who's who in the audience was President Sarvepalli Radhakrishnan. RL Sahni received him personally.

Besides a balcony, an air-conditioning system had also been added, making it one of the first cinemas to be fully air-conditioned. Odeon had now become unbeatable; in the past, it had let many a golden offering slip through its fingers but now it was an unquestioned winner. Raj Kapoor's *Sangam* came its way in 1964 because the Sahnis played for broke, leaving both Regal and Plaza, its immediate competitors, licking their wounds. In came Raj Kapoor and the rest, and Odeon was abuzz all over again. Soon, a 70 mm screen was added. With a blend of substance and style, the cinema had chutzpah like few else. Its billboards attracted attention and youngsters were swayed by them.

This popularity, though heady, was no fluke. It was built brick by brick over more than two decades. Even in its compact frame, the hall had played films like *Kohinoor* (1960), *Jhanak Jhanak Payal Baje* (1955), *Navrang* (1959) and *Naya Daur* (1957) to huge audiences. In the early '60s, the popularity of *Dosti*, the President's medal-winner, had no parallel. The same was true of Manoj Kumar's *Shaheed* (1965), that was booked for two weeks and stayed on for four more. Each of these films was a marvel of its time.

Odeon's unique identity was further forged with the patronage of Dev Anand—our own Gregory Peck. He was to Odeon what Dilip Kumar was to Excelsior or Raj Kapoor to Moti. *Hum Dono* (1961), *Jewel Thief* (1967), *Guide* (1965), all enjoyed repeat audiences, just like *Paying Guest* (1957) and *Munimji* (1955). Later, Chetan Anand's *Haqeeqat* (1964) evoked feelings of patriotism, more so because the film's screening was preceded by an airing of the national anthem.

So stirring was the response to these films that it seemed Odeon had achieved all it had set out to less than 30 years ago. It had a contemporary like Rivoli, healthy competitors in Plaza and Regal, toughies in the Old Delhi talkies and new challengers emerging in south Delhi. It continued to stay ahead in the game, though. For instance, Kamal Amrohi's *Pakeezah* (1972) opened here despite strong claims by others in the vicinity. Though it was a slow beginner, word-of-mouth publicity helped the film pick up strongly. With young Shyam Sahni learning quickly, Odeon was in fine hands, its sense of occasion and timing never letting it down. Hollywood receded and Hindi cinema occupied centre stage.

Black-marketeers also flocked here in droves; advance bookings which opened on Monday morning were all done by late afternoon. Yet, many preferred to lay their hands on a ticket in the black market than go to another hall or wait another week. Manmohan Desai's *Coolie* (1983) and KC Bokadia's *Pyar Jhukta Nahin* (1985), a surprise hit starring Mithun Chakraborty with Padmini Kolhapure and Danny Denzongpa, sold many tickets in black. Its songs, which often played on *Chitrahaar* on Doordarshan, helped the film pick up. Then came Sunil Dutt's Rekha-starrer *Yeh Aag Kab Bujhegi* (1991) and Raj Kumar Santoshi's Meenakshi Seshadri-starrer *Damini* (1993). Such was the craze for *Damini* that many who failed to find a ticket for the current show bought one for the next show, preferring to window shop in Connaught Place for a couple of hours and come back to watch the next show rather than go back home without watching the film. Even greater enthusiasm greeted Abbas-Mustan's *Chori Chori Chupke Chupke* (2001) that starred Salman Khan with Preity Zinta and Rani Mukerji. The film played to heavy police deployment. These films were a continuation of Odeon's efforts to attract the young, that begun with the screening of *Chashme Buddoor* (1981), a relatively low-key film starring Farooque Sheikh and Deepti Naval. The film worked wonders. The hall finally discarded its family destination image, cast in stone with films like *Saas Bhi Kabhi Bahu Thi* that opened here in 1971, and *Jeevan Sangram* (1974), whose tax-free status meant more people came to watch it.

Not only was Odeon brilliant with its choice of films, it could be combative too. Initially denied *Satyam Shivam Sundaram* (1978) and *Bobby* (1973)—both films went on to do record business at Regal—it decided instead to have a festival of RK films following the death of the maestro in 1988, making sure to include both those films in the line-up.

The path to Odeon's success was paved by its strategic location: of all the halls of Connaught Place, it was the most accessible, with first tongas, then *phut phut* rickshaws parked right near the cinema. Of course, there was a downside too—the bylane next to the cinema was often preferred by sex workers to woo their possible clients.

The hall took another leap into the future when Big Cinemas entered the fray in the early years of the new millennium, and it turned Big Cinemas Odeon. Quite an appropriate prefix for Odeon that was always big in heart, bigger on deeds.

4 PLAZA, Connaught Place

A little under a decade ago when Plaza downed its shutters, most assumed its epitaph had been written by the age of multiplexes. But it resurfaced a few months later, still as a single-screen theatre, with many skeptics raising their eyebrows. Established in 1933 and one of the oldest halls, it had been designed by British architect Robert Tor Russell, with a balcony on the first floor and columns on the ground floor. When it reopened in May 2004, the seats had come down to merely 300 but in this reinvention, Plaza offered new options to cinegoers, with a changed ambience and a different kind of audience.

Plaza has always more than just survived, as it did in 1952 and in the present times. Back then, business was only beginning to pick up. Shiela, Chanakya, Archana, Priya, all standard addresses for Hollywood movies, were nowhere on the horizon and Plaza played many blockbusters from Hollywood, its closest rivals being no more than a few feet away—Odeon, Rivoli and Regal. Together, the quartet brought to Delhi the experience of English summers years before the multiplexes enjoyed the adulation of fans with Spiderman series and James Bond movies. The four single screens in the prime part of Delhi rarely got a note wrong and this remained true for close to half a century. The value of Plaza went far beyond the few rupees they charged for the tickets; it was a question of pride to watch a film here or even be seen watching a film here. The management had deep pockets back then but it used this money to make the hall elegant, not ostentatious. Most enthusiastic cinegoers ensured they kept their dates with Plaza, arriving first by *ekka*s, then cycle-rickshaws and then cars. Plaza's juggernaut rolled on.

Back in the early '50s, when Delhiites were just settling down, Plaza played Cecil de Mille's *The Greatest Show on Earth* (1952); a movie with as lofty a name could scarcely have found a more befitting hall. The film was not widely publicised but word spread and it became one of the highest earners of the year.

The hall was renovated twice—first in the mid-'50s, then in the late '60s when a 70 mm screen arrived. In 1960, Plaza also added a jukebox and served cold coffee to its guests—among the first in the city to do so. For fans, this meant a better viewing experience; for the hall, it meant staying ahead of competition. The improved facilities brought along with it a little slice of history too as Plaza became the first to show Warner Bros films over seven days in 1964. Some still recall American actress Shirley MacLaine especially flying down to attend one of the shows.

Sholay, hailed as 'the greatest spectacle on earth' also opened here and Plaza was the only cinema to have a 70 mm print on the film's release in 1975. Amba had a 35 mm print, as did Novelty, which played the film about a month later. With each passing day, the craze for *Sholay* hit a new high. If other cinemas called it 'super', 'superb', 'supreme', Plaza resorted to no half-measures, simply labelling it 'smash hit of the decade'. As the film's craze showed no sign of subsiding, Plaza informed its patrons through newspaper insertions, 'Flames kiss the sky, sentiments reach the depth of the oceans...watch *Sholay* at a once-in-a-lifetime cinema'. Hyperbole for some, but that was the way Plaza was. The same hall played the gentle *Khushboo* (1975) just before *Sholay* and soon after it showed *Gharonda* (1977), showcasing the wide variety of its screenings. Topping it all were regional films, usually shown on Sunday morning.

Between *The Greatest Show on Earth* and *Sholay* in 1975, it showed *Battle for Berlin* (1973), *Crown of the Russian Empire* (1971) and *Fantomes* (1964). It also hosted a festival of Iranian films, and one for Japanese films. Then, at the height of Indo-Soviet friendship, Plaza had a succession of Russian films as part of the Soviet Film Festival.

In the mid-'70s, Plaza started concentrating more on Hindi films than foreign ones, partly because of the increased preference of movie watchers for Chanakya and Shiela and mainly due to the greater demand for Hindi films after the heady success of *Jai Santoshi Maa* (1975) and *Sholay* (1975). In came *Alibaba aur Chalis Chor* (1980), followed by *Sohni-Mahiwal* (1984). Soon after, *Mera Saathi* (1985) found many takers, as did *Jaal* (1986), touted then as Rekha's comeback film. The hall also played *Doosri Dulhan* (1983), Victor Banerji's early brush with Hindi cinema, and Kalpana Lajmi's *Ek Pal* (1986). Its special skills in choosing films was evident when it chose Anil Sharma's *Gadar* (2001) over Ashutosh Gowariker's *Lagaan* (2001)—the latter got all the encomiums while the former made history at the box office.

In the first decade of the new millennium, Plaza realised that mere survival wouldn't necessarily bring dignity. The multiplex boom had started impacting single-screen theatres. In the fast changing world, Plaza realised that the past, however, illustrious, brings only brownie points not redeemable at the box office. So, the hall went to the PVR chain and Joginder Sawhney—whose family had taken over from original owner Sohrab Modi—took a back seat. Today, Plaza, almost a mini theatre now, can look forward to the future with renewed hope and confidence, durability now entrenched as part of its character.

5 SHIELA, Paharganj

It was a delight to watch films at Shiela, more so in an age when calamities were neither rare nor brief, and challenges often existential. Life offered lesser sops. The immensely likeable Shiela was like a long-lost friend—you could walk in any day, any time, and you would be received warmly. No explanations sought on the long absences. Today, Shiela deserves the same love, care and affection that it has showered on its patrons for over 50 years.

On 12th January, 1961, when the air-cooled cinema threw open its premises to the public, it narrowly missed being Asia's first 70 mm screen. The honour went to Japan. That Shiela could not be the first cinema in Asia with a 70 mm screen, was not due to the ignorance of DC Kaushish, the proprietor and a former member of the Constituent Assembly, but because of lapses by the electricity department that dilly-dallied in granting the requisite permission. Shiela lost out the honour by two weeks but acquired the distinction of being the first 70 mm screen in India.

Shiela had neither the history of the Walled City talkies, nor the baggage of Partition. It was the product of an emerging nation that was beginning to express itself. With its signature big-screen logo, 70 mm screen and Luc Durand artwork on the façade and foyer, it was the cinematic equivalent of an art gallery. The 65-ft mural completed over three days especially for the hall, was crafted with bright and vibrant colours, imparting a joyful air to the surroundings.

All along, the cinema was frequented by the English movie-going crowd. Gradually, cinema halls in Connaught Place, which had been screening Hollywood films for several years, made way for Shiela, less out of deference and more in graceful acceptance of its superiority.

Shiela opened with *Solomon and Sheba* (1959). The Hollywood film heralded a new order that would remain unchallenged for over a decade. Often, Hollywood films would be screened at Shiela much before anywhere else in the country.

For almost the entire first year, Shiela operated on electricity supplied by a generator. With the war in 1962, like other cinema halls, it handed over its generator for a larger cause (these were taken to the North-East Frontier Agency) at the behest of the Indian government. Shiela closed down momentarily but the shows resumed within a few days. The electricity connection was sanctioned. For some time, there were instances of power breakdown. Then it was smooth sailing for the new hall.

Lovers of quality cinema were happy to return when it reopened. Among them were Morarji Desai, then Information and Broadcasting Minister in Jawaharlal Nehru's Cabinet, and Indira Gandhi with her little sons, Sanjay and Rajiv. Nehru himself took in a movie or two, and DC Kaushish's son, Uday, recalls sitting on Nehru's lap in the balcony to watch *Can-Can* (1960).

Can-Can had not been cleared by the Censor Board, so a special show had to be organised for Mrs Gandhi. After watching it, she gave it the nod, and *Can-Can* got the requisite Censor Board clearance.

Every day, for three shows, Shiela put out the best of Hollywood fare. It gave patrons a wide choice: one film ran for three days—Friday to Sunday—while the other got four days—Monday through Thursday. Not only was the audience spoiled for choice but had little time to decide what to watch and what to skip.

Back then, art-house offering *Bhuvan Shome* (1969) got the noon slot and BR Chopra's *Aadmi aur Insaan* (1969), struggling to find a theatre, was also given a screening here. The latter initially came for a week but stayed on for a month, a longer run prevented only by the hall's commitment to the next 20th Century Fox offering.

Shiela was pursuing a calling beyond the comprehension of other cinemas. Not just the layman, even the then President of India, VV Giri got it a bit mixed up when in his note for the cinema's souvenir commemorating its launch, he hailed the Kaushish family for providing a cinema in a working-class district. Be that as it may, Shiela regularly rolled out the red carpet for VVIPS, though it did pamper other classes with silks, velvets and piped music.

Till the 1970s, when Chanakya, Archana and Priya made their presence felt, Shiela was the cinema that spoke the language of the haves rather than of the have-nots, cheerfully engaging comrades and the right wing, with enough space for centrist forces too. The cinema was also a meeting ground for politicians of different leanings.

The mid-'70s marked a watershed for Shiela as its operations were hit hard by the Emergency. To an establishment looking for scapegoats, the hall was an irritant as the owners refused to buckle down to the demands for 'charity' of local bigwigs, arguing that these demands were akin to extortion. Under unsavoury circumstances, Shiela closed down, as government officials alleged that the hall was not fit for customers. This came within days of it winning the Best Cinema Hall of Delhi award. Witty, alert and agitated, Kaushish promptly issued newspaper advertisements, informing esteemed patrons that 'the best cinema hall in Delhi is shut due to unsanitary conditions'.

Shiela was the only hall asked to shut down during the Emergency, and there was an uproar. Two days later, Kaushish got a call from the Prime Minister's office. Mrs Gandhi, then on her way to Assam, had issued instructions for its prompt reopening. The officials who had ordered the hall's closure alleging it was not clean enough for patrons, came back to hand over letters of permission for reopening. Kaushish though took two days to reopen, arguing that dishonesty should not be encouraged.

Incidentally, some four years before the Emergency, on the completion of 10 years of Shiela entertaining over 10 million patrons, Mrs. Gandhi had sent her best wishes to Kaushish: 'May it (Shiela) long give good entertainment to the people of Delhi.'

The shows resumed. But the nature of the hall changed forever. It began playing Hindi movies frequently. Commerce demanded it, social pressures dictated it, and a film like *Jaane Bhi Do Yaaron* (1983) worked wonders. Thereafter, inexplicably, Shiela began showing skin flicks in the morning slot. Sleaze could not be camouflaged as business. The 1020-seater that once boasted of a silver jubilee run of *My Fair Lady* (1964) suddenly lost some of its bragging rights.

For much of the 1970s and '80s, business was heady. But in the changed times, black-marketeers began making a killing with their cries of '20 *wala* 50' (20-rupee tickets going for 50). Unthinkable for Shiela of the 1960s, it was par for the course in the '80s and '90s. The cinema no longer feared isolation, indifference or scorn. It was beyond approval and acclaim. The masses thronged to it and lapped up films like *Hero* (1983), *Souten* (1983), *Tarzan* (1985), *Shiva Ka Insaaf* (1985) and *Aakhri Raasta* (1986). Prayag Raaj's *Geraftaar* (1985) with the formidable trio of Amitabh Bachchan-Rajinikanth and Kamal Haasan drew such a thunderous response that in the melee, people tripped over each other, bringing down with them placards in the lobby. It became a favourite of the fans of Sunny Deol and Salman Khan. Sunny's films *Indian* (2001), *The Hero* (2003) and *Maa Tujhe Salam* (2002) were greeted with loud whistles and calls; Salman's *Jaan-e-Mann* (2006) and *Lucky: No Time for Love* (2005) had his die-hard fans coming all the way from Jodhpur, Alwar and Tonk to see the films on the first day of their release as the films had not released in Rajasthan at the time. An equally enthusiastic crowd greeted Farah Khan's *Om Shanti Om* (2007) though considerably fewer people turned up for JP Dutta's *Umrao Jaan* (2006) and Rakeysh Omprakash Mehra's *Aks* (2001) for which a special premiere was held here on a Thursday evening, a day ahead of the film's release. Interestingly, it played both Yash Chopra's *Deewaar* (1975) which attracted housefull shows for more than a month, and Milan Luthria's *Deewaar* (2004) which petered out after the first weekend.

In the mid 1990s , when the multiplex boom hit the capital and made running down single screens a favourite pastime, Shiela was disdainful of rivalry. Today, as an increasing number of single-screen halls make way for multiplexes, Shiela may have to give competition serious thought. Once, it played 'If You Miss The Train I Am On' for its valuable guests, waiting to enter the auditorium but today, its theme song might just be 'Ol' Man River'.

Shiela needs to make a choice.

6 IMPERIAL, Paharganj

In the days gone by, it could well have been a royal retreat or a rendezvous for the bold and bewitching. It played films like *Alam Ara* (1931), *Aurat* (1940), *Anarkali* (1953)—each a milestone in the annals of Hindi cinema. The hall was no less impressive than its films; it imparted a companionable and affable air. For many a weary passenger emerging from the New Delhi Railway Station, Imperial provided great comfort with it imposing yet dignified, formidable yet charming presence.

Launched in the pre-talkies days as a theatre, the balls it hosted were highly coveted and frequented by British officers and brown *sahib*s alike. Though located in a busy market hub, Imperial was a splendid address to share with anybody for an evening of leisure. In isolation, it was eye-catching; amid its surroundings, it was truly aristocratic.

With the arrival of Ardeshir Irani's *Alam Ara*, the hall bid adieu to its theatre days and turned into a cinema—probably the first to make the transition. Today, it stands as the oldest survivor of the silent-movie generation. It played the best of Hindustani cinema, many an A-grader from Hollywood, and was widely appreciated as much for its selection of movies as its ambience.

Well ahead of its time, it was air-cooled instead of naturally cooled, the way most cinemas were at the time. Its interiors and seating arrangement underwent a major renovation in 1952. Ever since, it has not undertaken any such task.

Partition had a major impact on Imperial, which was literally caught in the crossfire. On the one hand, trainloads of passengers arrived from Pakistan, relating unparalleled tales of horror while on the other hand, passengers waited to board the same train to Pakistan to avoid similar savagery in Delhi. Paharganj, then a Muslim-dominated area, changed in its demographic profile with the departure of Muslims to the newly created Pakistan, making way for Hindus from places such as Lahore and Peshawar. As displacement and replacement gradually gave way to reason and peace, Imperial's profile changed—from being a cinema that catered to the elite to one surrounded by new immigrants, including the deprived and the dispossessed. Since their most commonly spoken tongue was Punjabi, Imperial, sensitive to these subtle changes around it, started showing films in that language. The hall virtually ceased showing Hollywood films.

In the initial days, these newcomers, could not bear the thought of watching a Muslim social—so popular at other halls at that time—and Imperial was happy to oblige. It took to showing a series of Hindi mythologicals and Punjabi family dramas. The show, even if not always exhilarating, went on. If in the mid-'60s, there was *Jahan Sati Wahan Bhagwan* (1965), in the 1970s, there was *Bhakti Mein Shakti* (1978), Dara Singh's golden jubilee hit, and *Shiv Bhakt Baba Balaknath* (1972), which played at Sangam, Payal and New Amar as well. In the early '70s, *Saas Bhi Kabhi Bahu Thi* (1970) was screened at Imperial, as it was at Odeon. People residing in the vicinity came to Imperial, while at Odeon, people would arrive from beyond the immediate neighbourhood. Just as in the 1950s, Imperial showed *Yamla Jat* (1940) in re-run. The film was a major box-office success. Pakistani Punjabi films had screenings here as well.

For years, Imperial notched up the numbers. Denied big flicks on the day of their release, Imperial kept up the effort till all the popular films were eventually screened here. In the late '60s and '70s, many films arrived here a few weeks after their release in the city, and stayed long enough for the local audience to get familiar with them. Persistence proved to be Imperial's able ally.

Today, the booking clerk often doubles up as the usher, leading you into an auditorium where the seats are bereft of upholstery. Cigarette butts are extinguished against the backrest and *gutka* pouches and mint wrappers are strewn all around. The walls along the stairs leading to the auditorium have old but conspicuous marks of betel juice. Even though hardly any ladies frequent it, there is still a 'ladies cloak room', harking back to the old days.

Still only air-cooled, Imperial, with 580 seats and a maximum admission rate of Rs 30, is an important coordinate on the cinema map of the Capital. In a stinging reminder that the days of all-India hits cutting across class barriers are long gone, it caters to a niche audience of working-class men. In a city where tickets for select shows in multiplexes have gone up to a whopping Rs 1,500, this Paharganj cinema corroborates the adage—cinema is the best mode of entertainment for the common man. Its all-acquiescing patrons are the original cinema lovers—they ask for no Dolby digital sound or gleaming new prints in a perfectly air-conditioned hall. They have not heard of Mrinal Sen or Shyam Benegal, nor can they differentiate Karan Johar from Aditya Chopra. They are undemanding souls who turn up week after week for their heroes. At one time, they did so for Amitabh Bachcchan, and later, for Mithun Chakraborty. Now, as Imperial is unable to show either star's latest blockbuster, the audience laps up older films in the name of nostalgia, and men are often heard telling each other in the middle of a film, *'Ye film maine 9-10 saal pehle Moti par dekhi thhi'* (I had watched this film some 9-10 years ago at Moti). They have watched many Bhojpuri potboilers in four shows and seedy Hollywood flicks in the morning time.

Imperial has a past befitting its name but its future is doubtful. A hall of rare distinction, it deserves much better.

7 KHANNA, Paharganj

This cinema, which once played silent movies, fell silent in an indifferent world. Its existence preceded the arrival of talkies but no epitaph could convey the significance of one of the oldest addresses for cinegoers in Delhi. History proves it was once a fine entertainer, adept in the art of wooing audiences. With a bit of investment, Khanna could have been one of the heavyweight cinema halls in the city, rather than the bit-part player it was reduced to with the passage of time.

Its portals have been shut for long now. Today, the rain-lashed exteriors meld perfectly with the long-forgotten threshold, where a charpoy is placed and a goat tethered to the grill of the iron gates. Even the shop assistants in the busy market area all around don't have any idea of its exact location. *'Yahan kahin par hi thha Khanna'* (It used to be somewhere here), they say vaguely. There's not even a signboard with its name.

But the scene here was not always so dismal. There were years when Khanna was frequented by the rich, the connoisseurs, and the striving masses. Even as late as the 1980s, Khanna had not been completely done in by its failures. It needed one stand-out performance that would wipe away years of rejection, which happened with a mythological film, *Shiv Mahima* (1980) but that proved to be too little too late. However, since it made a good collection, Khanna survived, with the film going on to achieve a golden-jubilee run in the morning shows. Busloads of school students arrived from across the city, placing Khanna in the limelight again at a time when newspaper listings had all but stopped mentioning the hall. After stumbling for a long time, Khanna was on its feet again, like it had recovered many times before. The secret to its longevity indeed lay in constant reinvention.

Khanna's business was often confronted with challenges. In the 1930s, it did get to show movies made by top banners, but there were few people ready to travel here from either the Walled City or south Delhi. Even the regular *mushairas* in Old Delhi used to end fairly early in the day to facilitate safe travel back home for the audience. And Khanna was a couple of kilometres from the last gate of Old Delhi. It was not exactly close by for movie enthusiasts from other parts of the city either.

To address this problem, it gradually bid goodbye to big banners and new releases and concentrated instead on regional films which did not play at other halls in the vicinity. Marathi, Bengali and Telugu films would be screened here regularly. Gradually, people began trickling in from beyond the immediate neighbourhood, and schools with a vast predominance of students from non-Hindi speaking states arranged special trips so they could watch films in their mother tongue. Khanna didn't completely stop playing Hindi movies but the regional fare gave a definite fillip to the collections.

Occasionally, when Khanna did play a film by a top Hindi banner in the 1970s and '80s, it was with the knowledge that the same film would be showing in any of the four big halls in Connaught Place. Yet Khanna was confident of its target audience. It knew that those visiting Connaught Place travelled miles to watch a film, whereas its own audience just crossed from one lane to another to reach it! Hence, a film like *Jeevan Sangram* (1974) played at Odeon in Connaught Place as well as in Palace, Uphaar and Alankar, besides Khanna. When Mehboob Khan's now forgotten *Son of India* (1962) was released, it failed to recapture the glory of *Mother India* (1957), but at Khanna, the film's collections were better than at the infinitely more famous Regal where it failed miserably—Regal's fans were often better educated and well informed about films; Khanna's patrons often hailed from the economically weaker section of the society, hence usually not as well informed.

Like Imperial next door, Khanna too began as a theatre and showed silent films for a while. But it came into its own after the first talkie, *Alam Ara* (1931). Confident that there would be no looking back, Khanna bid farewell to its theatre days. Having played both silent films and talkies, Khanna went a step further in the 1940s by hosting the premiere of *Prithiviraj Samyogita* (1946) when Prithiviraj Kapoor himself graced the cinema. This was nothing short of a miracle since Prithviraj Kapoor was not known to go to cinemas other than Regal and Minerva.

A little over two decades after this film, Prithviraj's *Nanak Naam Jahaz Hai* (1969) rewrote box-office records and Khanna was fortunate enough to get a piece of the pie. The film was a precursor of things to come. A few years later, Khanna showed *Shiv Mahima* (1992), a long-running film which it sorely needed at the time, bringing into sharp focus the brief run of most films at this cinema.

Even in its heyday, Khanna, unlike halls such as Regal, Moti, Novelty, was not known for running films for a long period. A blockbuster meant a stay of only four to six weeks. Little surprise then that it proved a happy destination for banners like AVM and Gemini, whose films enjoyed a fine run here, often helped by curious tourists staying in budget hotels in the area.

The hall had some unusual patrons. After it was renovated, in the late 1970s and '80s, two women pickpockets would visit the hall in the evening shows. Inspired by the superhit *Seeta Aur Geeta* (1972), they would often try their luck near the booking counter, and on a couple of occasions, were caught by alert cinegoers. A few days later, the women were back to their tricks. Another patron was a man whose polio-stricken legs prevented him from standing. He would sit on a cart less than four inches above the crowd and push it himself with one hand. He would come to Khanna for every matinee show and wait for an usher to quietly allow him in, often without a ticket. His argument was that he occupied no seat. Learning from this experience, ushers started seating people with disabilities on the aisle seats, reserving six such seats till the show began.

Around this time, Khanna was also reduced to playing re-runs and fade-outs of yesteryear films, usually not the big hits. A while later, the films of Mithun Chakraborty and Dharmendra began enjoying a run here. With titles like *Policewala Goonda* (1995), *Bhai Thakur* (2000), *Khul-e-Aam* (1992), *Qatl-e-Aam* (2005) and *Jagira* (2001), Khanna had no pretensions to artistic sensibilities. The crowd's reactions to Dharmendra's *Jagira,* a film replete with *thakur*s, bad men, vulnerable girls, horses and bullets, clearly proved they enjoyed such hackneyed fare. As the hero entered astride a horse, the crowd whistled. When the heroine was thrown to the ground by the villain's henchmen, the viewers clapped in anticipation of her dancing in front of him, just like Hema Malini's character Basanti in *Sholay* (1975). That is the abiding memory of the last few years of Khanna's eventful journey. Today, it stands forsaken and forgotten.

II

Celluloid Charms Shahjahanabad

8 DELITE, Asaf Ali Road

During the Indo-Pak war, 1971, Delite remained steadfastly patriotic. At the time, cinema houses in the city were known to cancel their evening and night shows, under instructions to switch off their lights. But Delite was the rare theatre that played the latest news from the warfront during its regular shows. At the height of the war, when it showed *Upasna* (1971), a Sanjay Khan-Mumtaz-Feroz Khan starrer that did reasonable business, regular news despatches were aired at the beginning and interval of the film. The hall made provisions for two intervals, so that they could provide three updates during each movie. It pleased the patrons, who often said a silent prayer for the soldiers, and also emphasised the patriotic zeal of the management.

This ability to take on the odds was not a new principle of the Raizada family, which owned the cinema hall. Brij Mohan Lal Raizada led the way in the 1950s, despite having no prior experience of running a cinema hall when he founded Delite. He had largely been in dealerships with well-known automobile brands like Morris Minor. Yet, when he learnt that Prime Minister Jawaharlal Nehru wanted Delhi to have its own landmarks built by Indians after Independence, he went ahead with his plan. The government earmarked a plot of land on the periphery of Old Delhi for a fresh new cinema and Delite came up at the spot where once stood the age-old wall of the Walled City; the wall was demolished to give way to the cinema. This enterprise cost more than Rs 6 lakh. After that, the construction of the hall cost a further Rs 30 lakh. Most well-wishers advised Brij Mohan Lal against investing so much capital in a cinema which was neither here nor there—Delite was on the cusp of Old and New Delhi. But he stuck to his guns and Delite was built, with around 1,100 seats.

It opened in 1954 with Raj Kapoor's *Angaray*, which was widely promoted through loudspeaker announcements on cycle-rickshaws and *ekka*s. Soon, Delite came to be regarded as the loftiest cinema in the city, its building being counted among the tallest, its wide columns, its majestic pillars and its polka-dotted front, all became its signatures. The who's who of Indian politics and cinema such as President Dr Rajendra Prasad and Prime Minister Jawaharlal Nehru to Indira Gandhi, Morarji Desai, Babu Jagjivan Ram, came to the hall. Stars like Raj Kapoor and Nargis, Dilip Kumar and Madhubala, Meena Kumari and Dharmendra also visited Delite in the 1950s and '60s. For residents of south Delhi, travelling here meant a leisurely drive while those who came to Delite from Old Delhi wanted to watch a film in an ambience that was better than that of the Walled City cinemas.

With films like *Waqt* (1965), *Humraaz* (1967), *Vandna* (1975) playing regularly, Delite was never short of classy films. Sanjay Dutt's movies, from *Main Awara Hoon* (1983) to *Khalnayak* (1993) and others, ran to packed houses, as did Akbar Khan's *Haadsaa* (1983) and Raj N Sippy's *Qayamat* (1983). Subhash Ghai's films enjoyed a good run here too and Yash Chopra also made Delite the go-to hall for his movies. Among those who frequented Delite were also transgenders. From the 1990s, they opted for Delite as their favoured venue for watching films over the halls in Connaught Place. By this time, many Old Delhi cinemas had either shut down or offered the barest minimum amenities, with no top banner releases. So, many would come to Delite from near and afar to watch the first day-first shows. Among them were the *purdanasheen* women who would come here for matinee and evening shows. Delite offered both privacy and accessibility. In the early part of the millennium, a local women's organisation chose Delite as the venue for watching films. From as early as 2001, every Friday, the members would show up in a group of around 50, usually for family dramas or the NRI dreams peddled by Yash Raj Films.

Over the years, the hall created a little niche for playing regional fare in the morning shows. Bengali films, in particular, enjoyed a good run. Suchitra Sen's *Megh Kalo* (1970), which was booked for just one week, attracted such a rush that it eventually ran for eight weeks.

In 1994, when the movie business was down in the dumps, most cinema halls were reduced to playing forgettable potboilers, some even resorting to sleazy flicks. The films' posters used to be smeared with blue ink to arouse greater curiosity—a desperate attempt to bring in viewers. Only a handful of halls avoided such films. During these uncertain times, Delite's management decided to go in for an overhaul of the cinema: in came fresh seats (reduced to 900 from the earlier 1,100), better air-conditioning and revised admission rates. A wonderful cafeteria (which still offers its version of the Japani *samosa*—a large-sized savoury heavy enough for a lunch) was also built, along with swanky restrooms. With rare enterprise and an ability to take huge risks, Delite's management was able to turn the tide of insecurity prevailing in cinema halls at that time.

Rajshri Films, known for soft, gentle, family dramas, released *Hum Aapke Hain Koun...!* (1994) in a selective manner. Initially, only two prints ran, one at Sapna, the other at Delite, where it went on to complete a jubilee run. In hindsight, it was a masterstroke on the part of Shashank Raizada, Managing Director of Delite, since back then, *Hum Aapke Hain Koun...!* was a family film at a time when families had stopped coming to cinema halls. In the same spirit, Delite improved its facilities at a time when the returns were low.

For almost two decades, Delite has had the best ambience among single-screen halls in the city: plush interiors, marble flooring, a tasteful foyer and a canteen big enough to accommodate a crowd. A mini theatre, Delite Diamond, came up in the vicinity in 2006.

The 1971 war ended decades ago but war films continued to be screened at Delite. JP Dutta's *LoC Kargil* (2003) was shown, as was *Mangal Pandey: the Rising* (2005), Ketan Mehta's big budget dream. With *1971*, a Manoj Bajpai film released in 2007, the hall that had started with news of an actual war, had come a full circle. With crowd-pullers like *Bunty aur Babli* (2005) *Fanaa* (2006), *Chak De India* (2007), *Race* (2008), *Jodhaa Akbar* (2008), the show goes on uninterrupted, never mind the occasional *Mitti* (2001)—the film was taken off after three days—*Moksha* (2001) or *Jhoom Barabar Jhoom* (2007).

9 GOLCHA, Netaji Subhash Marg

It played many milestone films—*Mughal-e-Azam* (1960), *Chaudhvin Ka Chand* (1961), *Anand* (1971), *Khushboo* (1975), *Nikaah* (1982) and *Masoom* (1983). Each had thousands of takers, each struck a chord. Golcha played these films with the passion one reserves for special occasions. Lovebirds made it their perch when it screened *Mughal-e-Azam* and *Chaudhvin ka Chand*; children flocked to it when it showed *Masoom* with Gulzar's 'Lakdi Ki Kathi'. Golcha was different things to different people. But in the end, its worth went much beyond. As a hall of a kind, it was unique, affable, impressive. It created its own niche, charted its own path. The location itself became its strength—at the delightful cusp of Delhi, old and new, it assimilated the best of both, yet stood apart, like Hasan Kamal's lyrics in *Nikaah*, a film that played here for a year: 'Ye Qurbate, Ye Dooriyan'...(Such proximity, such distance).

The very mention of Golcha evokes nostalgia. A popular meeting point for the young, it was where dreams were made and many love stories blossomed. The films that were screened here went on to cultivate a long-term relationship with the hall.

Inaugurated by Dr Sarvepalli Radhakrishnan, later President of India, Golcha opened to the general public with

Sant Kabir in December 1954. With 850 seats, and attractive cement exteriors with a coat of pink, and each letter of its name cut out for vertical and horizontal display, Golcha came to be identified as the hall of the elite, the well read, the discerning.

Among the millions for whom Golcha was a rendezvous point is Shiraz Mirza, a leading rexine merchant of the city in the 1960s and '70s. As a strapping youth and die-hard consumer of romance, Avtar Singh*ji*, one of his business contacts from Punjab, wanted to watch Bimal Roy's *Madhumati* (1958). Shiraz, who had his fill of films only in Chandni Chowk, asked an employee to take the guest to Golcha. A few hours later, Avtar came back singing praises of the film but he did not stop at that. The guest from Punjab went on to describe Golcha: '*Kya khoob* hall *hai. Agar hamare* Punjab *mein aesa* hall *mil jaye, to log Dilli bhool jayen!*' (What a fine hall! If people could have such a hall in our Punjab, they would forget about coming to Delhi). Avtar*ji*'s words resonated in Shiraz's head.

It was, however, not until *Chaudhvin Ka Chand* graced Golcha that Shiraz found time to go to the hall. Once there, he was absolutely smitten, and not just because of the film. He had brought with him Zohra, his soon-to-be life partner. Shiraz fell in love with the film, its title song and the hall. He came back three days later for an evening show, then again a week later. Director M. Sadiq's film, however, had limited engagement with Golcha and was soon shifted to Jagat near Jama Masjid. Shiraz could not take Zohra there; the cinema was too close to the mosque, and if the faithful coming out from there spotted his soon-to-be wife, they would immediately think Shiraz was not marrying a *deendar* girl.

When Shiraz did return to Golcha with Zohra to watch *Mughal-e-Azam*, she was his wife. To mark the significance of the occasion, they had chosen the perfect film. K Asif's magnum opus, which took 16 years to make, arrived at the hall in a manner befitting royalty. For the first time ever, the film's print arrived on the back of an elephant. This honour was bestowed upon Golcha despite the film opening elsewhere too. The elephants were decked up, their trunks covered in velvet, their backs draped in a mix of satin and velvet. Their hinds had elongated bags attached to them just in case the animals had to answer nature's call during the procession.

Mughal-e-Azam proved to be every bit as grand as it was built up to be and went on to do smashing business. It brought people in by the hundreds and Golcha's balcony section, spacious and comfortable, became a second home for the lovebirds of Old Delhi. The film's subject and the hall's ambience meant that no show was less than housefull. Most tickets were booked in advance and many were sold in black. Films like *Dosti* (1964), *Guide* (1965), *Geet Gaata Chal* (1975), *Umrao Jaan* (1981) and *Ek Duje Ke Liye* (1982) were smash hits here, successfully attracting audiences to Golcha long after being taken off at other halls in the city. Even better was the feat of Raj Kapoor's *Ram Teri Ganga Maili* (1985), a film whose arrival was preceded by bare-dare trailers of the heroine, Mandakini. It aroused great interest among youngsters. Its golden jubilee run meant the film's hoardings had to be replaced thrice as the colours faded due to sustained exposure to the elements. Dilip Kumar-Raaj Kumar's iconic *Saudagar* (1991) evoked great initial interest, particularly pleasing its director Subhash Ghai, who, in the early years of his life, used to live not too far from the hall.

From its initial exclusivity, Golcha's appeal gradually widened and people from the lesser privileged section of the society too started frequenting the front and middle stalls. In fact, by the 1990s, it was their tastes that often proved a deciding factor in the selection of films. Hence, Salman Khan-starrers were much sought sought-after fare here. *Sanam Bewafa* (1991) was a roaring hit at Golcha, and even his mediocre films like *Tumko Na Bhool Payenge* (2002) and *Saawan* (2006) recorded fine initial collections, timed as they were to coincide with Muslim festivals. The boys from Old Delhi called him *bhai* and clapped and whistled when he took off his shirt on the screen to settle scores. Salman struck a chord with the stalls. For a while, his place as numero uno was occupied by Shah Rukh Khan, with *Dilwale Dulhaniya Le Jayenge* (1995), showing no signs of going away from the cinema. Two years later, the Shah Rukh Khan-Madhuri Dixit-Karisma Kapoor-starrer *Dil to Pagal Hai* (1997) with Uttam Singh's music evoked such hysteria here that pavement vendors on the adjacent road leading to Sui Walan started keeping its music cassettes, often attracting passers-by with their high-pitched cassette players.

Golcha was for a cool spring evening, a hot summer afternoon or a late night in the chilly winter. It was an all-weather cinema with grace and class. It still exudes those qualities.

10 JAGAT, Jama Masjid

Every afternoon, Afroz Begum secretly hoped that her husband wouldn't return home directly after his Zuhr prayers at Fatehpuri Masjid. He would, she hoped, catch up with the local *imams*, discuss issues of *deen* and *taleem,* and come back only after sunset. The husband, a *moulvi*, was no dictator, but he had banned movies from his and his family's life. Afroz Begum, though, desperately wanted to watch *Dayar-e-Madina* (1975), a film that was playing to a stupendous response at the nearby Jagat cinema. She could venture out to the hall only in his absence.

One day she learnt from a friend that the film was to be taken off on the upcoming Friday, but with the intervention of local clerics, who wrote to the management for a two-week extension, it got a longer run. The management of Jagat cinema heeded their request, happily answering their letters with words of grateful appreciation. *Dayar-e-Madina* went on to have an extended run at the hall, attracting bearded *maulana*s and women in burqas. Afroz Begum, too, sneaked out one day when work took her husband out of the city. Covered from head to toe, with her heart beating wildly, she went inside a cinema hall for only the second time in her life. The first time had been for a re-run of *Alam Ara* (1931), much before she had got married. She tried her luck again later with *Niyaz aur Namaaz* (1977), a Lalita Pawar-

Keshto Mukherjee film running at Kumar near Dariba Kalan in Chandni Chowk. But the hall located at the end of the jewellers' market seemed too far away for her. In comparison, the '*machhliwalon ka* talkies' (as many called Jagat due to its location close to the fish market) was more accessible, and she hardly took time to commute from her house in Urdu Bazar.

The faithful would arrive at the hall, remove their shoes and place them neatly on a rack made for the purpose, and only then watch the film. Some would bring along incense too! That was a different age at Jagat. Neither a bomb blast nor the Emergency could halt operations at the cinema of the masses where tickets cost less than a cola—a front stall ticket could be had for 75 paise and a cola came for Re 1!

Its proximity to the historic Jama Masjid meant the hall chose its films with great care. Similar sensitivity was displayed while deciding on the billboards to be hung on its façade. Films with any kind of skin show were a strict no-no. In the 1980s, the hall once showed *Shama* (1981), a Muslim social produced by seasoned artiste Kader Khan. He graced the hall during the first week of the release and a woman broke through the crowd to kiss his hand. Kader Khan was moved to tears.

Years before screening *Shama*, Jagat was witness to a couple of other rare scenes. Both involved tragedy queen Meena Kumari. It so happened that her film *Phool aur Patthar* (1966) was celebrating its silver jubilee at the hall and Meena Kumari had come to attend the function along with Dharmendra, the film's hero. Movie-watchers lined up on both sides of the road linking Jagat to Netaji Subhash Marg and as the crowd continued to grow, the hero and heroine had to leave their car at Daryaganj and walk down to Jagat, waving to the cheering crowds and signing autographs all the way. The same thing happened during the screening of *Laila Majnu* (1976), the

Rishi Kapoor-Ranjeeta love story that completed a golden jubilee at Jagat. Incidentally, for the film's jubilee week, a fresh set of hoardings was brought all the way from Bombay.

The second incident involving Meena Kumari provided equally compelling evidence of her effect on fans. Kamal Amrohi's *Pakeezah* (1972), opened with average collections but gradually picked up as news of her death spread. Viewers came out in hundreds to watch the film at Jagat as a tribute to their beloved artiste. Among them was Nawab Shariq, who stayed in an old *haveli* in Matia Mahal. Day and night, he would listen to the song, 'Mausam Hai Aashiqana' and hum along with the lyrics, 'Din ho gaye hain zalim, raatein hai qaatilana...mausam hai aashiqana.' Every Thursday, the nawab would step into a tonga which would stop on the carpeted streets of Matia Mahal only to carry him to Jagat, less than half a kilometre away, to watch *Pakeezah*. He would alight at the entrance and walk to the box at Jagat, not making eye contact with other cinegoers. The women of his family would follow in his footsteps, watching the film from the confines of the box reserved for the family—Jagat gave families the option of watching a public show of a film from the privacy of a small box and, at times, people reserved an entire box of six seats even though only three-four persons would be present. The nawab, in this case, would never watch the film in its entirety, staying on only for the song 'Chalte Chalte'. Once Gauri Shankar's choreographic masterpiece had played, he would shuffle out, the women again following him out. The entire family would return the following Thursday to watch the film all over again!

The love affair with *Pakeezah* went on for six months for the soft-spoken nawab, who was otherwise not known to patronise movies.

The air-cooled Jagat had other regulars who chose to see films here rather than go to Connaught Place where the halls offered air-conditioned comfort. Their constant support meant Jagat hardly ever experienced a low. Prakash Mehra, J Om Prakash, Pramod Chakravorty and Ramanand Sagar developed a special bond with the hall. Many of their films did outstanding business here, so they were generous enough to provide a bonus to the staff—15 days' salary.

Director Mukul Dutt's *Aan Milo Sajna* (1970) attracted housefull shows for a 100 days. Chandra Barot's Amitabh Bachchan-starrer *Don* (1978) completed a silver jubilee at Jagat but *Suhaag* (1979) fared better, running for 36 weeks. Prakash Mehra's *Muqaddar ka Sikandar* (1978), with which the admission rates were hiked, ran for 48 weeks—for the first 27 weeks, there was not a show that did not run to packed houses. Jagat prospered, happy to be a popular address for top-notch films from Hindi cinema, never taking a Hollywood detour. For fans who valued mainstream fare, Jagat was the hall that celebrated popular cinema.

Like most other halls, Jagat too was a theatre that turned into a cinema when silent movies gave way to talkies in the early '30s. Initially called Nishat, it was renamed Jagat in 1938. With movies like *Tansen* (1943), *Anarkali* (1953) and *Nagin* (1954) releasing here, it was smooth sailing for Jagat right from the beginning. Noor Jehan-Yakoob's *Zeenat* (1945) which also starred Naseem Bano, had a terrific run despite some of the shows being cancelled due to power failures. Incidentally, Pradeep Kumar and Beena Roy's *Anarkali* did not set the cash registers ringing initially, but as C Ramachandra's music scored with the masses, the film gained at the box office. Nandlal Jaswantlal's *Nagin*, though, shot to glory from day one as fans drooled over

Lata Mangeshkar's 'Mann Dole Mera Tan Dole', with men throwing coins at the screen during Vyjayanthimala's dance number. Ironically, when the film completed a silver jubilee, the entire star cast, except Vyjayanthimala, came to the cinema.

In 1956, an incident took place at Jagat. While Dev Anand's *CID* (1956) was playing, a crude bomb went off near the entrance of the hall soon after Shamshad Begum's number 'Leke Pehla Pehla Pyaar' had finished. The blast took place near the ticket counter, which used to open just outside the main complex towards the Murga Market. A portion of the hall was affected in the blast and it remained closed for a while before making a comeback as a renovated place of entertainment. It still had 650 seats, and the rates of admission went up to Rs 1.25. For the next 30 years or so, Jagat was a rock steady hall, showing films like *Rocky* (1981), *Jyoti Bane Jwala* (1980), *Vidhaata* (1982).

Like life, Jagat's innings too had to come to an end. For years, Jagat enjoyed great social patronage because of the well-established Muslim families who used to frequent the hall but over time, these families moved away, depriving the hall of much of its balcony audience. In their place came a floating population of working-class men, eager to watch sleazy films. After allegations of soft porn clips being inserted in a dubbed foreign film were levelled against it, Jagat had to shut down. The hall that once screened the finest of Hindi cinema, simply faded from public memory.

11 NEW AMAR, Hauz Qazi

In the good old days, every cinema hall was associated with certain banners and heroes. Some favoured Guru Dutt, Bimal Roy and, later, Gulzar and Hrishikesh Mukherjee, while others opted for Shakti Samanta, Nasir Hussain, Yash Chopra, Manmohan Desai, Prakash Mehra and Subhash Ghai. It was rare in those times for a hall to show *Mirza Ghalib* (1954) and *Kalicharan* (1976) in back-to-back shows, and then screen *Bobby* (1973). A hall that went beyond a 35 mm screen and a functional auditorium with a simple seating arrangement was also a novelty. New Amar did not just inform its patrons about the films being shown but actually sought them out. In an age when many halls resembled a theatre from the inside because of their early days as a venue for staging drama, New Amar was like an art gallery. At first glance, it resembled the work of an artist in stone while its insides were the result of a master craftsman at work. The elegant façade had a neat mix of soothing pale yellow and sky blue covering its engraved pillars, the tops of which sported elegant *pietra dura* work. There was an open balcony which was more like a Mughal age *jharokha* with intricate *jaali*s, which, during matinee shows, gleamed as the sun shone through the openings. The *jaali*s were painted white and seldom allowed to gather dust. Inside the hall, stained glass windows and crystal chandeliers took the audience back to the times when nawabs enjoyed the pleasures of life, and dancing girls provided company.

New Amar, which will probably go down as not more than a footnote in Delhi's cinematic history, was mindful of the social index when choosing its films or even seating its patrons. The hall used to have stalls which were informally reserved for the sex workers of Old Delhi, who made up a good chunk of the audience here. This was due to its location—just a few steps from the famous red light area of GB Road. New Amar was also less than a stone's throw from the age-old Mubarak Begum Masjid near Hauz Qazi. Ironically, the mosque itself was constructed by the mistress of a *mansabdar*.

The sex workers used to prefer the noon and matinee shows here and arrived in plain clothes without any make-up to avoid undue attention. Rather than soaking in a *Pakeezah* (1972) or a *Tawaif* (1985), the women preferred subjects with a strong female character, well-removed from the world of pimps and 'madams'. They satiated their appetite with films like *Mother India* (1957), *Mere Mehboob* (1963) and *Badal* (1951). It was largely due to these spectators that New Amar carved out a reputation for playing serious films. It did not quite play Muslim socials in the manner of Excelsior, located next door, but stayed clear of sleazy fare, which was no mean achievement as the hall was never the first choice of distributors looking for a screening in Old Delhi. That honour went to the cinema houses in Chandni Chowk, and New Amar had to bide its time before a 'new' film would be screened there, usually not earlier than the sixth week of its release. It was a 're-run' hall.

Nevertheless, it gave viewers many fulfilling experiences. *Badal*, a Madhubala classic, was suggested to proprietor Sushil Kumar by local distributor Ranjit Singh Seble but was initially turned down as it was black and white, and audience response seemed doubtful. But director Amiya Chakrabarty's film, which also had Prem Nath and Purnima, with tunes by Shanker-Jaikishen, was riding a wave of success after the duo's work with Raj Kapoor. Seble was able to convince the proprietors, and the film came to New Amar after a sustained publicity blitz. Almost a dozen rickshaw-pullers were hired and posters of *Badal* were pasted on three sides of the vehicle. In the centre sat a man with a loudspeaker telling passersby that *Badal* would be shown at New Amar shortly. For two days, a joker hopped and skipped in front of the rickshaws as they travelled through the lanes and bylanes of the Walled City. A day before the release, the film's pamphlets were distributed at shops and houses around the cinema hall, going all the way to Charkhewalan and GB Road, besides Bazar Sitaram and Choori Walan.

The film arrived at the hall in a manner befitting royalty. The hoardings came up on the cinema's front; there were special cut-outs of Prem Nath and Madhubala astride a horse. This shot was from the song 'Main Raahi Bhatakne Wala Hoon', rendered by Mukesh. The effort paid off as each and every show ran to a full house.

Similarly, New Amar paid plenty of attention to minor details when it showed *Mother India*, the Mehboob Khan film, after it had a long run at Moti in Chandni Chowk. By the late '60s and early '70s, New Amar was the preferred theatre for repeat-run movies. Distributors made a good profit and movie-watchers could take in good films at reasonable rates on a well-maintained screen. At times, though, New Amar also kept abreast of the bigwigs of the film distribution trade. For instance, *Daag* (1973) celebrated its silver jubilee here along with Minerva and Chanakya, admittedly in a single show in the latter. And *Jeevan Sangram* (1974) which had a tax-free status, was shown here while it ran simultaneously at Odeon, Paras, Alankar and Palace. In 1978, when Dharmendra's *Azaad* (1978) was being shown in daily four shows at many halls in the city, New Amar played Dilip Kumar's *Azaad* (1955) in the morning shows. A little later, it played Dharmendra's film too in the same slot!

Occasionally, New Amar stepped out of its tried and tested zone and screened films for children. These were usually in the morning when school students could be expected to come in droves with their teachers. *Toofan,* a film for kids, played in daily four shows here, but that was an exception. Otherwise, New Amar preferred to quietly cater to the majority.

When the Delhi Metro Rail project started, the site of the cinema was earmarked for the Ajmeri Gate Metro Station. Like Vivek in Patel Nagar, New Amar too was demolished, leaving behind nothing but a trail of memories.

12 EXCELSIOR, Lal Kuan

For much of the 1950s and '60s, Muslim socials ruled the roost. Films like *Anarkali* (1953), *Mirza Ghalib* (1954), *Mughal-e-Azam* (1960), *Chaudhvin Ka Chand* (1961), *Taj Mahal* (1963), *Mere Mehboob* (1963), *Gazal* (1964), *Bahu Begum* (1967), *Palki* (1967), *Jahan Ara* (1964) and, in the early '70s, *Pakeezah* (1972) and *Mehboob Ki Mehndi* (1971) became part of film lore. Every song, every ghazal, every stanza was analysed, the costumes appreciated and the sets admired. In the Walled City, it was not possible to pass by a lane without songs like 'Pyar Kiya Toh Darna Kya', 'Jo Wada Kiya Woh', 'Hum Intezar Karenge' or 'Chalo Dildar Chalo' wafting from a house, music shop or *paan-bidi* corner. Many stood mesmerised, soaking in the music. Business could wait. That was a more leisurely age—tastes were more refined and men were gentle and well-acquainted with Urdu, not regarded then as the language of any particular community. Even the working classes knew the difference between *mehtab* and *aftab; talaffuz* and *tarannum.*

When noted poet-lyricist Shakeel Badayuni visited Meena Bazar near Jama Masjid, he often had dinner at a local hotel to the accompaniment of the songs of *Chaudhvin Ka Chand,* which were his compositions. The music shops near the hotel played the songs completely unaware of the composer's presence in their midst. Shakeel's Old Delhi experience became even better as he stayed on for a few days to witness the opening of *Chaudhvin Ka Chand* at Golcha, where it attracted huge crowds. Soon, it came to Jagat, even closer to where Shakeel was staying, and completed a silver jubilee. Every evening, Shakeel would hear tales of people coming out of the hall and humming the title song. Every morning, he would wake up with stories of how the Jagat management had to close the booking counter within an hour of its opening as all the tickets were sold out. Then came *Mughal-e-Azam*, a film like none other; a film whose release, too, was a regal affair which further cemented Shakeel's reputation in cinema lore. Incidentally, *Chaudhvin Ka Chand* travelled in a near-straight line from one cinema to another over a period of three months, starting from Golcha in Daryaganj to Jagat near Jama Masjid and on to Excelsior.

In the Walled City, people embraced and raved about all Muslim socials; some cinegoers raved about Talat Mahmood's ghazals and Mohammed Rafi's songs, others queued up to see Meena Kumari or Madhubala, and yet more for Dilip Kumar. While Jagat released most Muslim socials or period dramas with pride and triumph, it was the good old Cinema Excelsior in Lal Kuan that captured the imagination of the faithful. From *Anarkali* to *Mughal-e-Azam*, *Mirza Ghalib* to *Palki*, *Taj Mahal* to *Jahan Ara*, it made up for not showing films on the day of their release by screening them all more than once. Most often, films here would arrive for a few shows and then be gone. But the audience remained faithful, waiting for the return, and return they did. *Mughal-e-Azam* played 17 times, *Anarkali* six times, *Palki* seven times and *Alam Ara*, a mind-boggling 21 times. Sometimes, they were shown in daily four shows, on others, thrice a day. They were screened at reduced rates in the mornings and there were special screenings for select audience members. All these factors combined to make sure that, for Muslim socials, Excelsior remained the most faithful theatre in Delhi.

From the 1930s when it began, up to the mid-'80s, Excelsior was a cinema that attracted the gentry in the matinee and evening shows—it was not uncommon to see women in *ghararas* sneaking in to see *Pakeezah* or *Mughal-e-Azam.* Occasionally, some of them would arrive covered from top to toe in a single-piece white burqa. The burqa would come in handy for some—they would take their child on their arm and wrap the burqa around him or her. This way they gained admission without having to pay for the child's ticket. Often, men clad in *kurta*-pyjamas would walk in with a pen and a little writing pad and request for corner or aisle seats. Once seated, they would use their pen and paper to write down the ghazals that played in films like *Mirza Ghalib* or *Jahan Ara.* Not everybody could afford LPs and with no Internet in those days, films offered the best chance to take down the words of a complete ghazal. The couplets were happily recited at subsequent screenings. Of course, the low admission rates at Excelsior helped. A pack of 20 cigarettes cost Rs 1.35 in the early '70s, while an LP came for at least five times the price. But a ticket at the cinema house could be purchased for a mere 10 *annas*! The facilities were basic—there were no seats with plush rexine covers, no stereophonic sound and no air-conditioning. Just two narrow-blade fans and a 35 mm screen.

Some cinegoers did not even pay that much. Among them was Mirza Shahid Baig, who, for years, ran a tea stall in Sirki Walan, near an exit gate of the cinema. While making tea at his roadside stall, Baig would keep his ears glued to the film playing inside, helped as he was by the fact that the hall did not have a stereophonic sound system which meant it was easy to hear the dialogues and sound sitting behind its closed creaky doors. Baig knew exactly when to step in to watch a song or a comic sequence, as movies here ran more than once. Keeping him company was Harbans Lal, the owner of a hardware shop nearby and a huge fan of Mohammed Rafi songs. He struck up a rapport with the ushers and guards and they would allow him to sneak in to watch a song. *'Tumharawala gaana aanewala hai,'* (your song is about to start) they would alert him. Lal, in turn, helped out when they put up new posters on Thursday night.

In its long history, Excelsior, with a seating capacity of 450, notched up a few interesting sidelights. When it showed *Alam Ara* (1931), it promoted the film as 'the greatest Muslim social with hit songs—full of ladies' sentiments'. It was among a handful of halls to play both *Mughal-e-Azam* and *Sikandar-e-Azam* (1965), Prithviraj Kapoor being the common actor. Then, it screened *Mother India* (1957) and *Son of India* (1962), two of Mehboob Khan's films that met with diametrically opposite responses at the box office.

As a hall that specialised in playing films with a dominant Muslim theme, Excelsior naturally had a festival of Dilip Kumar films. Dilip Kumar did not play any Muslim character of note till *Mughal-e-Azam* but the predominantly Muslim clientele of Excelsior regarded him as one of their own. The tragedy king was indeed a superstar here with a majority of his films finding a ready audience on opening, in re-runs, during morning shows and as part of film festivals. *Aadmi* (1968), *Kohinoor* (1960), *Sagina* (1974), *Ram Aur Shyam* (1967) and *Shaheed* (1965), all had multiple rounds. He always managed to pull in the crowds much better than contemporaries Dev Anand and Raj Kapoor.

However, for all its dalliance with history, the cinema is not as easy to locate from a distance. All along Sirki Walan road—a few quick steps from the Chawri Bazar Metro Station—one finds push carts lined up, with the occasional bullock cart thrown in. Hardware and sanitaryware shops are aplenty, not to forget those selling cauldrons, cages and *karchis*! With inter-meshed electric wires hiding the sky, Excelsior is easy to miss unless you keep an eye open for the old school-style film posters. Painted in red, blue and green, it is actually called Cinema Excelsior, a rare hall with the prefix 'cinema' attached to it, unlike the others which would call themselves 'talkies'. The lobby of the hall is like a mini gallery, with posters of the current film and those of the forthcoming one. On one wall, history is clearly visible—a poster of Dilip Kumar's *Vidhaata* (1982) and a small photo of *Naya Daur* (1957), BR Chopra's musical, besides one of *Gehri Chaal*, a 1973 film starring Amitabh Bachchan.

These days, the cinema is gearing up for renovation after playing re-runs of mediocre films. For the last few years, its audience was made up almost exclusively of blue-collar workers, those undemanding souls ready to watch a 20-year-old average film as a *'nai film iss hafte'* (the new film this week). They frequented the noon and night shows while the matinees were favoured by the girls from GB Road who used to visit New Amar. Inside, watching the film was no joy. The action on screen was often given competition by vendors who made their way inside the hall with cries of *'chai, chai, garama garam* bread *pakora'* (anyone for tea, freshly fried savouries?).

With the local Muslim gentry having shifted out of the Walled City and the area transformed into a business zone, it is time for Cinema Excelsior to start its second innings, possibly in a brave new avatar.

13 MOTI, Chandni Chowk

It's business as usual in Chandni Chowk. On a balmy winter afternoon, a man sits on the edge of the pavement, picking wax from someone else's ear. Barely 10 yards away, people crowd around the shop selling the popular Japani *samosa*, big enough to be a light lunch. Two yards further down sits a one-legged old man, a leprosy-stricken beggar with fingers not much longer than stubs. He rests his back against a wall covered by two posters: one of a Bhojpuri film, *Nagin* (2013), obviously inspired by a popular Hindi movie of the '70s; the other of a dubbed Telugu film, *Ek Naya Tiger* (2013), a title clearly borrowed from Salman Khan's *Ek Tha Tiger* (2012). On the other side of the wall stands the historic Moti Talkies, a cinema that screened the very best that tinsel town had to offer, and one called 'talkies' even in the age of multiplexes.

When cinema was in black and white, Moti treated the discerning to the masterpieces of Bimal Roy, Mehboob Khan and Guru Dutt. Both *Mother India* (1957) and *Madhumati* (1958) attracted housefull shows for weeks on end, with Mehboob Khan's film running for 31 weeks and Bimal Roy's completing a silver jubilee. Viewers came in happy droves, some from the timeless *kucha*s and *katra*s of Chandni Chowk, others from the *mahal*s, *sarai*s and *haveli*s of Jama Masjid, and yet others from central and south Delhi.

Moti was built in a blend of Victorian and Mughal architecture, its half-dome a standout symbol before a more utilitarian, less ornate style was adopted after it screened *Barsaat* (initially released in 1949) in the late 1950s. It had been a theatre until the 1938 takeover by distributor CB Desai. He did away with the stage and side wings and the ridiculously low admission fare of 4 and 7 *anna*s; people had to have at least a rupee to purchase a ticket. Projection equipment was imported from Germany in 1940.

Keeping in mind the high-profile audience, Moti even played Hollywood films in the pre-Partition days and in the early years of Independence. These were usually slotted for the Sunday noon shows, On some weekends, movies from across the world were also shown, including the best of Japanese, Iranian and French films. By the late 1970s, these films gave way to an occasional offering from Indian parallel cinema but that was for a very niche clientele.

Even those brought up on a staple diet of Hindi mainstream cinema didn't get a reason to complain at Moti as the hall had regular screenings of all films released under the RK banner. There was also a special association with Manmohan Desai, the man who believed people came to watch a film to escape the grim realities of life. From Bimal Roy's neo-realism to Manmohan Desai's escapism, Moti showed all kinds of films, something that endeared the hall to many.

A film that released at the then air-cooled Moti was immediately put in a separate bracket. Especially memorable was the scene at the release of Sohrab Modi-Mehtaab's *Jhansi ki Rani* in 1956; the queue stretched all the way to Sunehri Masjid and Fawwara, leading to Old Delhi Railway Station. The film was uniquely promoted: there was a procession of guards in Chandni Chowk every day, dressed in *churidar* pyjamas and carrying swords to signify the latest release on the Indian revolutionary. In such small but unforgettable ways, Moti connected with both cinegoers and filmmakers. Raj Kapoor was one of the big names who would visit Moti for the premier of his films, staying at Imperial Hotel on Janpath and arriving at the hall in a simple Ambassador as he was not comfortable with big cars. With him would be an entire entourage, including Shanker-Jaikishen, Hasrat Jaipuri, VP Sathe, Khwaja Ahmed Abbas and Radhu Karmakar. All of them would be at Moti, like Raj Kapoor's extended family, on the first day of the release of films like *Awara* (1951), *Jagte Raho* (1956), *Barsaat* (1949), *Jis Desh Mein Ganga Behti Hai* (1960), *Sangam* (1964) and *Mera Naam Joker* (1970). When *Awara* was being screened, two queues would form at the exit turnstiles—one would snake out of the hall towards Dariba Kalan, the jewellery market nearby, and the other would proceed towards Fawwara. People waited for hours to get a ticket for the film, for any show. Similar enthusiasm marked the arrival of Mehboob's *Aan* (1952) here.

Later, in the 1970s and '80s, Moti became the chosen venue for Manmohan Desai for releasing his big budget films. *Desh Premee* (1982) had a stupendous run here, as did *Coolie* (1983) and *Mard* (1985), the former especially significant as it was the film in which Amitabh Bachchan had a near fatal injury during a shot opposite Puneet Issar. Even his son Ketan Desai's *Allahrakha* (1986) was released here, the film's name derived from the name of the bird in *Coolie*.

In those times, other halls also played A-grade films, with many of them enjoying long runs on their screens. But among the halls of Chandni Chowk, Moti stood out for its class and sensitivity to its audience. Till about a decade ago, it was the preferred address for family audiences, who rarely went to

Kumar next door, while the Muslim gentry in the area mostly patronised Jagat near Jama Masjid. Cutting across religious, cultural and regional barriers, people flocked to Moti, where the films were selected with extreme care. The management kept in mind the prevailing social norms even while selecting the billboards and set-ups, usually placed a day before the release of a film, on Thursday evening. At the Chandni Chowk entrance, prominence was given to the hero, with all other actors reduced to miniatures. No skin show was allowed; the hoardings didn't mislead the masses to attract more people to the film. For instance, the hoardings of *Jis Desh Mein Ganga Behti Hai* were all in black and white, tasteful and sober, with no character portrayed in colour to avoid giving out a misleading impression. In 1979, when K Viswanath's *Sargam* released at Moti, the hoardings showed Rishi Kapoor with the famous *dafli* from the 'Dafliwale, Dafli Baja' song. As for the heroine, Jaya Prada, only her face was captured, with special stills procured from the filmmaker as local artists were not familiar with the face of the debutante. Inside the hall, cut-outs of the heroine's dance shots were put up, accentuating her silhouette but without any revealing clothes. The idea was to appeal to the audience, not to titillate. It worked. The film started on a low key but gained in popularity as its music hit the charts and its dance numbers became a rage.

Similar care was taken at the release of *Coolie,* with boards on the hall's façade showing Amitabh Bachchan with a load of suitcases on his head. Inside, there were specific hoardings of the fight scene in which Bachchan got injured. Rishi Kapoor, the film's second hero, was dwarfed in comparison. Black-marketeers had a field day on all such occasions, and cries of *'2 wala 10, 5 wala 25'* (Ticket of Rs 2 for Rs 10, of Rs 5 for Rs 25) frequently rent the air. They would often book chunks of tickets in advance when the plans opened on Monday and sell tickets on the weekend.

Since the theatre was first converted into a talkie, Moti forged a bond with cinegoers across generations. As a talkie, it opened with *Sant Gyaneshwar* (1940), the precursor to other mythological movies like *Bhakta Raj* (1943), *Ram Rajya* (1943) and *Har Har Mahadev* (1950), each of which had a fine run at the hall in the early years. Many movie buffs, carried away by the devotion on screen, brought incense and marigold, and offered these before the set-ups near the entrance.

In latter years, Moti's proximity to Lajpat Rai Market spawned other businesses. The market, known for shops selling audio-visual discs and cassettes, was also home to many bands which played in the city on weddings and birthdays. Whenever a film with super-hit music played at Moti, the bands would gather outside the hall and play tunes from the film, the idea being not only to get a few rupees from the more generous visitors but also to showcase their skills in the hope that they would be hired by the wealthier movie watchers.

Moti was good as long as it lasted, and it lasted close to 50 years. Slowly, however, its fate nosedived. In the 1980s, the gentry of Old Delhi started leaving the Walled City for more spacious avenues elsewhere in the city. As a result, family audiences, Moti's main strength, began thinning. Partly because of the beginning of this migration, a film like *Naya Kadam* (1984), director K Raghavendra Rao's take on illiteracy in our villages, collected only modest numbers here though the film did better elsewhere.

The people who were left began veering off towards the state-of-the-art technology that multiplexes offered. Chandni Chowk was reduced to a mere commercial hub frequented by businessmen from smaller towns who would occasionally catch a movie for a few rupees. Blue-collar workers, shop attendants and rickshaw-pullers would give them company. Ticket sales indicated they did not have the eye or the patience to watch a Guru Dutt or K Viswanath saga unfold; they wanted their entertainment in an instant in a language they spoke. Moti's management read the writing on the wall, and out went *Pyaasa* (1957) and *Sargam* (1979), making way for Bhojpuri films, among them *Sasura Bada Paise Wala* (2003)and *Panditji Batai Na Biyah Ka Hue!* (2005), and dubbed versions of Tamil and Telugu potboilers such as *Ek Naya Tiger*.

The show goes on, but the spotlight has shifted to a different category of films and patrons. Moti, often called 'Pattharwalon ka talkies' due to its proximity to the stone engravers' market opposite the historic Red Fort, continues to mark time.

14 KUMAR, Chandni Chowk

Kumar, with its black marble floors and steel railings at the entrance, was a tasteful understatement for those who found Majestic too ornate or Moti too grand. With a façade that was easy on the eye, it stood at the gateway of Bhagirath Place, its slanting roof a testimony to the days when most halls in Uttar Pradesh were similarly built. It seemed to be a quiet oasis amid the clamour of Chandni Chowk, but when it came to screening the big films, Kumar had to wait its turn while Moti and Majestic had the pick of the best. Yet, Kumar played pleasing films that appealed to the masses, and held some housefull first day-first shows—crowds preferred to watch a new film on the Friday of its release, the banner and the production house being immaterial. The night shows used to be a hit with men, who would gather here at the end of a long day's work. The matinee and evening shows did not draw much of a crowd as most patrons were busy earning their wages for the day.

But the location of this cinema hall posed a unique problem. Adjacent to it was a public toilet where men would frequently queue up, most of them on their way to the ever-busy Bhagirath Place market to buy electrical goods and pharmaceuticals. Offering neither privacy nor hygiene, the toilet stank, keeping hundreds away from Kumar even when a film like *Chhote Nawab* (1961) or *Qaidi* (1957) was screened. In the late 1980s, when the cinema started screening movies which did not cater to family audiences, the management found an ingenious way of using the lavatory. At eye level of the visitor to the toilet, two film posters would be pasted: one of the film coming up the following week and the other of the one playing in the morning show. That was the time films with a good mix of action, songs and dances like SS Ravichandra's *Qaidi* (1984), K Raghavendra Rao's *Himmatwala* (1983) and *Hoshiyaar* (1985) did good business.

Kumar did make something of a name for itself, providing predominantly male cinegoers who were not so well off, memorable films at affordable rates. At times, even niche films found space on its screens. Its admission rates, which were merely *'aath anna'* in the 1970s, meant even daily wagers could watch a film here while Majestic and Moti remained out of bounds. It became the regular address for Padmalaya films and later for the movies of KC Bokadia, briefly hailed for his Midas touch in the 1980s.

Once inside the hall, the audience that braved its stinking surroundings, enjoyed its air-cooled comfort, its screen and audio system that provided a rich viewing experience. Besides regular crowd-pleasers, Kumar also showed films like *Daag* (1952), the Dilip Kumar-starrer that ticked all the boxes at the turnstiles, and *Raat Ke Andhere Mein* (1969) with Mohammed Rafi's timeless hit, 'Agar Bewafa Tujhko Pehchaan Jaate'. HS Rawail's *Pocket Maar* (1956) arrived as a re-run and stayed on for a full six weeks. These films, which convinced families to visit Kumar, helped the cinema widen its appeal, but the 'working-class' tag did not go away completely. Thanks to a judicious film selection, though, Kumar was able to tap serious audiences as well.

Like most others, this hall was initially a venue for staging plays. In the 1940s, when it turned into a cinema hall, the word 'talkies' was added to its name and locals would call it Kumar Talkies. It stayed that way till the cinema downed its shutters about a decade ago. But this closure was not permanent; it rose again as Abhishek Cineplex with reduced seats and increased admission rates.

Times have changed vastly. There is a conspicuously busy McDonald's outlet. The entire area could be mistaken for just a big eatery. But step a little to the side and the Bhagirath Place market is still there, chaotic as ever. The toilet is there too, separated by a few steps from the staircase of the now fully air-conditioned Abhishek. The steps are of green granite and the fare on offer ranges from potboilers to the occasional seedy flick. The giant billboards which once covered its façade or garish films posters on tripods in the lobby of the past are now replaced by banners. Today, there is simply the name of the film, along with its certification. For a better-informed audience now, perhaps that suffices.

15 MAJESTIC, Fawwara, Chandni Chowk

In one of the ironies of life, Majestic hosted two radically different kinds of audiences: families with children in tow, and men looking for seedy entertainment. The former, mainly the Chandni Chowk gentry, were attracted by top directors like Yash Chopra, Nasir Hussain, HS Rawail, Manoj Kumar and SK Kapur. Until about 20 years ago, with its timeless *havelis*, *kuchas* and *mohallas*, Chandni Chowk used to be the residence of noted businessmen, freedom fighters, poets, descendants of *mansabdars* and well-heeled nawabs and pandits. Every now and then, these families would frequent Majestic to watch A-grade offerings from Hindi cinema's dream merchants. The advance bookings would open on Monday for a film to be released the next Friday. By afternoon, balcony seats for the first week would all be taken as many families reserved seats in blocks. General Talkies, the company which ran the hall, chose films with care, making sure they catered to the tastes of the gentry. In fact, as the company ran cinema halls in Lucknow, Kanpur, Saharanpur and Meerut too, it was able to strike a good bargain with most top-notch banners and hence scored over Kumar, one of its closest rivals. Films chosen with such care usually paid dividends as they ran for many weeks and attracted housefull audiences. Among them were *Deewar* (1975), *Dus Numbri* (1976), *Yaadon ki Baraat*

(1973), *Pehchan* (1970) and *Upkar* (1967). One of its finest achievements was the stellar run of *Mahal* (1949), with its evergreen song, 'Ayega Aanewala'. People used to come to watch this Khemchand Prakash classic at Majestic from far and near, for weeks on end, with many inviting friends from other parts of the city to watch the film as its sound system was better than that of many other halls. The man himself, though, did not live to see *Mahal*'s popularity.

If Majestic became a popular avenue for watching films and meeting near and dear ones with *Mahal*, in the early 1980s, it charted its way into history with the Sanjay Dutt-starrer *Mera Faisla* (1984). When Majestic was showing the film in daily four shows, Jubilee, next door, was wooing the Dutt fans with billboards of *Main Awara Hoon* (1983), and Kumar sought to do the same with posters of another Dutt film, *Bekaraar* (1983). The posters were put up on the wall of the public toilet outside the hall.

The hall's proximity to places of worship—Gurdwara Sisganj Sahib and Sunehri Masjid were within earshot—meant that it showed neat and clean family fare that also attracted a colourful audience. Homosexuals were said to frequent a public lavatory near the bus stop in front of the cinema. The open air lavatory was like a meeting point for homosexual men in the area and many would stand for long hours waiting for a possible friend. Once they found a friend, they would head straight to Majestic's turnstiles and purchase tickets for the stalls (till the late 1970s, the stall tickets could be purchased for less than a rupee whereas balcony prices were double). In the rear section, as revealed by OP Katyal, an immensely popular man from the film distribution market nearby, the men who had just met a few minutes earlier would get cosy even as people around them stayed oblivious to what was going on. Majestic rather than Jubilee was preferred for such activities because at the latter, there were hardly any family audiences. At Majestic, the families stayed in the balcony area and most of the staff tried to make their stay comfortable. The stalls, hence relatively less policed, provided a safer option. Thus, two segments of society gathered under the same roof to watch films, with their areas tacitly demarcated.

Like many others, the cinema hall that began as a theatre in pre-Independence days, had a location befitting its name. For Jubilee, you had to walk a few metres from Fawwara. Kumar (now Abhishek) had too narrow a façade to grab instant attention and Moti, for all its grandeur, could be approached better from Lala Lajpat Rai Market. But Majestic could not be missed: right in the middle of the Mughal street with the famous Bhai Mati Dass Chowk or Fawwara in front and Gurdwara Sisganj across the road. The deep niches, alcoves, *chhatri*s and *jharokha*s gave Majestic an appearance which took you back in time. Inside the hall, it was much the same with two parallel walls tending to meet at one end where statues of Radha and Krishna adorned the walls.

The *chhajja* behind the first floor balcony was utilised for more than one purpose. It acted as an advertisement vehicle for forthcoming films at the hall with giant billboards placed across the façade, overlooking the busy street. Regular patrons looked forward to new hoardings every Thursday. For unlettered folks, the hoardings were a signal of the next film and giant cut-outs of big stars gave the name of the film away. As the hall, with about 750 seats, often played films for a long stretch, some hoardings fell victim to the weather. The much-talked about *Deewaar* (1975), which completed a silver jubilee here, had its hoardings blown away by a thunderstorm within two weeks of the film's release and an artist had to be called to fix Amitabh Bachchan's popular '*billa* number 786'. Something similar happened with Manoj Kumar's cut-out from the film *Dus Numbri* (1976). Its digit in the title along with the hero's goggles had to be restored. A half-broken board or a faded one was taken as a sign by patrons that the film was not doing well, so the producer or exhibitor was not ready to spend any money on it. Such was the case with Rishi Kapoor's *Bade Dil Wala* (1983) and Rajiv Kapoor's *Ek Jaan Hain Hum* (1983), and Rajesh Khanna's *Agar Tum Na Hote* (1983). The films did not exactly create box-office records and the hall had to make do with smaller set-ups than usual after the initial big ones toppled over.

Every Republic Day, though, the billboards were cleared so that patrons and guests could take in the parade from the cinema. Even as soldiers marched past and troupes from various states exhibited their talent, people would sit on the *chhajja* of Majestic and watch the glory of independent India unfold before their eyes. There was no morning show on such occasions and the cinema hall happily played hosts to patriots.

In September 1993, Majestic made way for a Sikh museum in deference to the wishes of the large Sikh community in the vicinity. Majestic in life, it was graceful in departure.

16 JUBILEE, Old Delhi Railway Station

It's 7 o'clock on a freezing winter morning. The fog has barely lifted and there is not much movement on the road. The only noise is from a bell at a temple under a peepul tree, located outside the Central Bank. At the historic Gurdwara Sisganj Sahib on Fawwara Road, a dozen or so Sikh women, most of them in white, have their heads draped with *dupatta*s and shawls. Their lips quiver as they recite the name of the divine.

A little distance from the gurdwara are young men in a queue barely in their 20s. Most look like they are blue-collar workers. A security guard tries his best to put in a semblance of order but he is fighting a losing battle. The men reach the booking counter only to find it closed and still two hours away from issuing the day's first ticket. But that does not deter them from their purpose—to book a ticket for the Sanjay Dutt-starrer *Main Awara Hoon* (1983), hours before the sun lights up the hall's slanting slabs. For the moment, they have to make do with the giant billboards perilously placed on the first floor of the hall. *'Bhai, isne kya gaadi chalai thhi* Rocky *mein'* (Brother, how he rode the bike in *Rocky*), a fan remembers.

Of course, not all of them are here for Sanjay Dutt. A handful want to see Raj Babbar—*'arre Dilli ka hai'* (He is from Delhi). *'Heroinay nayee hai'*, (The heroines are new) another chips in. 'Heroines' mean Rati Agnihotri and Jaya Prada, both relatively new to the industry at the time. They are almost dwarfed on the billboards.

These were the scenes at Old Delhi's Jubilee cinema hall. In the early days, it had Majestic cinema on its left and just a few metres down the road stood Kumar and Moti. Each had their distinguished patrons and Jubilee, over nearly the last three decades of its existence, catered to daily wagers and others who sweated it out for a living. After *Main Awara Hoon*, Jubilee played Girdhar Art International's *Be-Abroo* (1983), a film that raised quite a storm in film circles. At Jubilee, though, the most prominent sound was of the cash registers ringing. The 1983 winter release was initially booked for four weeks but went on to have a seven-week run due to persistent demand.

The hall had a specific purpose. Majestic, almost opposite the gurdwara, had to keep in mind the sentiments of the devout who frequented the area. Moti also had a reputation to protect. Most top-notch distributors opted for either of these two cinemas in Chandni Chowk and the crumbs were left for Kumar. Jubilee, though, had to wait for the middle and lower rung banners and distributors. A film that could not be screened at Majestic because it was booked in advance was often screened here. The hall, with a capacity of 663 seats, made a killing as it played housefull shows from noon to night. With a mixture of action flicks and others with a degree of nudity, Jubilee catered to the whims of men removed from their families, eager to see their fantasies played out on screen in the anonymity of the metropolis.

Contrary to its name, not too many films had a jubilee run here. The young men who were its regular patrons hated monotony and the kind of extended runs that films enjoyed at Novelty, not too far away. Not for them the serenity of

Majestic which usually dished out family fare. Jubilee was 'their' hall; films had to come and go fast. They had to come loaded with action, a Silk Smitha number or even scenes of criminal assault which were, unfortunately, often shot with the purpose of titillation. Ajay Devgn's bike stunt in *Phool aur Kaante* (1991), which enjoyed a six-week run here, was lapped up eagerly. Even the cut-outs of Sunny Deol put up before the release of *Angarakshak* (1995), caused such a frenzy that they came tumbling down. The cut-outs had zero-watt bulbs around the hero's head to give him an aura as the masses' avenging angel! These, however, could not help the film in having a great run.

Occasionally, a distributor would play smart with his films and evoke a sense of nostalgia among the male patrons, many of whom stayed in bachelors' accommodations in the vicinity or simply slept at their place of work. Tarachand Barjatya decided to play the much-lauded *Nadiya ke Paar* (initially released in 1982) in its golden jubilee week here. It spoke the language of the audience and the ploy worked.

Incidentally, the men made their own 'arrangement' with the ushers and guards at the hall. Whenever a song would play, some men would step out to go to the toilet while others would step out of the hall itself and bargain for peanuts or fruit *chaat* with the vendors outside. A few minutes later, they would be right back inside, no questions asked. Those were days with fewer security concerns.

Jubilee closed down in 1998 due to safety issues, when the authorities were clamping down on all cinema halls in the city after the unfortunate Uphaar tragedy. Jubilee did not have an overhead tank for dousing flames in case of fire and so did not meet the safety requirement. After toying with the idea of giving a facelift to the hall, General Talkies, whose five-year lease was expiring soon after the ruling, decided against extending the lease. Thus, the air-cooled Jubilee, which had started as Radha Theatre before Independence, met a quiet end. Gone with the hall were tales of the days when Jubilee played films like Nitin Bose's *Mashaal* (1950), Roop Shorey's *Dholak* (1951), Nanabhai Bhatt's *Sindbad the Sailor* (1952), and the day Manna Dey visited it and was virtually forced by the audience to sing a line or two of 'Upar Gagan Vishal.'

Nobody knew back in the late '70s that when Shakeel Badayuni's song from *Mela* (1948), which played at Jubilee in the morning shows, 'Yeh Zindagi Ke Mele Duniya Mein Kam Na Honge, Afsos Hum Na Honge' would prove a harbinger of days to come.

17 NOVELTY, Old Delhi Railway Station

The timeless charm of Novelty, a cinema at a stone's throw from Old Delhi Railway Station, attracted a dedicated clientele for each of its daily four shows. Novelty ran just one film a year or at the most two, as most movies that graced its screen went on to complete a silver or golden jubilee. Not just movie-watchers, this cinema was the preferred abode for the first-day, first-show screening by a host of banners, filmmakers and stars like the house of Gemini, the family of the Barjatyas, Manoj Kumar, Dharmendra, Rajesh Khanna and Sunil Dutt.

Due to its lofty status, the hall's authorities could make decisions that seemed completely absurd at the time, like turning down GP Sippy's *Sholay* in 1975 because they were happy with the collections of Dulal Guha's *Pratiggya* (released in June, 1975). Eventually, *Sholay* did come to Novelty but not without a hint of controversy. The film had opened at Ajanta cinema without making too much noise at the box office and hence it did not seem to be a very smart idea to bring in a movie that was far from being a blockbuster. It came to Novelty after a four-week run at Ajanta, and surpassed the collections of *Pratiggya,* going on to have a record run of 75 weeks at the 929-seat hall.

Novelty began as a theatre called Elphinstone and was renamed when Jagat Narain Seth took over in 1935. It rapidly gathered a reputation for playing films chosen with such care that they usually set box-office records. Going back to pre-Partition days, when *Rattan* (1944) and *Anmol Ghadi* (1946) played to housefull shows, right up to *Sholay* and the rest, not a single movie had a short run. There are instances of Novelty's famous advance booking, which opened on Monday with advertisements in local dailies, being the scene of unruly crowds. Usually within a couple of hours of the counters opening, the balcony tickets for the first week would be sold out!

The cinema had a dedicated clientele for each of the daily four shows. The noon show was frequented by the university crowd, though the sex workers from GB Road would occasionally be there too. The matinee show was preferred by ladies who arrived after completing household chores. The night was for families, with local shopkeepers heading home in the evening, having dinner and then bringing their wives to the cinema. The evening show was the poorest in attendance with the market around it closing down and not enough residents around to fill the hall. But that was a minor aberration.

The admission rates at Novelty began at a measly 10 *anna*s and went up to a maximum of Rs 3. These were revised only after 1971 but business was not affected by the hike. If *Sholay* completed a 75-week run, Manoj Kumar's much-talked about *Roti, Kapda aur Makaan* (1974) ran for a year, as did *Kranti* which was released in February, 1981. Such was the *Kranti* craze among fans that the owners themselves were virtually locked out of the hall. BR Chopra's *The Burning Train* (1980), starring Dharmendra, Vinod Khanna, Jeetendra, Hema Malini and Parvin Babi, worked better here than at most other places, at least partly because Novelty's audiences preferred star-driven sagas. Oddly, K Asif's *Mughal-e-Azam,* released in

1960 ran for only six weeks at Novelty. In fact, it was only on Asif's request that the hall played the film. The dacoit drama, *Mujhe Jeene Do* (1963), which did roaring business at Novelty, grabbed attention for more daring reasons. Film lore has it that dacoits themselves came to watch the film here, though as honourable lovers of cinema, purchasing their tickets, watching it and leaving.

At times, things went way beyond expectations. In the week that Noor Jehan's *Anmol Ghadi* (1946) completed its silver jubilee, the line of fans outside the hall reached up to 100 metres. The legendary singer-actor's popularity knew no bounds and super-hit songs like 'Awaaz De Kahan Hai' and 'Jawan Hai Mohabbat' attracted one and all. Similar adulation and hysteria marked the arrival of *Rajputani* (1946) and *Dillagi* (1949), notable for its memorable song 'Main Tera Chand Tu Meri Chandni'. Such was its popularity that youngsters walked all the way from Chitli Qabar near Jama Masjid to the hall to watch the film.

Zohrabai Ambalewali, who sang 'Akhiyan Milake Jiya Bharmake Chale Nahin Jaana' for *Rattan* (1944) ensured a repeat audience for that film. It was this ability to get repeat viewers that helped Novelty notch up a first for a North Indian cinema hall. In 1948, it screened Gemini's *Chandralekha* (1948), the first South Indian film to be dubbed into Hindi. The film did such good business that from there on, Gemini would call up the proprietor about six months before the release of any new film to book the hall.

A little later came *Andaz* (1949), the Raj Kapoor-Dilip Kumar-Nargis starrer for whose premiere the superstars paid a visit. Dilip Kumar's *Leader* (1964) was screened in the mid-'60s with which the management embraced the 70 mm culture, calling it a wall-to-wall screen.

Besides Dilip Kumar or Raj Kapoor-starrers, Novelty became the favourite destination for Amitabh Bachchan-starrers. Sultan Ahmed's biggest hit, *Ganga ki Saugandh* (1978), starring Bachchan and Rekha, completed a silver jubilee here. Prakash Mehra's *Sharaabi* (1984) went a step further—the Bachchan-Jaya Prada starrer not only raked in the riches at the box office, but increased the profits of the cinema's sweepers too. Bappi Lahiri's music and songs like 'Mujhe Naulakha Mangade Re' and 'De De Pyar De' would enthuse the audience so much they would throw coins at the screen, which were collected by the sweepers at the end of every show. Not so successful was the screening of Kunal Goswami-Sridevi's *Kalakaar* (1983).

However, the demographic profile of Old Delhi was undergoing subtle changes all along. The posh nawabs, the well-off businessmen and *mansabdar*s had started trickling out of the Walled City to areas less congested around Preet Vihar and Nizamuddin, and with them went the balcony crowd at Novelty. A little later, when the local authorities clamped down on small industries operating out of residences, the working class began shuffling out too. Only students and passengers from the nearby railway station remained as patrons. Housefull shows became a mere memory. And big banners were no longer affordable. The hall tried to stay in business for a while by playing smaller films or re-runs of big banners but slowly lost its charm before quietly fading away from public consciousness.

18 WEST END, Sadar Bazar

The Chitnis family owned two theatres in Old Delhi, West End and Excelsior, both of which carved out a distinct reputation. Excelsior concentrated on Muslim socials while West End played mainstream films with a clear preference for the biggest banners. In the morning show slot, the two halls willingly inter-changed their fare—a film that showed at Excelsior one week went to West End the following week and vice-versa. It helped viewers too; if they missed the film at one place, they caught it at the other the next week.

Like most cinema houses in Old Delhi, the 654-seater West End started off in 1935 as a theatre. At that time, it staged Parsi plays and was identified as a popular hangout for the upper crust of society. However, when talkies became a rage with the arrival of *Alam Ara* (1931), West End switched to showing films. Its exteriors were changed immediately to give it the look of a cinema but the insides remained largely the same. In 1938, it became a full-fledged cinema hall, showing films like Mehboob Khan's *Aurat* (1940) and Sohrab Modi's *Sikandar* (1941). In the years to follow, both films played a crucial role in the way West End shaped up as a cinema hall. *Aurat* inspired Mehboob Khan's timeless saga *Mother India* (1957), which opened here as well and *Sikandar,* with the legendary Prithviraj Kapoor in the title role, did so well here that it paved the way for the beginning of the Kapoor clan's love affair with the cinema hall. Raj Kapoor, in particular, made sure that all his films found a platform here. As a result, Moti in Chandni Chowk and West End in Sadar both showed the same film, as well as the greatly valued Regal in Connaught Place, which too used to open regularly with Raj Kapoor's films.

Raj Kapoor's bond with West End went back a long way. He used to arrive from Imperial, make a stopover at Moti and then be at West End in time to watch the first show of his films. It used to be immaculately timed. Moti would start the first show about half an hour before West End, which gave the star time enough to make his presence felt at both places. The evenings were reserved for Regal. At West End, every time his car stopped at the hall, many queued up just to see and touch him. Often, he had to use the side entrance along with the manager of the hall to avoid the crowds. Over a period of time, a special entrance was made for VVIPs.

Raj Kapoor loved West End's unique architecture, which stemmed from its theatre days. Until its renovation in 1958, West End had two wings in the balcony and the audience would sit in two sections with the space between the wings left bare. The lowest admission fare was 63 paise and the highest touched Rs 2. Predictably, most of Raj Kapoor's films like *Jagte Raho* (1956), *Shree 420* (1955) and *Mera Naam Joker* (1970) did fine business here for many weeks though *Sangam* (1964) attracted huge crowds for much longer. *Bobby* (1973) did excellent business too, the film having opened here alongside Regal, Moti, Chanakya, Amba, Vishal and Sapna.

Dilip Kumar's films were popular as well. *Aan*, India's first truly international release, was shown here in 1952. Some locals even claim the film's international premiere was held here. For BR Chopra's *Naya Daur* (1957), the cinema had a long queue of young men in their 20s trying to replicate Dilip Kumar's hairstyle and mannerisms from the song, 'Ude Jab Jab Zulfein', waiting to get in on the first weekend. Back in the 1950s and '60s, West End, with its Victorian architecture, aesthetic sensibilities and choice of films, was an attractive option for an outing. With films like Sohrab Modi's *Raj Hath* (1956), Devendra Goel's *Ek Phool Do Maali* (1969), Guru Dutt's *Kaagaz Ke Phool* (1959), Yash Chopra's *Dhool ka Phool (*1959) and, in the 1970s, SK Kapur's *Apna Khoon* (1978) under its belt, West End became known as a cinema for housefull movies.

These films enabled West End to appeal to family audiences. Before them, West End often attracted the devout with mythologicals. Till the late '50s, mythological films as a genre were quite popular with fans and in the '60s, when most central halls failed to provide a screening to *Shankar-Sita-Ansuya* (1965), West End stepped in, successfully showing the film for weeks on end in 1965. The film made good collections like *Hanuman Janam* (1954) had a decade earlier, attracting not just men, women and children but, as many liked to believe, even the 'monkey god'. One seat was kept 'reserved' for a monkey who would come unannounced and quietly occupy a seat in the balcony, watch the film till the end and depart with the rest. He disturbed nobody.

Not all films were accepted by everyone, though. When action movies like *Daku Mangal Singh* (1966), *Samson* (1974) and *Rustom* (1982) played, the audience was made up mostly of men.

But for more than 50 years, West End was among the prized halls with its convenient location, good banners, clean environment and affordable rates. However, the onslaught of satellite television affected its business, with most patrons preferring to stay indoors and watch movies. This was followed by the heightened competition and escalating prices for big-budget movies. The morning shows stopped in the mid-1990s and West End was reduced to waiting for leftovers.

The present holds out little hope but the past continues to play the loveliest songs, reminding you of Faiz Ahmed Faiz's gentle *ghazal*, immortalised by Noor Jahan, 'Mujh Se Pehli Si Mohabbat Mere Mehboob Na Maang.'

19 MINERVA, Mori Gate

Blessed with a quaint charm and unique ways of attracting patrons, Minerva, unlike most talkies of Old Delhi, had a chequered history, its moments of achievement interspersed with periods of denial and dejection. It shared its lofty name with its namesake in Bombay where GP Sippy's *Sholay* (1975) played for an inordinately long time. Delhi's very own Minerva, though a baby of Sohrab Modi, failed to convince the distributors to even release *Sholay* here; that honour went to Plaza and Amba, with Novelty close by showing the film a little more than a month after its release. Truly, Minerva was often left to scrounge for crumbs.

In pre-Independence times, Minerva used to be a theatre called Roxy, admired by many for the Parsi plays it would stage. Sohrab Modi, credited with bringing Parsi theatre to the common man, was responsible for transforming the arena into a cinema hall when he took over in the early 1960s. He renamed it after the banner—Minerva Movietone—he had established in 1936. Around that time, Goa was about to be formally inducted into the Indian Union and distributors in Delhi thought it ideal to rouse patriotic feelings. They revived Modi's 20-year-old film *Sikandar* (1961), which was based on the conquest of Alexander in 326 BC.

The early days, though, had been encouraging. Besides Prithviraj Kapoor's *Sikandar,* it showed Mehboob Khan's

Aurat (1940), both landmark films in the annals of Hindi cinema. Minerva's best moment came when Dilip Kumar's *Gunga Jumna* (1961) completed a silver jubilee here. The film's star cast did not make it to the hall for the screening but the occasion nevertheless warranted a celebration. In the first show of the 25th week, sweets were distributed to the audience. Its success was also boom time for black-marketeers who would sell a ticket priced at Rs 2.50 for Rs 15 and two tickets at the concessional rate of Rs 25.

In 1971, *Johnny Mera Naam* also ran at Minerva for 25 weeks, a laudable achievement as Golcha was screening *Anand* (1971)at the same time. Two years later, Yash Chopra›s *Daag* (1973) celebrated its silver jubilee here alongside Chanakya and New Amar but this wasn't as unexpected an achievement as the former had only a single screening a day while the latter was not considered a prestigious hall.

. But by the late '70s and '80s, Minerva was reduced to a poor cousin of the more preferred halls in Chandni Chowk. It was always second even in a two-horse race with Ritz next door. For years, the hall was caught in a no man's land, unsure whether to appeal to the discerning viewers or the masses, the middle class or the working class. Most cinema houses in the Walled City had their faithful heroes, directors and distributors but these were absent in Minerva's case.

Some nuanced films aside, Minerva was left to pick up the scraps, which essentially meant *masala* entertainers with little artistic pretension. In the late '70s and early '80s, it showed films like *Daku Aur Jawan* (1978) and *Sitamgar (1985)* and before that in the mid-'60s, it played *Daku Mangal Singh* (1966), an out-and-out action film. Even though Ritz, next door, was showing *Mera Saaya* (1966) at the same time and films like *Dil Ne Phir Yaaad Kiya* (1966) and *Love in Tokyo*

(1966) were doing stupendous business, *Daku Mangal Singh* outlasted them all.

Action movies, the kind that attracted housefull shows on the first day, were also screened at Minerva. Movies starring Dharmendra, Shatrughan Sinha, Vinod Khanna, Mithun Chakraborty and Rajinikanth found takers among young men. *Boxer* (1984), *Insaaf Kaun Karega* (1984), *Insaniyat Ke Dushman* (1987) and *Hathkadi* (1982) garnered good numbers, helping the hall keep its head above water.

However, the management of Minerva had not always aimed to simply survive. In the 1970s, it took some innovative steps to overcome the challenge of bigger banners, and not through the usual methods of radio publicity or big hoardings at traffic intersections. It relied on word of mouth. A film like *Deen Aur Imaan* (1979) helped woo the young men of the Walled City, studying to be *maulanas*, who often came to Minerva for the night show as its distance from the historic Jama Masjid meant the community elders did not know of their whereabouts. A door to the balcony from the rear side was informally 'reserved' for these would-be clerics. They played safe too, staying inside the hall during the interval to avoid being seen. Soon, the monopoly of men was broken with burqa-clad women from Ballimaran and Chitli Qabar. It was easier for them to come here than go to Jagat where the chances of being seen by a neighbourhood elder and thus inviting ignominy were higher.

Around this time, Minerva, along with Ritz became quite a favourite of women from the Walled City, who would gather at Purdah Bagh, the women's only park in Daryaganj, and take a cycle rickshaw to the hall. This was again a ruse to hoodwink the conservative sections of society who thought it improper for women from decent families to watch films at a cinema.

However, a movie hall's business cannot be built on a stealthy audience. Gradually, as the area came to be known for its automobile spare part shops, the middle-class patrons started staying away.

Almost a decade after Sohrab Modi breathed his last, the hall closed down in 1993, among the earliest ones to call it a day.

20 RITZ, Kashmere Gate

Among the more glamorous halls of Delhi, Ritz was first called Capital in 1932 and renamed Ritz only in 1942 with the screening of director PC Barua's Hindi film *Jawab* (1942) on 1st November, 1942. The cinema started amid predictions of doom. Though Ritz was adjacent to the Inter-State Bus Terminus (ISBT), it also lay on the path to Nigambodh Ghat, a crematorium. Matters of bereavement and entertainment could not co-exist, many argued. Life had to lose to death, they felt, so the cinema would have to fold up. *'Agar ye cinema chal gaya to Nigambodh Ghat par bhi chal jayega'*, (If this cinema works, then one at Nigambodh Ghat could work too) a trade hand told Jagat Narain Seth, its proprietor. Seth, though, did not listen to their doomsday predictions and set about establishing a hall that made a name for itself over time.

Ritz played A-grade Hindi films to family audiences who came from far and wide to the hall. It offered boxes for a family. Like at Jagat, well-heeled families would book these sections and enjoy the privilege of watching the film on the big screen in privacy. Among the audience were also women viewers from Old Delhi. Back in the 1950s and even up to the '70s, women from respectable families were either not supposed to watch films, or watch them alone. A few die-hard fans in the Walled City found a solution: they would not watch a film at a hall closest to their *haveli, mohalla, kucha*. But they were not confident enough to go out too far either, so they opted for halls in the vicinity of Jama Masjid and Chandni Chowk. On the one side, Golcha and Delite cashed in on this, as did Minerva and Ritz on the other. Ritz, with its private box, gave them greater freedom and safety. Women would gather in groups at Purdah Bagh near Daryganj and then proceed to Ritz in tongas or cycle-rickshaws. The Ritz management under proprietor VN Seth reserved seats exclusively for them. They paid Rs 1.25 though the stall tickets were priced as low as 5 and 10 *anna*s.

Keeping in mind the profile of the audience, Ritz usually concentrated on neat and clean family films though occasionally films with skin show were shown too: these films were for the wayfarers, the travellers, the crowds which boarded inter-state buses from the terminus close by. A large space was reserved for putting up hoardings of the current and forthcoming films, even taking care to write the week of the film's run at the hall. While it played top mainstream films in daily four shows, its morning show was the most prized one for several reasons. Art films made their presence felt here, as did Hollywood movies. Even controversial films ahead of their times like *Mann Ka Aangan* (1979) had a fine run in the morning slot. Incidentally, morning shows used to be a weekly affair till 1968, with screenings only on Sunday. Then they became a daily feature.

It also screened the occasional adult film. In the 1950s and the '60s, most films with an 'adults only' certificate used to flaunt the 'A' sign in bold fonts. While this was done partly to keep away younger cinegoers, the major aim of the display was to titillate the audiences and lure them with the unsaid promise of a film with 'scenes'. It was generally not thought that a film could get an 'A' certificate because of too much violence or an adult subject needing sensitive handling. For many, an 'adult' film could mean only one thing—nudity.

Youngsters often found ingenious ways of getting into the hall for an adult film. Many would rise on their toes at the time of check-in to appear taller, others wouldn't shave for a few days before the show so they could point at their stubble, still others would talk loudly about college to give the impression that they were not in school. Winters provided an easier alternative: cover your face with a shawl or a blanket and sneak in quietly.

It was an option exercised by one teenage boy to watch *Bob and Sally* (1948) at Ritz. The film was said to be *'garam'*—with hot, steaming bedroom scenes. For the night show, he went covered with a blanket from top to toe and easily fooled the gatekeeper to gain an entry. However, in those days, even an entry did not guarantee watching the film in its entirety. In every adult film screening, the torchman used to throw light every now and then at audiences in a bid to catch any under-age viewer. The boy watched a good part of the film from a tiny opening in his blanket that covered all his body except his eyes, looking very much like a woman in a burqa. Closer to the end, though, an usher came to him, saying, '*Beta*, you have watched the film almost fully. Now take off that blanket!' Embarrassed, he took off his 'veil'. This boy, GK Sharma, would later be the manager of Amba cinema, where he started as an usher, then a booking clerk and gradually progressed to the top.

Sharma was not the only one with a story at Ritz. The hall was strategically located next to the ISBT and was just a kilometre from the railway station. It was an option for men who had only a few hours to idle away before taking their bus or train. A number of Hollywood flicks and Hindi films with objectionable scenes raked in the riches.

Ritz was renovated in 1961 with the release of *Junglee,* which ran here for 33 weeks. Similarly, the Farouque Sheikh-Poonam Dhillon starrer, *Noorie* (1979), was initially booked for four weeks. Following good performance at the box office, the film was extended to 36 weeks. In the early 1980s, KC Bokadia's *Pyar Jhukta Nahin* (1985), the classic poor boy-rich girl tale, cocked a snook at the doomsday pundit's predictions. Bokadia and director Vijay Sadanah went against the action-hero image of Mithun Chakraborty and cast him as a loverboy and the turnstiles could not take the rush of audiences who flocked to see the film for six months. Before this, there had been Shakti Samanta's *Awaaz* (1984), a half-baked, belated attempt at capitalising on Rajesh Khanna's *Aradhana* (1969) magic. Incidentally, the film was initially conceived with Dilip Kumar and Anil Kapoor; later Rajesh Khanna and Rakesh Roshan did the roles. As the film's music started doing the rounds, people came in droves to watch it, me among them. Then a teenager, I stealthily boarded a public transport bus from my house in Lajpat Nagar and came to Ritz without the fear of being seen by a neighbourhood elder, much like those self-effacing ladies of Old Delhi. Around such experiences was woven the magic of Ritz, used as a fine tool for revival by Rajesh Khanna in the '80s. Clearly outwitted by Amitabh Bachchan in the race to the top, Rajesh Khanna attempted to recast his image. *Awaaz* was a step in that direction, as were films like *Aaj ka MLA Ram Avtar* (1984) and *Maqsad* (1984). For the former, an artist came from Meerut to carve out a figure of Rajesh Khanna as a politician; for the latter, a local billboard artist Lakshman made a special hoarding of Rajesh Khanna showing a fist of fury with Jeetendra.

Ritz shut shop briefly in the early years of the new millennium before coming back a stronger player in the cinema hall game. The stealthy viewer of *Bob and Sally* is now a doting grandfather and the kid from Lajpat Nagar has a grey beard, while the women who reached here from Purdah Bagh are now in their dotage. But Ritz still has stories to tell and it does so away from the limelight.

21 DELITE DIAMOND, Asaf Ali Road

This cinema was a new concept—a mini theatre adjacent to the main theatre, which was Delite in this case. The two theatres have separate entry and exit points, separate admission structures and invariably screen different films so they couldn't jointly be called a multiplex. From inside, Delite Diamond which started on December 8, 2006, is regal with its half dome making it a standout theatre. It has fire-proof drapery, Egyptian carpets and beautiful glasswork on the ceiling. Its seats are decorated with brocade and have an attached brass holder for drinks. This 148-seater hall has chandeliers imported from the Czech Republic and Victorian lampposts near the entrance.

The cinema often plays films which are a little off-beat and draws a crowd of discerning viewers. Of course, that does not prevent it from running dubbed Hindi versions of Hollywood biggies too. It has played the best of commercial Hindi cinema, going back to *Baabul* (2006), director Ravi Chopra's film that aimed to reap a harvest following the windfall called *Baghban* (2003).

The film met with limited success. Better fate awaited Mani Ratnam's *Guru* (2007) and Rakeysh Omprakash Mehra's *Delhi-6* (2009).

III

Talking Films Up North

22 PALACE, Roshanara Road

Amid Barf Khana, Tope Khana, Ghanta Ghar and Peshawariyon ka Akhara—a conspicuous part of social discourse 50 years ago—stood the grand old Palace cinema which, for more than a decade, was the biggest in the city. Its impressive façade, the appealing cut-out of a dancing girl in front and ample open space on either side, was endearing to many. Palace was quite a favourite of Hindi cinema's top banners that often picked it as the cinema of choice in north Delhi. Movies like *Mera Saaya,* (1966) *Aradhana* (1969) and *Jeevan Sangram* (1974) played here to housefull shows. *Jeevan Sangram*, in particular, attracted crowds that went well beyond the cinema, extending right up to the neighbouring Barf Khana. Ticket sales were even more because of its tax-free status but Palace, which had a unique two-part monogram with the letters 'PC' written in between, could not show the film for long. It expressed its regrets through an insertion in local newspapers which read, 'Due to prior commitments, the film will be discontinued after this week.' The same happened with *Mera Saaya,* which had been hailed as 'a good picture with an entertaining story'. Again, the management lamented, '*Mera Saaya* will be discontinued after only two weeks due to the previous commitments of the exhibitors.' When a film opened here, it usually ran for an average of six weeks, though some did stay long enough to celebrate jubilees.

In the over six decades of its existence, there were just a handful of moments when Palace failed to show anything but the best. One such instance came in September 1975 when *Sholay* opened at Plaza and Amba and gave Palace a miss. To rub it in, Amba aggressively promoted *Sholay* with the tagline, 'Super, superb, supreme'. Almost in a huff, Palace played Dhirubhai Desai's *Daku Aur Bhagwan* (1975), a forgettable film simultaneously released at Gianand, Kumar and Khanna. But it shared the glory accompanying the screening of *Jai Santoshi Maa* (1975), which played at Palace before GP Sippy's multi-starrer, and drew massive crowds. For seven weeks, the cinema knew not an empty seat—huge billboards inside the complex, devotees as viewers inside the auditorium and music bands playing *bhajans* outside the hall. This film sparked off a trend of devotionals at Palace: soon after came *Shiv Bhakt Baba Balak Nath* (1972) which opened in the Walled City but had special screenings here. A couple of years later, in November 1978, arrived Dara Singh's biggest hit, *Bhakti Mein Shakti* (1978). The film smashed many records as the local population, Sikhs displaced from Punjab in Pakistan, turned up in hundreds.

The hall, with 1,200 seats, withstood Partition, survived the Emergency and the communal violence in the aftermath of the assassination of Indira Gandhi in 1984. The last event did see a mob attempting to vandalise the hall but the timely intervention of security personnel ensured it remained unscathed. Palace, like many others in the city, remained closed for four days and opened its booking windows only when peace had been restored in the city. Fittingly, it played *Dosti* (1964), a film it had played earlier too.

Palace took all the setbacks in its stride and continued to be a favoured hall of the classes. Away from Old Delhi, it played the best of Hindi films. Its 70 mm screen, said to be the biggest in Delhi besides Shiela's, and interiors were renovated in 1984. It hosted the International Film Festival of India when it was held in the early '80s in New Delhi and was the only hall in the capital with a special family stall similar to the box available at halls like Regal, Jagat and Ritz.

In the 1990s, Palace also drew housefull crowds for Sooraj Barjatya's *Hum Aapke Hain Koun...!* (1994) as well as Yash Chopra's *Mohabbatein* (2000). These Hindi films were interspersed with Punjabi films like *Nanak Naam Jahaz* (1969), *Chhan Pardesi* (1980) and *Putt Jatta De* (1981) as Palace repeatedly played these films to popular local demand. It often screened Punjabi films in the morning shows. Interestingly, though the hall has been shut for more than a decade now, its faithful viewers, including shopkeepers in the vicinity vividly remember their Palace experiences. One of them, Urmail Singh, claims to have watched *Gadar* (2001) at least 20 times, having paid to watch it only the first time. Another remembers bringing along his aunts and uncles, who all hailed from the undivided Punjab, to watch *Nanak Naam Jahaz* when the film played here on re-run.

It was no surprise that Anil Sharma's blockbuster, *Gadar*, dealing with the violence around Partition, had a record-breaking run here. But that was the last hurrah for a distinguished hall rich in cinematic history. It folded up in 2001.

Today, pigeons flock to the good old cinema like movie lovers in the years gone by. Some find a comfortable perch on the impressive name on the façade. Others fly to the passage leading to the parking to eat *bajra*, usually scattered by someone in the vicinity. Dogs too laze around in the Palace complex, most of them favouring the parking near the exit point. The booking windows of the cinema relate a similar tale—just a pair of shoes gracing the 'current' booking counter and a gallon of water with a couple of glasses at the 'advance' booking counter. The board announcing 'next change' is covered with soot and grime.

Palace, among the biggest cinema halls in the city, is clearly overrun by the sands of time.

23 AMBA, Clock Tower

Amba is an oasis amid chaos. Blaring horns and road rage incidents are frequent as buses, cars, carts, bikes and rickshaws vie for every inch of space available. The Subzi Mandi is right in front and an *akhada* of *pehelwan*s close by. Every morning, daily wagers sit on the road in front of the hall, waiting for somebody to give them employment for the day. Some help out at local shops by unloading goods from trucks, others are unskilled or semi-skilled labourers, masons and painters. Not too far away are wholesale shops of sugar, wheat, rice and the like. In fact, the entire street is one large granary. Amid this swirl stands Amba, solitary and majestic, its perfectly manicured gardens and beautifully tiled sidewalks looking even more impressive from a distance. In the years gone by, the large walls on its sides with iron frames have hosted a number of set-ups as artists came up with special hoardings for Amba cinema in north Delhi. On one side used to be the hoardings of the film showing at the cinema, on the other, relatively smaller ones, were hoardings of the forthcoming film.

The cinema's façade with a concrete impression of the silver screen remains visually brilliant, its polka dot front adding to its appeal. Inside, the patchwork of black and white marble leads to white marble stairs with gleaming steel railings, further onto a hall that progressed from reels to UFO, to the state-of-the-art technology approved internationally. All this without the hall having undergone any major renovation since the time it opened to the public on 5th April, 1963 with the screening of OP Ralhan's *Gehra Daag* (1963), a Rajendra Kumar-Mala Sinha starrer for which the lead cast was present. India's future Prime Minister, Morarji Desai, was also present for the inauguration, the beginning of a long and successful innings for a hall that, in recent years, has resisted the march of the multiplexes by providing equally good viewing experience at more affordable rates. With the maximum rates of admission going up to Rs 90, the 1,153-seater Amba caters to the young Delhi University students besides the middle-class families staying in areas such as Kingsway Camp and Shakti Nagar. The working-class men who toil for long hours at neighbouring markets frequent the stalls and prefer evening and night shows at the hall which sticks to the tried and tested formula when it comes to movie selection. Movies with explicit content are a no-no and films catering to family audiences and youthful romances are fairly popular.

When it opened as a 1,001-seater hall, the minimum rate of admission was 10 *anna*s and balcony tickets came for Rs 2.50. The pricing was on the higher side compared to Palace nearby and other halls in the Walled City. Slight corrections were made in the pricing structure within the first two years of its inception to make Amba accessible to many more.

Amba carved out its own niche gradually. The hall, which specialised in Hindi films, started playing Hollywood movies every second Saturday in the morning show, and a further slot was added in the form of every fourth Sunday. As a result, the morning shows came to be much coveted. Warner Bros' films became a regular affair, and even when mainstream Hindi fare was playing, the films invariably notched up impressive numbers. The Sunil Dutt-Nutan starrer *Milan* (1967) completed a silver jubilee as did Vinod Khanna's *Mera Gaon Mera Desh* (1971) and *Pocket-maar* (1974). Rather than single men in blue collar jobs who made up a chunk of the morning-show audience at many halls in the capital, families started frequenting Amba in the mornings.

The success story was repeated in daily four shows as families filled the balcony of Amba almost regularly. As the hall's reputation grew, one by one, Dharmendra, Meena Kumari, Sadhana, Shakila Bano, Raaj Kumar, Dara Singh, Madan Puri and later Sanjay Dutt and Akshay Kumar graced the shows. In fact, its 76-year-old manager GP Sharma, whose association with the cinema goes back to the beginning, claims to have lifted, cuddled and fed a young Akshay during his childhood, which was spent in the famous Paranthewali Gali in Chandni Chowk. Even local political bigwigs like former transport minister MB Barot and top-notch bureaucrats would often be seen at Amba, having booked their seats in advance.

In the early years, hit after hit was the norm. *Dil Hi Toh Hai* (1963) and *Geeta Mera Naam* (1974) ran to housefull shows for weeks on end as did *Mughal-e-Azam* (1960), which came here in a repeat run, having released three years before the hall was opened. Later, films like *Johnny Mera Naam* (1970), *Prem Pujari* (1970) and *Laila-Majnu* (1976) drew big crowds for long stretches. Like elsewhere in Delhi, *Jai Santoshi Maa* (1975) broke many a record, even though its collections here were without the element of drama which accompanied the film's screening at Moti and Paras. The first jubilee, though, was registered almost inevitably by GP Sippy's *Sholay* (1975). Half a decade later, its heady success was replicated for the first few days by Ramesh Sippy's *Shaan* (1980). The collections tapered off soon enough as the film did not have lasting appeal to enjoy a repeat audience. No such handicap dogged Manoj Kumar's *Kranti* (1981) which completed 100 glorious days at the cinema. A step behind it were Raj Kumar Kohli's multi-starrer *Jaani Dushman* (1979) and Manmohan Desai's *Coolie* (1983).

Today, Amba no longer runs a film for 100 days; the maximum run is a couple of weeks. The audience these days has far too many alternatives, including the screening of many films on television within six weeks of their box office release. But Delhi University youngsters and the middle-class crowd still show up here. The students have their fill in the noon and matinee shows while the families take over in the evening. Neither the anti-Sikh violence of 1984 nor the tension following the demolition of the Babri Masjid in Ayodhya in 1992 had a lasting impact on the hall. It was almost abnormally calm in front of all the life-threatening challenges.

At Amba, it is business as usual even 50 years after its inauguration.

24 ROBIN TALKIES, Old Subzi Mandi

In pre-Independence Delhi, it was rather unusual for a commoner to have a watch. Those who had one kept it as a prized possession, usually in their pocket. In 1941, a few good Samaritans of the city pooled in their resources and came up with the Clock Tower at Old Subzi Mandi in north Delhi. It had four huge clocks facing north, south, east and west, and became popular in the area as Ghanta Ghar.

A little over two decades later, Amba was established on the same road. However, much before Amba came up in 1963, there was Robin in Old Subzi Mandi, a few steps away from the Clock Tower. As Robin's front gave the impression of an iron-mesh grill at the entrance of a lane in Old Delhi, Robin was often referred to as Ghanta Ghar *par gali wala* cinema—the Clock Tower lane's cinema. Much like the more celebrated cinemas of Chandni Chowk, Robin had the 'talkies' suffix attached to it. Set up by a British gentleman in the pre-Partition days, it was initially called Blue Bird theatre. At that time, it also had a dance floor. After talkies became the way to go, it was renamed Robin Talkies, after the son of the proprietor. The ownership changed many hands—first it was a Delhi University academic, then a builder, followed by a film magnate who passed it on to a real estate giant.

The cinema had all one could ask for in terms of accessibility, affordability, camaraderie. It was more like a little *adda* in a small town. On one side were shops selling spices—turmeric, chillies, coriander, all in jute sacks left enticingly half open—on the other side, sweatmeat shops with mouth-watering *jalebi*s and piping-hot *samosa*s. There were vendors selling 'Firozabad *ki choodiyan*' (bangles of Firozabad), *bindi*s and necklaces. Across the road, community elders would sit on charpoys, with a goat or sheep tethered to its stumps. In the middle of this chaos were hoardings advertising movies at Robin Talkies.

The talkies too treated its patrons with respect; they could sneak out in the middle of a movie, have a *paan-bidi*, oversee business for a few minutes and come right back. During interval, a water-seller would arrive outside with a *mashq* on his back, jingling bowls and calling out to thirsty souls. At Robin, there used to be both: plenty of cinegoers and lots of thirsty souls as the talkies was only air-cooled. That too was an improvement as in the early days, a good portion of Robin was naturally cooled, a delightfully affirmative term for the absence of artificial cooling. As the water-seller called out from the road, cinegoers extended their hand from behind the meshed-grill of Robin to take a bowl, each of which cost 10 paise. The water-seller was never admonished by the guards but the *chaiwala* was not so lucky. Often, he would be shooed away as the guards realised he was cutting into the business of the canteen that was located on the first floor.

The canteen was right outside the balcony and could be reached by climbing a wide staircase of thick red sandstone, which had portraits of Sohrab Modi, Raj Kapoor and Dilip Kumar and the likes hanging on the walls. The balcony was divided into three parts with chairs in ascending number, set one behind the other. This did not necessarily mean that each patron had a specific seat; the policy of first come, first served was followed here.

Robin attracted a varied audience: some long-time residents lived with their families in little lanes all around while others had moved in here from undivided Punjab, Uttar Pradesh and Bihar. Most of them worked as shop assistants or set up their own little stalls by the streetside. They came for evening or night shows after a long day's toil. They were far from their families.

In the early '80s, when Jaya Prada in a yellow sari and a long plait lip-synced to 'Tum Mere Swami Main Tumri Daasi', men turned up in large numbers. Many missing their wives, found in the screen projection of the song of *Kaamchor* (1982) a reflection of their feelings. Because of the response, Robin, which usually played movies for one week only, was forced to continue director K Viswanath's film for an extra week. The same thing had to be done for Subhash Ghai's *Hero* (1983), where the viewers persistently requested the projector room manager to replay Reshma's soul piercing song, 'Lambi Judaai'.

Lonely men longing for the warmth of their families made up a good chunk of the audience of Robin till the late '80s. Sachin-Sadhana Singh's *Nadiya ke Paar* (1982), which spoke their language, a mix of Hindi and Bhojpuri much before Bhojpuri cinema became the rage, also did well here. Interspersed with such fare were *Tiranga* (1992), *Mujrim* (1989) and *Coolie No. 1* (1995) as the predominantly male audience had a taste for action movies and comedy fare. Sundays and Mondays attracted better business because the market nearby was closed and workers were free for the day.

Robin had only a 35 mm screen and greeted its patrons with a little gallery that had black and white pictures of Madhubala and Meena Kumari and garish ones of Govinda, Mithun Chakraborty and Madhuri Dixit. Always known as a hall that played re-runs of films, Robin showed the best of Raj Kapoor, Dev Anand and Dilip Kumar. Later, Mithun Chakraborty and Govinda enjoyed great popularity, easily beating Aamir Khan, Shah Rukh Khan or Salman Khan. It never hosted a premiere but the hall does have a few anecdotes to share too. Kishore Kumar was once brought here by his chauffeur while *Padosan* (1968) was showing on the screen, even though his intended destination was actually Palace, which was playing *Door Ka Rahi* (1971).

Robin's business stayed steady till the Old Subzi Mandi shifted and the next generation of immigrants moved out of the vicinity. Films became more expensive, and it was no longer feasible to run the hall. Today, Robin stands closed for more than half a decade. Even the water-seller who frequented it stopped coming about a decade ago, his *mashq* being no match for mineral water bottles. Meanwhile, the Clock Tower's clock facing the Old Subzi Mandi has stopped ticking, though the one facing Amba still works.

In reality, what has stopped ticking is a way of life.

25 ALPNA, Model Town

When Jugal Kishore Paliwal and Mahendra Kumar joined hands to set up a cinema hall on a plot of about 3,000 square yards in Model Town, they did something rather unusual. Instead of calling it a glitzy name or using the surname of the owners, Kumar released a newspaper advertisement inviting suggestions. Many names did the rounds until the partners settled for Kalpna. But on second thoughts, they considered Alpna a more artistic and poetic name, and that was how the legacy began in 1967. A place rich in anecdotes, within each story lies another.

Alpna, though, faced teething problems. It was easier to build a hall than to fill it with patrons. In those days, north Delhi was neither densely populated (except the area around Subzi Mandi) nor was it considered safe late in the evening, personal cars being few and public transport elementary. The management came up with an ingenious plan to bring in cinegoers from far and near, hiring buses to fetch viewers from the Inter State Bus Terminus at Kashmere Gate and Old Delhi Railway Station. The buses would start from these points about an hour before the show, take the audiences to Alpna and drop them back at the end of the movie. Occasionally, local bands accompanied the travellers, playing tunes from the current film. *Mehrban* (1967), the Ashok Kumar-Sunil Dutt-

Nutan starrer, was released at the hall amid such fanfare. The film arrived with a horde of artistes, loads of fans and went on to do good business. This way, Alpna, which had three ticket categories—front stall, A-class and balcony—started on a sound footing.

Rajendra Kumar, the king of romance, was one of the stars of the show here, with *Talash* (1969), *Aap Aaye Bahaar Aayi* (1971), *Gora Aur Kala* (1972) and *Sunehra Sansar* (1975) enjoying a warm reception. Alpna hosted the premiere of *Talash*, the OP Ralhan film. Besides Ralhan, his lead cast, including the irrepressible Madan Puri and Tun Tun, came for the show. It was advertised for its budget which exceeded Rs 1 crore. Three years later, Kamal Amrohi's *Pakeezah* (1972) was screened, and the premiere was attended by music director Naushad. He arrived in a black Mercedes, sending viewers into raptures. The film, which was a slow starter at most places, did good business here from the first day, its collections improving with each show. After Meena Kumari's masterpiece, the hall did away with the complementary bus service for viewers, now confident that they had successfully created their place in the minds of cinegoers. Alpna went on to become the top hall in north Delhi with only Amba as a competitor. Batra came up much later; Vijay and Robin did not appeal to family audiences and Palace concentrated too much on potboilers.

The hall was seldom short on glamour. As more and more Hindi film biggies started making Alpna their halt, even Joginder, popular with front-benchers with his action flicks in 1970s, felt it necessary to show his film *Ranga Khush* (1975) here (the film derived its name from a dialogue in an earlier film, Shibu Mitra's *Bindiya Aur Bandook,* released in 1972*)*. He arrived for the premiere accompanied by popular actor Nazneen and mouthed the dialogue all over again, leaving the masses asking for an encore. The film, predictably, was a hit.

Hit after hit, buses after buses, Alpna's fortunes got better still when the biggest hit in the history of Haryanvi cinema, *Chandrawal*, released here in 1984. Initially, though, many sniggered at the then 17-year-old hall. How could a Haryanvi film with a completely rustic background be screened at a posh cinema located not far from Delhi University? Some took it as a sign of bad times for the still young hall and began preparing its epitaph. The film came here with nil expectations, except from a small circle of people from Haryana who lived on Old Roshanara Road, and in pockets of Rana Pratap Bagh.

But the box-office performance of the film turned out to be an unexpected surprise, turning the tide in its favour. Cinegoers arrived by the hundreds from across north Delhi, some hiring private buses and tempos. They arrived early morning to procure tickets for the noon show and spent the intervening hours sitting on charpoys they had carried from home! For months on end, these charpoys covered the vast open space in front of Alpna as fans of Haryanvi cinema got to taste a rare film in their language. They would bring in their hookahs, play *pachisi* and if they failed to get tickets for the noon show, they waited for the matinee. While the housefull crowds kept turning up, the cast and crew arrived here to a tumultuous reception. It was like a village fair that went on for weeks. The film that was supposed to write its epitaph had become an epiphany.

The hall became known for its intrepid selections. In the mid-'70s, Alpna played Mithun Chakraborty's first ever Hindi film, *Mrigayaa* (1976), again after being advised not to show it. Nobody knew Mithun at that time and director Mrinal Sen was not known to deliver box-office winners either. But the film did reasonably well in its initial three-week run. Later, when Mithun reinvented himself as a popular hero, Alpna played his films regularly. In came *Suraksha* (1979), followed by *Boxer* (1984). Years later, *Vivekananda* (1994) had a special screening. It was like a rediscovery of the *Mrigayaa* hero.

In the late '60s and early '70s, the peerless Dev Anand had towered above the rest, with Navketan Films finding a captive audience in this part of the city. Films like *Hum Dono* (1961) and *Kala Bazar* (1960) were released much before Alpna came into existence but their re-runs were gladly lapped up by the audiences as were those of *Guide* (1965) and *Jewel Thief* (1967). Incidentally, morning shows at Alpna were remarkably removed from the fare often on offer elsewhere, with a number of Navketan Films productions like *Shaheed* (1965) and *Himalay Se Ooncha* (1975) on offer at reduced rates. That time slot did far better at Alpna than at its closest competitors—Batra, and later Aakash. Interestingly, while the families trooped here for matinee and evening shows, students would come for morning shows and occasionally, the night ones too. On their demand came a film like *Enter the Ninja* (1981) in the morning time slot and re-runs of niche art-house fare like *Gaman* (1978) and *Chakra* (1981).

The rapport that had been established with Mithun faded when he moved away from mainstream cinema and began acting in movies like *Chandaal* (1998), *Jallad* (1995), *Gautam-Govinda* (2002), *Dada* (2005) and the rest in the '90s. At a time when his charm had reduced considerably, Alpna played Rajshri's record-breaking *Hum Aapke Hain Koun...!* (1994), which arrived here after six weeks of its release and completed a golden jubilee, the only such instance in the history of this cinema. Salman Khan became the new craze and Madhuri

Dixit's attire from the song 'Joote De Do, Paise Le Lo' was copied by many young girls in the vicinity.

With such varied fare on the platter, Alpna could afford to not feel threatened by multiplexes and be dismissive of rival single screen theatres. But things began to go downhill after differences cropped up among the partners. What was once a fine business strategically located in a residential area came to an ugly halt in 2008. There is a possibility that business might resume, even though Alpna may be no more than a small auditorium with about 300 seats. Be that as it may, a fresh start can only add to its rich history.

26 HANS, Azadpur

Here is a cinema that does not bask in the spotlight, a cinema that has been openly indifferent to the multiplex-hopping crowd and of late, even wary of the traditional middle-class viewers. Hans has been impressive in its understated ways, a bit of a quiet, maybe, even brooding loner in an expanse of chaos. Located in Azadpur, Hans has, over the years, undergone a complete transformation, lost its original name—it was called Vijay earlier—but always managed to keep its audience steadfast. Standing almost solitary, Hans has gone about its business in its own way.

Surrounded by halls like Amba, Palace, Batra and Alpna, each more upmarket, Robin, easily more affordable and Aakash, more sophisticated, Hans' fate has been similar to that of a climber—each successive step has been less about attaining glory, and more about survival. That it has managed to stay afloat is a feat laudable in itself. That it stands poised for better times is truly remarkable, more so when the infinitely better endowed Palace and Alpna have shut shop and many others have often teetered on the brink. With a permanent theatre tag attained recently after years as a temporary or semi-permanent structure, Hans is beginning to appreciate the rewards of a journey.

Today, as hundreds of fans queue up at the turnstiles to watch the latest Bhojpuri flick in Friday noon show, Hans presents a pretty busy, happy picture. With its simple stone slabs and concrete with a dash of a colourful paint, it makes the façades of the halls in Old Delhi or Connaught Place seem a luxury best avoided. It has been that way for quite a while. Over the past decade or so, Hans has become the centre for the release of Bhojpuri films. More like Moti in Chandni Chowk, Hans has found a new lease of life, courtesy Bhojpuri cinema. And unlike Moti, Hans is not just about breathing. It is up and running.

In the early 2000s, screening Bhojpuri films seemed a high-risk venture. Hans, after all, had a history of playing the best of Hindi films, including the much talked-about *Gadar* (2001) which had an 11-week run here in mid-2001. Men who defy convention are more easily lauded than cinemas that do so. Hans' fate was surprisingly different. And viewers who had begun to stay away from the hall following a series of re-runs of films like *Jallad* (1995), *Mawali No.1 (*2002), *Munnibai* (1999), *Dacait* (2000), starring the well-past-their-prime Mithun Chakraborty and Dharmendra, came rushing back. After more than five years spent watching quickies of Mithun and Dharmendra in the late 1990s and early years of the next decade, Bhojpuri films seemed to have a nice identifiable ring to them, and viewers embraced them without reservations. Hans was back to happy times.

Thirty years earlier, this enthusiasm had been generated by Prakash Mehra's Feroz Khan-Sanjay Khan starrer *Mela* (1971), which completed a diamond jubilee in its repeat run here—a unique feat. Subhash Ghai's *Gautam Govinda* (1979) also had a fine run as did out-and-out entertainers *Rampur ka Lakshman* (1972), *Jangal Mein Mangal* (1972) and *Dharma* (1973). Hans held its own even when other cinemas were playing the same films—*Azaad* (1978) went on and on at Swarn cinema but had a strong showing here as well. Such was the case with *Phandebaaz* (1978) too, which played simultaneously at Delite. Later, when Jaya Prada's saris and Sridevi's *matka*s in *Tohfa* (1984) had the city on its feet for a while, Vijay, as Hans was called then, belatedly joined the party. They all showed here without great hype or even stars gracing the hall. Simple word of mouth publicity and elementary modes of information did the trick. When most halls have gone online and often use merchandise to publicise their wares, Hans still relies on a cycle-rickshaw covered with film posters on all sides.

Yet, in its trusted and traditional ways, Hans takes India closer to the heartbeat of Bharat. It has age-old patrons sans the cola-sipping crowd and members of the bubblegum brigade. Bishwas Singh, a vegetable vendor from the market nearby, is happy with Hans and its decision to change films almost every week. 'Who wants stale fare in the market?' he says. Raju, a rickshaw-puller, is another patron: 'It is not the place for sahibs and memsahibs. *Yeh hamara hall hai*' (This is our hall).

It is indeed a familiar place that generates a certain warmth and easy acceptance among less privileged audiences. From the outside, it's a stately, stolid structure; inside, the cinema is more of an inclined plane with a slanting seating arrangement from the balcony to the front stall. The more you pay, the higher you rise—balcony admission is Rs 35 and the stalls down below are for Rs 20. The 900-seater plays host to regional cinema in four shows, usually reserving a solitary morning show for Hindi blockbusters of yore. Even today, the morning shows are at reduced rates. A sum of Rs 15 may not buy you a cola at a multiplex, but at Hans it buys you the right to watch the best of Mahesh Manjrekar, Anil Sharma and the rest. Thanks to its staple diet of

Bhojpuri cinema and Hindi action flicks in morning shows, Hans carries on cheerfully.

Azadpur Mandi may not be the best place to come across pockets of old world charm. And Hans, with its leisurely ways, may appear a bit of an oddball, but it belongs to an unhurried passage of time. Quiet, unhurried and sober.

27 AAKASH, Azadpur

Neither well-known nor illustrious, not even among the chosen few with history and tradition written all over its walls, Aakash goes about its business with no fuss. This hall, part of the government's plan to develop cinema houses as part of local commercial complexes, is among the bigger ones in the city and needs 1,000 viewers for the housefull board to be displayed outside. That, though, has not been witnessed in recent times.

Back in 1987, when Aakash opened with *Insaaf ki Pukaar* (1987), a Dharmendra-Jeetendra-Bhanupriya film, it seemed to be a sign of things to come. Not only did the cinema register great business with the film, it heralded the kind of fare that was likely to rule the roost here. The cinema played mainstream commercial potboilers and escapist fare, riding out on the names of the stars and not subjects or directors. These films were box-office gold at Aakash, attracting long and disorderly queues. Giant hoardings and colourful posters were plastered on bare walls, outside public conveniences, next to notice boards of Resident Welfare Associations, tea stalls and *paan-bidi* shops to announce the film playing here. All posters had a single-line addition in gaudy blue ink, *'Ab dikhaya jaa raha hai rozana 4* show *Aakash mein'* (now showing in daily four shows at Aakash). Occasionally, local newspapers carried a notice about the current show.

Aakash was strategically located, at the intersection of Adarsh Nagar and Azadpur. With its giant deep brown and golden brown façade and slim pillars, it was difficult to miss even from a bus. It had a 70 mm screen and, after a while, Dolby Digital sound. It sold three categories for admission: front stall, upper stall and balcony. Later, the dress circle category came up as well. All films arrived on a limited engagement, seldom lasting more than three weeks which meant that movie-watchers could expect new films often and stay clued in to the latest. Even though hardly any premieres were held here and few stars ever visited, the hall did steady business, thanks to the people living around the cinema.

The hall was able to tide over the slump in business in the early '90s with a fine cocktail of films having a mix of action, comedy and romance interspersed with occasional shows of yesteryear super hits. A film like *Ek Phool Do Maali* (1969) was promoted on a grand scale, as was *Do Kaliyan* (1968) but those were exceptions. Indeed, Aakash barely put a wrong foot forward in its chosen market—it knew what the front-benchers wanted and supplied as much. It ran regular morning shows too, but these screenings did little for the cinema's reputation. Often, they were sleazy Malayalam flicks or the occasional Hollywood film, the focus always being on explicit scenes. These films ran on reduced rates, too, as little as Rs 10 until five years ago. But then, the growing popularity of the internet, which had much more material for those looking for cheap thrills, played a hand in drying up the morning shows.

In the early years of the new millennium, two other events occurred which had an impact on the hall's future. The night shows also began being cancelled, particularly in winter when fewer people ventured out. Then the hall started playing Bhojpuri films, the new sunshine industry.

First came *Sasura Bada Paise Wala* in 2003, followed a little later by *Daroga Babu, I Love You* (2005). It made for sound economics and common sense. A significant portion of the audience here spoke Hindi with a dash of Bhojpuri; they were usually immigrants from eastern Uttar Pradesh and Bihar and eked out a living doing small jobs in the market or the age-old Azadpur Mandi. They were happy to see Ravi Kissen and Manoj Tiwari speak their language.

Aakash continued collecting good numbers, even more so since it no longer had to compete with Alpna or Amba to play top drawer Hindi cinema. In Bhojpuri cinema, it had few competitors in the area and was a clear winner. Today, the 1,000-seater hall still stands nice and quiet. Every monsoon, its impressive building loses some of its sheen because of pot-holes around the entrance and pools of stagnant water just off the approach road. But it continues to have its loyal patrons, the ones catered to by the peanut-sellers outside the hall every winter. And the ubiquitous *shikanji*-sellers in summer.

28 SAMRAT, Britannia Chowk, Shakurpur

With the rare offering of air-conditioned comfort for a low price from the day of its inauguration in the 1980s, Samrat caught the eye of many, though its location in a resettlement area did prove a bit of a dampener. Nevertheless, those who came to the hall in the 1980s could watch a morning show for as little as 10 *anna*s on a 70 mm screen, and it was with these economics that Samrat came to play a crucial role in the life of north Delhi's movie watchers.

The hall was launched with a lot of fanfare with *Suhaag* (initially released elsewhere in October, 1979) an Amitabh Bachchan-starrer that completed 50 days, something unheard of in that part of the city. Soon after came *Muqaddar Ka Sikandar* (1978) in a re-run, which also went on for 50 well attended days. Bachchan was the crowd-puller; the lesser privileged men could identify with the characters he played, usually an upstart hero who fought 'their' battles and did things on the screen that they probably imagined doing themselves. With most of the crowd in the vicinity of Samrat comprising migrant workers, it was easy for Bachchan to strike a chord by playing a small-town boy lost in a big city of corrupt men. Samrat barely had a show which was not housefull when it played a Bachchan flick. Things took a turn for the better with *Coolie* (1983), the Manmohan Desai blockbuster. The news of Bachchan's accident during the shooting had reached before the film, and posters happily pointed out the incident as well, not in print but in garish blue ink. Released in November, 1983, *Coolie* ran like no other film, completing a 100-day run.

The Haryanvi film *Chandrawal* (1984) completed a silver jubilee here in 1984, an extremely rare occurrence for a city that embraced Hindi films like few others, leaving only a small gap for Punjabi flicks in certain pockets, and hardly any for films in other Indian languages. Yet in the early and mid-'80s, Haryanvi films found many takers in north and east Delhi just as Garhwali films found an eager audience in south Delhi. Egged on by this formula, Samrat played a few more Haryanvi flicks in its morning shows where even the balcony ticket came at a princely sum of Rs 3.20!

In the early days, when it screened Bapu's *Hum Paanch* (1980), noted actress Shabana Azmi visited the hall, as did co-star Kanwaljeet. They waved at the fans, smiled, and left after some polite chit-chat. In its daily four shows, Samrat cultivated an image for playing mainstream action films.

In the 1990s though, as fewer people from the neighbouring middle-class colonies visited Samrat, the management decided to renovate the cinema. For a while, business in the balcony seats was steady but the real bucks for Samrat continued to pour in from the front, middle and rear stalls. Soon, the management decided to go full throttle to cater to the wishes of the viewers looking for instant gratification. As fewer women frequented the hall, men's tastes dictated the choice of films. Mithun Chakraborty became the presiding deity of Samrat; all his action movies had a great run here. Whether they were re-runs of films like *Suraksha* (1979), *Kasam Paida Karne Wale Ki* (1984) and *Boxer* (1984) or those he did with TLV Prasad and Rajiv Babbar, all worked magic at the box office. Cinema lovers in other parts of Delhi did not come to know but *Jallad* (1995), *Chandaal* (1998), *Guru* (1989), *The Don* (1995), *Gautam-Govinda* (2002) set the screen on fire at this hall. No English newspaper mentioned these movies in its cinema lists, no music channel played their songs and no critics reviewed the films, yet they all ran full house to an audience that knew what it wanted. Samrat's success briefly emboldened even Liberty cinema on Old Rohtak Road to play *Yamraaj* (1998), a Mithun-Jackie Shroff starrer.

The hall also played films starring Joginder, whose *Yeh Hai Basti Badmashon Ki* (originally released in 1999 but revived in 2002 on local demand) and *Bindiya aur Bandook-2* (2003) held their own even in weeks when Sanjay Leela Bhansali's *Devdas* and JP Dutta's *LoC* were released. He made a 'star' appearance at the hall on one occasion, answering the whistles of his fans by throwing flowers at them and doing a little jig. Joginder, a trained pilot, had also worked with former Prime Minister Indira Gandhi. This combined with the success of these popular films meant that even local MLAs and MPs visited Samrat once in a while to endear themselves to prospective voters. Even in the 1990s, it used to occasionally try out Bhojpuri films in morning shows, as it tried screening Tamil and Malayalam films, most of them dubbed Hindi versions of the original.

But like most halls in resettlement areas, Samrat also took to showing Bhojpuri films of Ravi Kissen and Manoj Tiwari in the first decade of the new millennium. The films, though never losers at the box office, failed to get a similarly warm response, which forced Samrat to go back to screening time-tested mainstream action fare from Bollywood.

Today, the hall charges at least Rs 20 for admission rights, an astronomical amount compared to the 63 paise of yore, but it is still more affordable than the Rs 90 tickets at many single screen theatres, and Rs 200 at multiplexes.

29 BATRA, Mukherjee Nagar

The cinema that opened with producer GP Sippy's *Ahsaas* (1979) back on 2nd November, 1979, has had a distinguished run, skilfully tiding over the lows. From the very beginning, Batra has sought to combine the niche appeal of art-house cinema with the popular appeal of *masala* entertainers. In a city where only a handful of halls have made space for cinema beyond stereotypes, Batra consistently showed films of Shyam Benegal, Goutam Ghose, Mrinal Sen and Bhimsain in the noon show in the 1980s. It also played the standard in-demand films—the Manmohan Desais, the Prakash Mehras, the David Dhawans and the Karan Johars. Its noon and night shows have been great hits with the student community. Subhash Ghai's *Hero* (1983) attracted better footfall at night than evening! For every *Gehrayee* (1980), *Dooriyan* (1979) or *Doosri Dulhan* (1983), there have been scores of *Dabangg*s and *Hums*. Over the past decade or so, Batra has confined itself to only mass entertainers.

30 DEEP, Ashok Vihar

Like Ajanta, Deep also had a brief period of glory in the Ashok Vihar-Wazirpur belt. It was inaugurated on 30th April, 1971 by then Lieutenant Governor of Delhi, AN Jha, in the presence of Ram Niwas Mirdha, later to be a Union Minister. A fully air-conditioned hall from the first day, Deep had a 70 mm wide screen and the latest equipment. When the hall opened with *Reshma aur Shera* (1971), it even advertised DTC bus routes that touched the cinema. It was considered extremely far away 40 years ago and special buses ran from Sabzi Mandi to Deep and back. It often played films similar to those running at Liberty, among them *Rani Aur Lalpari* (1975), which was screened at the end of 1975. It did not last for long though, ceasing to be a cinema hall 20 years ago after playing a number of super hits like *Jeevan Sangram* (1974), *Loafer* (1973), *Prem Pujari* (1970), *Love In Tokyo* (1966) and *Mera Saaya* (1966).

31 KALAMANDIR, Mangolpuri

In 1979, when Kalamandir opened its doors with a string of action movies, the working-class residents of Mangolpuri were thankful for a cinema in their midst that showed their favourite fare at low rates. After Manmohan Desai's *Naseeb* (1981) became a roaring hit here, the bigwigs of the trade started choosing Kalamandir for their movie releases. For years, this hall's name was taken in the same breath as the ones in Connaught Place and Old Delhi.

In its initial years, people from nearby villages used to frequent Kalamandir. Today, it is preferred largely by blue-collar workers, most of whom are immigrants from eastern Uttar Pradesh and Bihar. Action films work better and Salman is the most popular Khan. In the past, Bachchan and Sunny Deol have ruled the roost. This hall is among the more resilient ones in the city. Yet little is known about its existence even among the charmed circle of cinegoers beyond its immediate neighbourhood.

32 KUSHAL, Jahangirpuri

Kushal had a limited run for about two decades. Located in the resettlement colony of Jahangirpuri, the hall had, predictably, basic amenities. It showed films, offered no add-ons and kept the ticket pricing on the lower side. The films too were usually the latest action flicks, the kind Mithun Chakraborty and Sunny Deol starred in with relish in the late '80s and '90s. They attracted good crowds for a while but Kushal failed to make a lasting impression on the circuit and made a quiet exit.

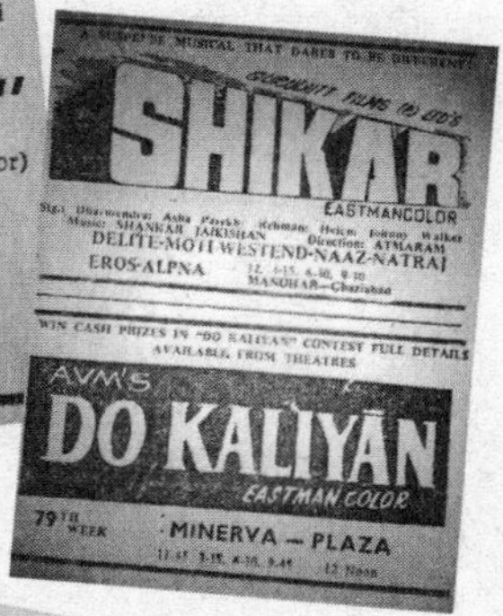

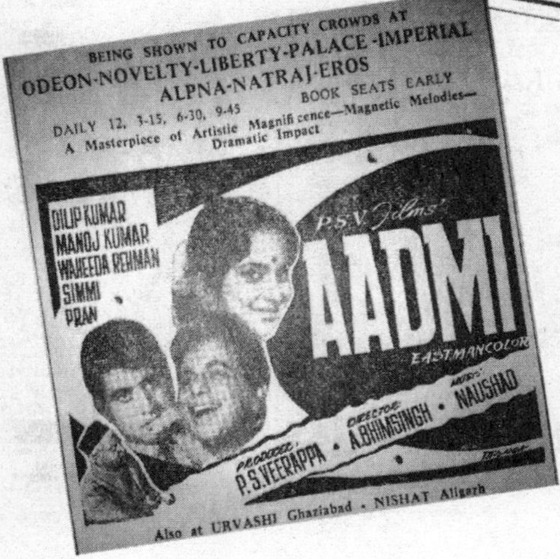

Film advertisements in *Patriot* in 1968. The newspaper was popular with movie-lovers looking for information on forthcoming films. All the advertisements began with the name of a cinema in or around Connaught Place.

Film advertisements in *Partap*, *Milap* and *Qaumi Awaz* in the '70s. These Urdu dailies carried many such advertisements on Fridays, the day new films are released in cinema halls.

The '90s were the last years of the exclusive single-screen experience. These advertisements show only the names of single-screen theatres showing films like *Joru Ka Ghulam* (2000), *Hadh Kar Di Aapne* (2000) and *Josh* (2000). The only exception was PVR Anupam.

Meena Kumari at Regal in Connaught Place for the premiere of *Phool Aur Pathhar* (1966).

Raj Kapoor's *Satyam Shivam Sundaram* (1978) had a silver jubilee run at Regal.

One of the leading cinema halls of central Delhi, and a favourite of Raj Kapoor, Regal was known to play big banner films for a long time.

Located in Connaught Place, Odeon's façade when it showed *Bhabhi* (1957), starring Balraj Sahni, Nanda and Durga Khote.

Naseeruddin Shah at Regal for the premiere of *Woh Saat Din* (1983).

Come September was released at Odeon in 1963. The hall had been closed for six months and re-opened with the film.

Mr RL Sahni, the owner of Odeon, receiving Dr Sarvepalli Radhakrishnan, former President of India at the screening of *Come September.*

In the late '70, young Shyam Sahni (centre) gave a new direction to Odeon and Rivoli cinemas.

In the early years of the new millennium, good old Odeon turned Big Cinemas Odeon.

Known for its Hollywood fare, Rivoli, another prominent cinema hall in Connaught Place had a definitive change of profile in 1969 with Shakti Samanta's *Aradhana.*

In 1956, Sohrab Modi's *Jhansi ki Rani* drew huge crowds at Plaza in Connaught Place. Here curious passersby stop in front of the hall to take a look at its hoardings.

The first cinema to serve cold coffee, and offer add-ons, Plaza was always the top choice of film exhibitors and stars. It continues to be a favoured haunt in its new avatar as a small theatre.

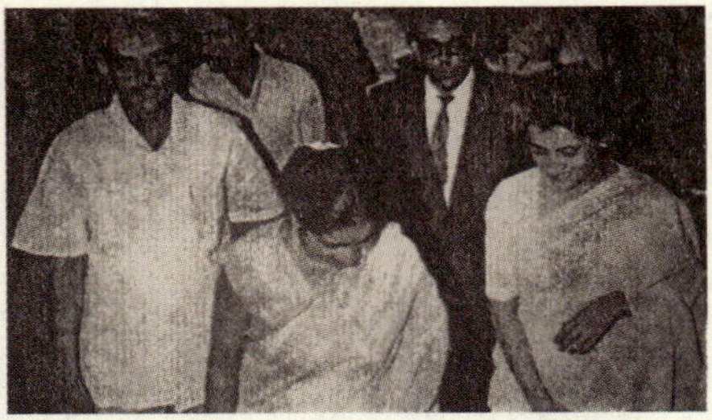

Shiela in Pahar Ganj narrowly missed out on being Asia's first 70 mm cinema but it hosted prominent political leaders such as Pandit Jawaharlal Nehru (left, right) and Indira Gandhi (top, right).

Luc Durand in the foyer of Shiela where he had designed a 60-ft long mural in 1961. A Canadian artist, he was recommended by noted architect, Habib Rahman. Durand designed the mural on the spot and finished it in three days, using a vibrant mix of yellow, red and blue. The bright abstract work sought to impart a joyous feeling to cine-goers.

Delite, located on the cusp of Old and New Delhi, capitalised on it unique location to attract viewers from across the city. It opened in the '50s with *Angaray* (1954) and continues to play top banners even today.

In the '50s, Dr Rajendra Prasad, President of India (left), and Pandit Jawaharlal Nehru, Prime Minister of India (2nd from right) accompanied by grandson Rajeev Gandhi (right) watch a film at Delite.

(Below starting 2nd from right) Premnath, Manoj Kumar, Prem Chopra (back row extreme left) and Anita Guha (right centre) and others enjoy a screening of *Tipu Sultan* (1959) at Delite.

Nigar Sultana's *Magroor* (1950) was a rare film that released at Plaza, and Cinema Excelsior in Hauz Qazi, simultaneously.

Cinema Excelsior was known for playing Muslim socials till the 1980s.

Located in Chandni Chowk, Moti, which once played mythologicals, was a favourite with Bimal Roy, Guru Dutt and later Manmohan Desai. Over the last few years, it has been showing Bhojpuri and Telugu films dubbed into Hindi.

(Left to right) Deepa and Udit Narayan with SS Rajkamal and SK Pankaj, veterans of Delhi's Bhagirath Place film circuit, at the premiere of Bhojpuri film *Kab Hoi Gavna Hamaar* (2005) at Moti.

Jubilee at Chandni Chowk has given way to a pavement market.

If you missed a film at Excelsior, you could catch up with it at West End at Sadar Bazaar, and vice-versa.

Dilip Kumar, Vyjayantimala (top, 2nd and 3rd from left) and Naushad (top right, 2nd from left) at the silver jubilee of *Gunga Jumna* (1961) at Minerva in Kashmere Gate.

Though never in the same league as the Connaught Place and Chandni Chowk halls, Minerva earned its stripes by playing super hit films like *Gunga Jumna* (1961), *Hamraaz* (1967), and later, *Daaku Aur Jawan* (1978).

At its launch in Kashmere Gate, many pundits wrote off Ritz but the Seths were firm that cinema hall would work. And work it did, becoming a favourite of Rajesh Khanna by showing films like *Maqsad* (1984), *Aaj ka MLA, Ram Avatar* (1984) and *Awaaz* (1984).

Palace in Roshanara Road played mainstream popular films that the local crowd lapped up. It closed down soon after showing Anil Sharma's *Gadar* (2001).

Unknown to most cine-goers who opt for central and south Delhi's halls, Hans in Azadpur has carved out a niche for itself by playing Hindi films in the morning shows and Bhojpuri films in daily 4 shows. *Photo Courtesy: The Hindu*

Hans has found ingenious ways of promoting its films—a fully covered cycle rickshaw with the posters of the films hung on the sides.

Robin in Subzi Mandi was less a cinema and more a popular haunt for local residents who could walk in and out of the film at their pleasure.

Amba in Kamla Nagar, though frequented by Delhi University students, always appealed to family audiences. With its 70 mm screen and affordable pricing, it has withstood the multiplex boom.

Veteran actor Pradeep Kumar's *Taj Mahal* (1963) did well at Amba and many other halls across the city. Here he is seen with GK Sharma (extreme left), manager of the hall.

Amba was a rare hall chosen for the premieres of big banner films like *Phool Aur Pathhar* and *Rocky.* Dharmendra (2nd from right) arrives for a screening of *Phool Aur Patthar* in 1966.

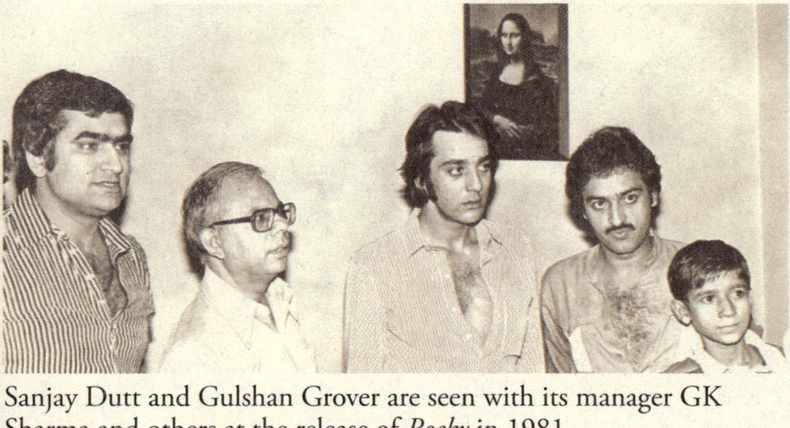

Sanjay Dutt and Gulshan Grover are seen with its manager GK Sharma and others at the release of *Rocky* in 1981.

Madan Puri at a screening of *Talash* (1969) at Alpna in Model Town. The hall's name was decided on suggestions invited through newspaper advertisements.

Joginder (extreme left) and Nazneen (3rd from left) at the showing of *Ranga Khush* (1975) at Alpna.

Sanjay Khan (4th from left) with Sri Ram Talwar (2nd from right) at Alpna in 1980.

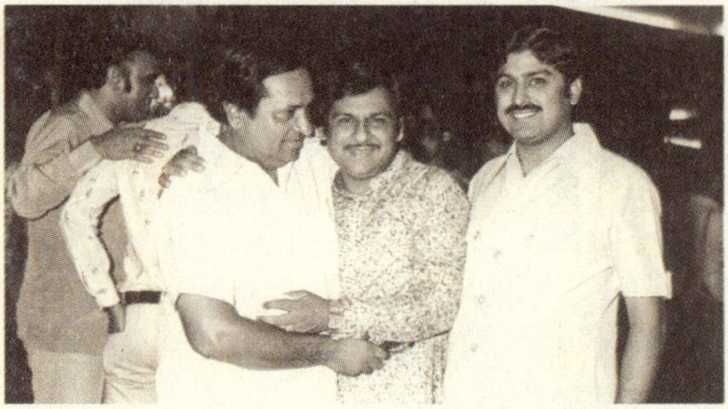

Illustrious ghazal exponent, Ghulam Ali (centre), at Alpna.

In the initial years, Alpna provided free bus service to its patrons. Rajendra Kumar, and in later years, Joginder and Mithun Chakraborty, often graced the hall with their presence.

Mrs Rajeshwar Prasad of Liberty Cinema in Karol Bagh, presenting a cheque of Rs. 4012 to the wife of Gulzarilal Nanda after a charity show of the opening film, *Pooja Ke Phool,* in 1963.

In the early years, Batra, located in Mukherjee Nagar, struck a fine balance between arthouse and mainstream cinema. Today it concentrates only on *masala* entertainers.

Kumar Gaurav (2nd from left) and Vijayata Pandit (3rd from left) arrive at Batra for the showing of *Love Story* (1981).

Deepti Naval (top, extreme right) Shabana Azmi (top, 4th from right) and Amrish Puri (left, right) at Batra for the premiere of *Hum Paanch* (1980).

Starting as a temporary hall in Badarpur, Seble had a chequered history before becoming a permanent hall. In the 1984 anti-Sikh riots, it was reduced to ashes but was up and running within six weeks.

The Sebles established some of the early halls in Rawalpindi and Peshawar before bringing to Delhi the concept of moving theatres — they established a cinema on a stretch of land for about three months before moving on. Seen here are the men behind the temporary theatre movement in Delhi: (left to right) Shri Marwah, LS Puri, RS Seble, Surjit Singh and Manjit Singh Seble.

Raj Kapoor (left) and Mukesh (right) with RS Seble (centre) after the screening of *Barsaat* (1949) at Seble.

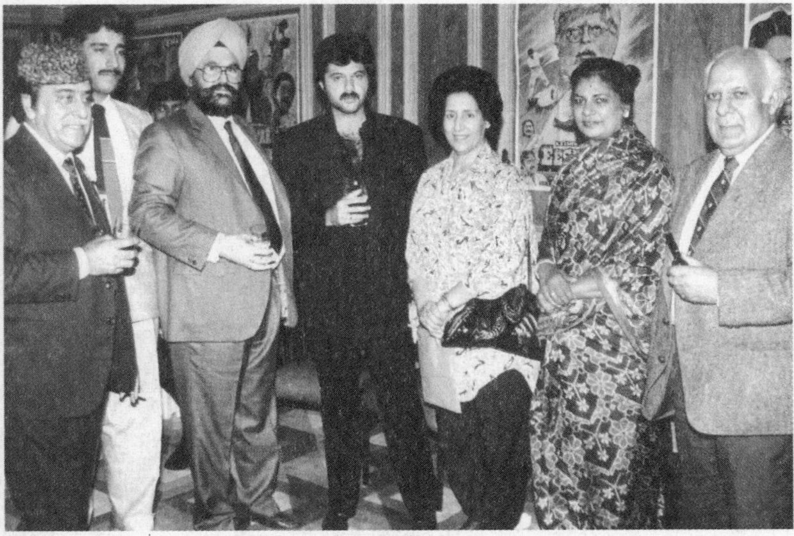

Anil Kapoor (centre) at the premiere of *Eeshwar* (1989) in the Capital with RS Seble (3rd from left).

Basking in the success of *Murder* (2004) (right to left) Anurag Basu, Emraan Hashmi Mahesh Bhatt, Mallika Sherawat, SR Talwar and his staff at Vishal cinema in Rajouri Garden.

Kumar Talkies in Chandni Chowk, which once played pot-boilers, shut shop for a few years before making a comeback as Abhishek Cineplex. Today, the number of seats has been reduced, amenities improved, and the show goes on.

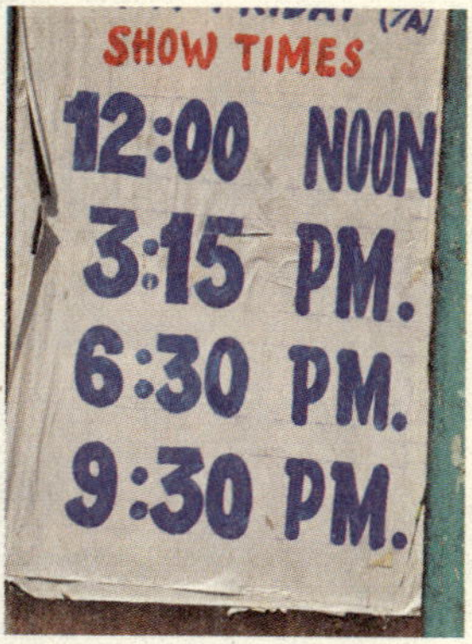

Abhishek Cineplex still sticks to the daily 4 shows routine.

Unlike *Mother India* (1957), Mehboob Khan's *Son of India* (1962) failed to attract cine-goers at most cinema halls across the city. However, Khanna in Pahar Ganj registered good footfall.

Kachche Heere (1982) was a hit with the masses at cinema halls in Delhi. The film was a black marketeer's delight at several places like Vivek in Patel Nagar, Filmistan in Karol Bagh and Kamal in Safdarjung Enclave.

Some of the earliest temporary talkies, which were often not much more than tin sheds, came up in places like Zakhira, Subhash Nagar and Model Town.

These halls played only three films a day but managed to get top-rung films. Keeping in mind the sensitivities of people, the names of films were, at times, written in four languages, namely Hindi, Urdu, English and Punjabi.

Rehana's *Lajawab* (1949) had a good run at old Delhi talkies but was not so successful in the other parts of the Capital.

Dacoits are said to have watched Sunil Dutt's *Mujhe Jeene Do* (1963) at Novelty in SP Mukherjee Marg. Here the star (2nd from left), accompanied by his wife Nargis (4th from left), is seen enjoying the film with its cast and crew.

K Asif's *Mughal-e-Azam* was released at Golcha, Darya Ganj, in its black and white (1960) and colour (2010) versions. On both occasions, the film ran to packed houses.

Chandra Barot's *Don* (1978) enjoyed a jubilee run at Jagat near Jama Masjid.

Dostana (1980), Amitabh Bachchan and Shatrughan Sinha's tale of friendship attracted huge crowds at Gianand in Shahdara.

D Ramanaidu's *Tohfa* (1984) worked wonders at the box office because of its super hit music. The film was lapped up by the audiences at Raaj in Tilak Nagar where it was shown a few weeks after its release elsewhere in the city.

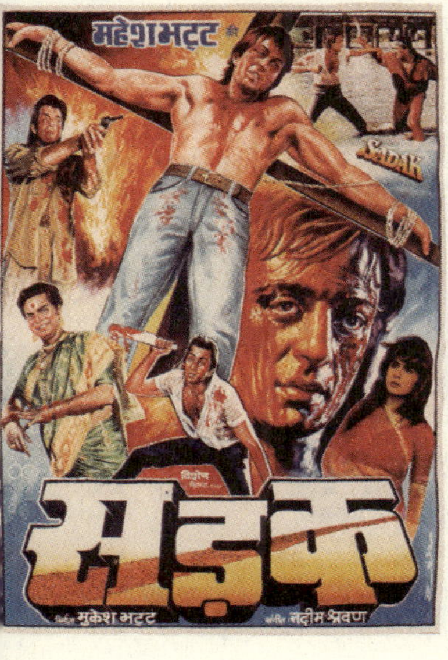

Mahesh Bhatt's *Sadak* (1991) was a rare Hindi film which gave prominence to the villain on its posters and hoardings at cinema halls across the city. In this poster, (left to right, foreground) Sadashiv Amrapurkar, Sanjay Dutt and Pooja Bhatt enjoy equal billing.

GP Sippy's *Aatish* (1994) had a very succesful run at Vivek in Patel Nagar.

Watching a film at Sapna in East of Kailash was a pleasure for the local residents. Govinda's *Sajan Chale Sasural* (1996) was a hit here.

IV

Cameras Rolling Westward

33 SURAJ, Najafgarh

In the summer of 1975, from May to September, hundreds of people would gather four times a day to watch *Jai Santoshi Maa* (1975) in the 'naturally cooled' Suraj, then a newly-built hall offering nothing more than the barest minimum. It had a roof, walls, chairs and a screen; no air cooler, fans or carpets. Yet cinegoers stuck it out, indeed sweated it out, braving the notorious Delhi heat. Director Vijay Sharma's film was supposed to run for only four weeks but such was the demand that it got a month's extension, followed by another, then another. Women used to be a good chunk of the audience, many of them doing *Namaskar* in obeisance whenever Santoshi Maa would appear on the screen. Some would bring *aath aana* (50 paise) and *ek rupaiya* (one rupee) coins tied to the ends of their sari or *dupatta* and toss them at the deity, almost like fulfilling a vow.

Suraj had begun screening films in 1974 as a temporary cinema, its licence being renewed every month for the first 10 years of its existence. The hall, in fact, fulfilled the need of the local population of Najafgarh, where there was no cinema hall for a distance of 20 kilometres. The only mode of entertainment was a moving troupe which enacted folk songs for the local populace. Unlike Connaught Place and Chandni Chowk, where a cinema hall graced the landscape every few steps, Suraj filled the gap here. It came up on a plot of one acre, and locals, mostly Sikh Jat and Hindu Jat communities, embraced it with open arms.

In the initial days, a cycle rickshaw, covered on all four sides, would move around Najafgarh, with a man at the centre announcing the name of the film being screened and playing snatches of the movie's songs. Children would run after the rickshaw, often wondering about the man inside. At times, the man would be dispensed with and a tape-recorder would play.

Unlike many halls in the city, Suraj was the preferred venue for middle-class viewers. As most people were unaccustomed to the subtleties of cinema, Suraj concentrated on playing action and comedy films. There was little space for romance as love stories were against the prevalent social norms in the area and as a result, films highlighting teenage romance were a no-no but those with images of macho heroes were hugely popular. Sunny Deol became the darling of the masses, many of whom identified with him as a Jat and did not mind watching his films more than once. *Ghatak* (1996), *Ghayal* (1990), *Ziddi* (1997) and *Jeet* (1996), all played at Suraj many times over and always notched up impressive numbers. The best, though, was reserved for *Gadar* (2001), the Anil Sharma film that was released in June, 2001. When people got to know that Sunny Deol was in Delhi to promote the film, they pleaded with the management to invite him to the hall as they wanted to 'touch' him once. Suraj had earlier had a brush with stardom when veteran actor Jagdeep with his son, noted comedian Javed Jaffery, came to the hall for the premiere of *Soorma Bhopali* in 1988. The locals, who had not seen many stars in their life, turned up in huge numbers to welcome the duo.

Sunny Deol's popularity rubbed off on his brother, Bobby Deol, as well. *Soldier* (1998) was screened here more than once. Other actors equally popular here have been Sanjay Dutt, Ajay Devgn and Salman Khan, but none has been able to rival the zest with which Sunny is greeted in these parts of the city. There have been only stray occasions when films without any of them have done good business here. One such moment was provided by the Haryanvi film, *Bairee* (1987) which ran for 10 weeks with all 28 shows every week playing to packed houses. When Sooraj Barjatya's much talked about *Hum Aapke Hain Koun...!* (1994) finally graced Suraj's screen, more than two months after it opened at Sapna on 5th August, 1994 in the city, the frenzy was the same. For six weeks, Suraj saw no unoccupied seat with, even women from conservative families in the vicinity calling up to book tickets in bulk.

For almost 40 years, Suraj provided a valuable option to those eagerly awaiting Hindi film screenings in and around Najafgarh. In the early days, the cinema was patronised by only the middle class population but from the late 1980s, the working class formed part of the audience as well. The hall improved its facilities, turning from a 688-seater to one with 519 seats, the number reduced to provide a space of at least 30 feet between the screen and the front stall. In the early days, Suraj charged as little as 70 paise for admission rights to stalls and the fare went up to Rs 1.40 for the balcony audience. Today, the same categories go for Rs 25 and 80, respectively. Along the way, the naturally cooled hall has given way to an air-cooled one and the tag of a temporary cinema has been shed too, with the hall getting a permanent licence in 2003, renewable every 10 years. And it may not be long before Suraj, like many other single-screens, turns into a multiplex.

34 AJANTA, Najafgarh Road

When Ajanta opened on 24th June, 1966, it was hailed as a 'showhouse that was fully air-conditioned and fitted with imported machines'. It had a restaurant and push-back seats and was the epitome of luxury when it played OP Ralhan's *Phool Aur Patthar* (1966), a Dharmendra-Meena Kumari starrer that was also released at Regal, Jagat, Palace, Naaz, Vivek and Radhu. The film's booking for the noon show started at 8 in the morning and it did fairly well at Ajanta and the hall came to fill a vacuum in the Najafgarh Road area. Soon, with films like *Sasta Khoon Mehnga Pyar* (1970), *Nai Umar Ki Nai Fasal* (1965), *Daku Mangal Singh* (1966), *Putlibai* (1972) and *Taj Mahal* (1963)—the last of these doing stupendous business in the repeat run—Ajanta became a hall that offered popular films in a fine ambience. Its stall were better attended than the balcony. However, Ajanta was not destined to be around for long. It shut down a few years ago due to financial difficulties.

35 RAAJ, Tilak Nagar

Raaj cinema began with temporary moorings—it was one of the many halls owned by the Sebles, who would set up makeshift cinemas for a few months, then dismantle and establish them elsewhere. But Raaj stayed the course. In the 1960s, its highest admission rate was not much more than Rs 1.25. And the lowest fare was less than half of that.

Those were the days when the government was not very keen to give licences to cinema halls in the heart of the capital and permission was more likely to be given for faraway areas like Subhash Nagar, Tilak Nagar and Vishwas Nagar. Temporary theatres sprung up here, which ran a film for a few weeks, shut shop and moved on. Then they found another barren piece of land and put up their structures all over again. Most such cinemas closed down by the late 1960s, giving way to permanent cinema halls. Raaj was a fortunate beneficiary that didn't perish in that culling. But it did face teething troubles. Unlike other cinemas in the city, it began as a weekend hall, playing movies only three shows a day for a couple of days a week. Over time, business picked up as more and more people started living in Tilak Nagar. Gradually, there were enough prospective viewers for the hall to turn into a daily affair, showing three films a day. In the 1970s it transformed into a daily four shows theatre. It showed *Chaudhury Karnail Singh*,

(1960), a National Award winner and one of the earliest films of seasoned actor Prem Chopra; later, it showed Mahipal's popular film *Nagdevta* (1962). The films struck a chord with the predominantly Punjabi-speaking audience.

Raaj became a semi-permanent hall in 1973 and a permanent theatre in the 1980s. If earlier it had three classes of admission, now it became a 680-seater with the modern-day classification of front stall, rear stall and balcony. The prices for tickets also changed with the times, the permanent hall's lowest rate being Rs 10 and the highest Rs 25 before it closed down. It registered better business in evening and night shows, whereas its noon and matinee shows were not as popular.

In the mid-'80s, Raaj experienced a boom. A succession of films hit the bull's eye at the low-profile hall, taking veterans back to the thunderous receptions that once greeted Dara Singh—considered a real *mard*. The men who lived in and around Tilak Nagar, a substantial part of the audience, identified with him and eagerly waited for films like *Sikander-e-Azam* (1965), *Rustom* (1982), *Faulad* (1963) and *Raka* (1965). A little more than a decade after his last mega hit, *Bhakti Mein Shakti* (1978), it was time for a new object of adulation. Men still constituted the principal audiences at Raaj but their tastes had changed from the brutal physicality of Dara Singh to the more cheerful face of Jeetendra. The elder part of the audience thought it was not the done thing for a man to dance, except a step or two of *bhangra* but the next generation of immigrants—mostly from Pakistan's Punjab province—was ready to step beyond stereotypes and Jeetendra of Jumping Jack fame became quite a favourite of the crowd. Nearly all his films were greeted with whistles, claps and impromptu live dancing by the audiences. In 1980s, films like *Mawaali* (1983), *Himmatwala* (1983),

Tohfa (1984) and *Majaal* (1987), were gleefully accepted as Sridevi and Jaya Prada caught their fancy with songs like 'Nainon Mein Sajna', 'Ooi Amma Ooi Amma' and 'Gori Tere Ang Ang Mein'. Many threw coins at the screen and demanded an encore. All mega hits reaching Raaj a few weeks after doing the rounds elsewhere in the city, meant that viewers had already been swaying to the film's songs for a while. Many came to Raaj specifically for the dance numbers, not dismissed then as 'item numbers'. Each was a gem for the audience. This musical wave at Raaj was very different from a similar wave earlier at cinemas like Golcha, Jagat and Excelsior where cinegoers used to turn up for films for their sheer melody. Here the songs were appreciated, not so much for their lyrics or music, but because of the physical energy and sensuality of the actors. It was no celebration of poetry while running around the trees. Rather, the men here liked the women for an uninhibited expression of their sexuality through dances in songs.

In the 1970s and '80s, while many men in the balcony sections of halls in south and central Delhi went out for a smoke during songs, they did not do so at Raaj. They were happy that when Sridevi hummed 'Naino Mein Sajna', the camera focussed everywhere except on the eyes. A similar reaction was evinced when Jaya Prada danced to Asha Bhonsle's 'Ooi Amma…Aane Lagi Mujhko Haya' in a poolside shot.

For as long as Jeetendra ruled the roost in the mid-'80s, Raaj had very few poorly attended shows or cancelled night shows. Many films made a comeback too on popular demand. With the comeback of melody in Hindi cinema through films like *Aashiqui* (1990), *Dil Hai Ke Maanta Nahin* (1991) and *Saajan* (1991), Raaj's fortunes nosedived, its patrons not as happy with films whose songs drew heavily from romantic poetry. About a decade ago, Anil Sharma's *Gadar* (2001) played here to packed houses. Again, the film that related a love story of a Sikh man and a Muslim woman against the backdrop of Partition touched a chord here. And men in the audience loved Sunny Deol's larger-than-life persona.

Many called Raaj a *'dabba'* while others referred to it simply as 'talkies' but for a long time, business was good despite competition changing colour and form. It could hold its own with a certain segment of the audience.

The elite went to the balcony and dress circle of south Delhi and the Connaught Place halls which played Hollywood films and the middle class favoured the balcony sections of A-grade halls showing the latest of Hindi cinema. The working class went to a hall like Raaj. However, the bubble burst when satellite television made inroads into every house. Soon, the hall could only play faded prints of old films and worse, dubbed versions of Hollywood and Korean films. Plans are reportedly afoot to turn it into a multiplex. The quiet little theatre might just get a new lease of life.

36 VISHAL, Rajouri Garden

In the 1980s when *Chhota Chetan* (1984) was released at Vishal, the local residents came out by the thousands to watch the film. What's the big deal, one would ask. Wasn't that normal practice in an era when many films went on to do silver or golden jubilee and even average films ran for at least 50 days? But this was the dubbed version of India's first 3-D film, *My Dear Kuttichathan* (1984), and viewers were as enthralled by the content of the film as by the way of watching it. They were provided special 3D glasses rented out at 50 paise, which had to be returned at the end of the show. Everybody in and around the cinema would talk of the '*chashme wali* film' (film to be watched with spectacles). Curious men and women who used spectacles in everyday life quietly enquired about how they could use the glasses. '*Kya apna chashma utaar kar pehenna padega*?' (Do we have to remove our glasses to put on these spectacles?). Only when the booking clerk or an usher gave a practical demonstration were they convinced.

As word spread, fans started driving down 20-25 kilometres, to catch a show of this film at Vishal. The film did not show elsewhere in the city for the first seven weeks, in stark contrast to the practice then, when every A-grade movie released at 10-12 cinemas. It helped that Vishal with 1,401 seats was the largest cinema in Delhi. In film circles, its Friday night shows were considered 'silver shows' and Saturdays were 'golden nights'. There was no ebb on the weekends. *Chhota Chetan* pulled in the crowd even for the noon shows, never a strong point in these parts after the first weekend.

This 3D film turned the spotlight back on Vishal as the cinema that treated cinegoers as valuable guests. The gleaming marble staircase, the brass vases on every turn, teakwood railings and a huge lounge in front of the canteen meant that Vishal lived up to its name. It was indeed *'vishal'* or larger-than-life in every sense of the term and it had been that way since the time it opened with the premiere of *Heer-Ranjha* (1970), the Raaj Kumar-Priya Rajvansh film in 1971. The star cast, with director Chetan Anand, came to the hall, which had been decked up in marigold, and sweets and snacks were generously distributed.

Vishal was owned by JR Sood of the Eros group and stayed in the family when his son, Ajay Kumar Sood, took over. He is of the belief that the cinema has to move with times in terms of technology but doesn't need to compromise on its single-screen status.

Its admission rate in the early days was on the higher side at Rs 1.25 because Vishal was air-conditioned from day one. But that proved no deterrent to cinegoers; they had been starved of films until this cinema was opened. On a stretch of 13 kilometres, between Alpna cinema in Model Town which opened in 1967 to Rajouri Garden, there was not a single hall of any stature. Viewers had to travel far and wide to get their fill. Vishal filled that void.

Heer Ranjha whipped up magic at the box office and its success paved the way for innumerable mainstream films, most of which appealed to family audiences. While *Mughal-e-Azam* (1960) and *Taj Mahal* (1963) raked in the moolah in re-runs here, *Jai Santoshi Maa* (1975) marched into a league of its own. Initially supposed to be a small-budget film, it was released with only six prints but the awe-inspiring box-office performance meant this was soon doubled. Men, and especially women, fell in love with the film which evoked devotional fervour like none other in the past. After that, only Dara Singh's *Bhakti Mein Shakti* (1978) came close to replicating the passion. Even then, the latter did better business in the morning shows while *Jai Santoshi Maa* had a successful daily four shows run.

Yash Chopra's epic *Deewaar* (1975) got off to a blistering start on its release here, a feat replicated by *Amar Akbar Anthony* (1977) a couple of years later. Raj Kapoor's *Satyam Shivam Sundaram* (1978), which encountered a lot of problems at other cinemas in Delhi because of the skin show it featured, faced no such issues here. Even the film's set-ups were left untouched as the middle-class viewers, most of them Punjabis and middle-level businessmen with antecedents in Peshawar, Rawalpindi and Lahore, accepted the film. Though it did not go on to become a smashing hit, it proved that movie watchers had varied tastes and did not regard skin show to be necessarily vulgar.

Most of the time, though, Vishal played family or action flicks. Dev Anand used to be a guest here and his films, including *Des Pardes* (1978), did remarkably well. Both Amitabh Bachchan and Mithun Chakraborty also had their fans here—if Amitabh Bachchan starrers like *Deewaar*, and *Amar Akbar Anthony* set new records, Mithun's *Suraksha* (1979) and *Boxer* (1984) among others appealed to many. Interestingly, once Mallika Sherawat graced the hall and was sporting enough to enter the current booking section to have over tickets for viewing *Aap kaa Suroor*, her 2007 film with Himesh Reshammiya.

Today, Vishal is among a handful of single screens to have successfully survived the onslaught of multi-screen halls and is still sought after by top banners. Business, though slightly reduced, remains positive. And Vishal, with the little fountain at the entrance, well-lit marble staircase and spacious canteen, continues to hold its own.

37 JANAK, Janakpuri

When Prakash Mehra's *Muqaddar Ka Sikandar* released on 27th October, 1978, Janak was the talk of the town. It was the inaugural film at this fully air-conditioned hall with a 70 mm screen and stereophonic sound. It turned out to be a hit. Then came *Sholay* in re-run, a little over three years after its initial release in 1975. Janak promoted it in a unique fashion: the cinema's advertisements consisted of the film's hit dialogues. Since the film was longer than most Hindi films, shows were advanced by half an hour with the noon show starting as early as 11.30 a.m.

This was followed by *Bhakti Mein Shakti* (1978) and the hall enjoyed good business again. The fare at Janak was always mainstream, with no time or inclination for Mrinal Sen or Shyam Benegal. Everything was smooth till the anti-Sikh riots in 1984, when the hall was badly affected by fire. It closed down till normalcy returned to the city. The management then decided to renovate the cinema before relaunching it a couple of years later. Janak's has been a chequered history, never short of drama. Now, it is among the preferred halls with facilities comparable to the cream of the crop.

38 LOKESH, Nangloi

Among the bigger halls in Nangloi and surrounding areas, Lokesh is seldom frequented by audiences not living or working in its immediate vicinity. It caters to the local population's need for commercial cinema and no more. It has screened blockbusters like *Ganga Ki Saugandh* (1978), *Suhaag* (1979), *Naseeb* (1981) and, much later, films like *Indian* (2001), *Gadar* (2001) and *The Hero* (2003). If in the 1970s, Amitabh Bachchan ruled the roost, in the early 2000s, Sunny Deol's films drew huge crowds. Salman Khan was the crowd-puller after *Wanted* (2009) and *Dabangg* (2010).

Lokesh has screened films in their second run as well with *Azaad* (1978) and *Mujhe Jeene Do* (1963) having particularly memorable stints. With its impressive seating capacity, Lokesh is able to attract top banners and run actions flicks for more than a week too.

39 MILAN, Karampura

The good old Milan cinema that still carries on with its operations opened at the same time as Deep and turned out to be more long lasting. Over the years, the fully air-conditioned cinema proved a better judge of viewers' tastes. It opened with *Nanak Naam Jahaz Hai* (1969) and understandably so, considering a lot of people in the vicinity were immigrants from Punjab in Pakistan. Later, it did good business screening many mythologicals, including *Har Har Mahadev* (1950).

Over time, it came to be identified as a middle-rung hall that offered new films at affordable rates. Occasionally, though, Milan, like almost all other halls in the city, played re-runs. When it showed Dilip Kumar's *Sunghursh* (initially released in 1968) the film did well enough at the box office to merit another run here a few years later. That was the case with Shakti Samanta's Shammi Kapoor-Sharmila Tagore starrer *Kashmir Ki Kali* (1964) too in re-runs.

After being in the doldrums at the turn of the millennium, Milan reinvented itself to stay in business. *Bachke Rehna Re Baba* (2005), a rare film starring Rekha and Mallika Sherawat together, released here in 2005 and not at any of the more illustrious halls of Connaught Place or Old Delhi. With better amenities and better films, Milan's relationship with cinegoers has stayed firm and true.

40 NATRAJ, Moti Nagar

For the residents of Kirti Nagar, Shadipur, Karampura, Guru Arjun Nagar and even beyond, Natraj was a household name, its yellow exteriors as identifiable from a distance as the biggest building in the area. It played blockbusters with zest and steered clear of art-house fare, specialising in films like *Bindiya Aur Bandook* (1972), *Dharma* (1973) and *Azaad* (1978). It made room for both Muslim and Hindu devotionals, being a rare hall in Delhi to show both *Dayar-e-Madina* (1975) and *Jai Santoshi Maa (1975)*. Interestingly, in 1978, it played two films of Sanjeev Kumar at the same time by screening *Devata* (1978) in daily four shows and *Manoranjan* (1974) in the morning slot.

A little under a decade ago, it gave way to Fun Republic, the first multiplex in and around Moti Nagar in West Delhi.

41 PAYAL, Naraina

Among the earliest cinemas outside the charmed circle, this hall was comparable with most upmarket halls preferred by middle-class residents of south Delhi. It had a distinguished existence in south-west Delhi from the 1960s till 2002 when it gave way to a PVR multiplex. If as a single screen theatre,

Payal concentrated on Hindi films high on entertainment quotient, as a multiplex too it favours Hindi movies though it keeps a little window for Hollywood offerings too.

While it was up and running as a single-screen cinema, Payal revelled in its night shows and registered better footfall in those time slots than at matinees. The screenings were frequented by industrial workers who queued up for a film at the end of a long day. Among the notable films it played was Rajshri's *Dulhan Wohi Jo Piya Mann Bhaye* (1977), which graced its hall in the golden jubilee week while it was playing simultaneously at Chanakya. Payal was once ravaged by fire in the '80s but came back stronger.

42 RACHNA, Rajendra Place

Rachna hit the headlines as the new favourite of youngsters in the late '70s. Though it had Liberty and Vivek close by, Rachna hardly put a foot wrong forward in its initial years. *Ek Baar Phir* (1980), Deepti Naval's much-talked-about film, ran for seven weeks here, creating quite a stir with lyrics by Vinod Pande and music by Raghunath Seth, and misplaced talk of skin show.

However, a few years before that, Rachna had run Raj Khosla's *Main Tulsi Tere Aangan Ki* (1978) with distinction. The film pitted opposite big star films like *Muqaddar ka Sikandar* (1978) and *Devata* (1978) was promoted in an unusual way, appealing to audiences to choose it after they were through with the rest. The advertisement claimed, 'When you have forgotten all other blockbusters, you will remember this for its sheer beauty and nobility of human emotion.' What blotted its book was that it often played seedy films in the morning shows and there were allegations of even smuttier stuff being interpolated on films. As a result, their license was revoked in the '90s.

Rachna shut down many summers ago, its lasting memory being a film like *The Birds, the Bees and the Italians* (1966).

43 SATYAM, Patel Nagar

These days, the name of Satyam, Patel Nagar, evokes visions of a multiplex that is high on style. However, it is actually a successor of the good old single-screen cinema that screened films for about a couple of decades. Back in 1980, when it was founded, Satyam was a breath of fresh air. It brought people the latest films in a clean ambience, and respected the privacy of viewers—no vendors were allowed inside, unlike Vivek close by. The ticket pricing was relatively on the higher side, so often only those genuinely interested in the movie would be part of the audience. The hall was not known to play seedy flicks either. Its balcony crowd was brought up almost exclusively by the residents of Patel Nagar while the stalls were patronised by those from Ranjit Nagar and Guru Arjun Nagar, the two colonies being less expensive than Patel Nagar. In 2002, it was converted into a four-screen multiplex.

44 SHOBHA, Sultanpur Road

Among the first established halls in and around Nangloi, Shobha did well for some time. The toiling masses for whom Shobha often played formula action films, populated its stalls; the balcony section, preferred by family audiences, came in numbers during family dramas. Both combined to make Shobha a good business enterprise some 40-odd years ago. Many people preferred to watch a film here even if they worked in the heart of the city, say Connaught Place. It had everything to do with the affordability factor as also Shobha's ability to get new releases alongside the more illustrious halls. Manmohan Desai's *Parvarish* (1977), starring Amitabh Bachchan and Vinod Khanna, attracted such a huge crowd that the film had to have another run. Bachchan had a great fan following here as well, with *Ganga ki Saugandh* (1978) and later *Kaalia* (1981) registering a good footfall. In between, there were films like *Apna Khoon* (1978) and *Seeta Aur Geeta* (1972) in repeat runs.

For a little over a decade, Shobha did decent business, before finally making way for commercial establishments.

45 SONIA, Vikaspuri

Even younger than Grandlay, Sonia was among the last single-screen cinemas to be established in Delhi. Its foray was short and largely incident-free. Sonia played regular mainstream fare to a largely middle-class audience from the neighbouring Vikas Puri and Tilak Nagar belt. While the facilities could compete with the more celebrated halls of south Delhi, Sonia was never on the radar of movie-watchers from beyond its immediate neighbourhood. In 2002, it turned into a multiplex, opening with the Anil Kapoor, Abhishek Bachchan and Fardeen Khan multi-starrer, *Om Jai Jagadish* (2002). Though it concentrated only on Hindi movies as a single-screen theatre, it plays Hollywood films and even occasional Punjabi flicks in its multiplex avatar. It registers decent footfall and its non-English shows are better appreciated.

46 VIVEK, Patel Nagar

A trip to Vivek always involved a high degree of luck—you needed a lot of it to lay your hands on a ticket. You could turn up half an hour before a scheduled show, and stand in a queue at the current booking counter, yet find it closed within a few minutes of opening. Tickets disappeared as soon as they appeared! If you didn't procure tickets in the morning for a noon show, you could forget about watching a film. Alternatively, touts could be approached but for that, deep pockets were essential, as was a keen eye. They all dressed alike in jeans and T-shirts, sneakers and shades. The going rate according to them was at least twice the original amount and could go up to five times more. They made a killing here, coming in unannounced and going away as quietly. In between, their eyes would search for fans desperately looking for tickets for the next show. A quick and furtive deal was struck, tickets and money exchanged hands and cinegoers went inside, relieved at getting admission. The black-marketeers would go straight to the *paanwala* or the puncture-*wala* and share their stories. A couple of hours later, they started afresh.

Apart from being a blink-and-you-miss-the-chance kind of theatre, Vivek belonged to the rare class of halls without a balcony. Its seating arrangement was such that the lesser you paid, the lower was the level of your seat and as the price went up, so did the distance from the screen and the height of the seats. The cinema was smart with its film selection, going in for blockbusters and playing them only for a few weeks to keep the audience interested enough to lap up the tickets, and also ensured brisk business for the black-marketeers.

When Subhash Ghai's *Hero* (1983) was released in the early 1980s, it attracted housefull crowds everywhere. Even though the hall was more than 10 kilometres from where I lived, Vivek was a possible option. However, the prospect of discovering a new cinema and watching a hit film was too alluring to ignore. Four of us reached the hall a full hour before the matinee show but all the tickets were sold. Crestfallen, we were returning when the alert eye of a 'facilitator' fell on us and, realising our predicament, he sold us the tickets at nearly *10 times* their printed rates. We watched the film, choosing to forego a meal, which proved difficult at a hall like Vivek. In most halls, if you did not want to eat anything during the interval, you could just avoid going to the canteen but here, vendors came inside during the interval and dangled their wares in front of us hungry souls. Sales inside the hall were a common feature here and the guards and ushers were very 'cooperative'.

In the days when security was not an overriding concern, fans smoked inside the hall while others would exit during a song, attend to their private business and come back. Shopkeepers around the hall often came to Vivek just to use its conveniences and some of them doubled up as ticket hoarders too. Nobody complained. Vivek was an acquiescing kind of hall.

Vivek was among the oldest cinema halls outside the charmed Connaught Place-Old Delhi circle. Rachna and Satyam, its immediate competitors, came in much later, as did Natraj and Milan further down the road. With films like *Phool Aur Pathar* (1966), *Bobby* (1973), *Deewaar* (1975),

Kaalia (1981), *Maqsad* (1984), *Hero* (1983) and *Elaan-e-Jung* (1989) under its belt, it had a repertoire that was not easy to match. From the 1970s, it was a destination only for star-driven shows with *Reshma Aur Shera* (1971) leading the way. But in the early days, it did make room for more discerning fare. A film like *Nai Umar Ki Nai Fasal* (1965) enjoyed a fine run here as did *Jagriti* (1954) in various repeat runs. In the early '80s, a niche offering, *Bin Maa Ke Bachche* (1980) ran in a single show daily for close to two months. Shah Rukh Khan and Dibakar Banerji were among its patrons before they became formidable names in Hindi cinema.

The running of the hall, however, was not always smooth. Its decline began much before the multiplex boom. A little more than a decade ago, it was demolished to make way for the Delhi Metro, the second hall after New Amar to meet this fate. And Vivek, often careworn, not always well looked after, became history.

47 LIBERTY, New Rohtak Road

Liberty was an early entrant in the business in this part of the city, its history dating back to 1956 when it was under the ownership of Seth Amolak Singh. He, however, was not very successful at improving the fortunes of the hall as the area was not regarded particularly safe at that time. This changed in 1962 when Rajeshwar Prasad took over; his family had established at least five cinema halls in the undivided Punjab in places like Chandigarh, Ambala, Hisar and even Gurgaon which was then part of the Punjab only as Haryana had not yet been founded. Taking over Liberty cost Prasad Rs 1,00,000 at a time when a booking clerk did not make more than Rs 60 a month. Two years later, the cinema was closed for six months for renovation and it returned a 959-seater, centrally air-conditioned hall with a 70 mm screen which used a Russian projector. It was inaugurated with *Pooja ke Phool* in 1964, which went on to make history. A special charity show was organised to raise funds for the National Defence Fund—until then no filmmaker had had a charity show of any film in the week of its release. An amount of Rs 4,200 was raised, the cheque handed over to the wife of Gulzarilal Nanda, the then Home Minister, Government of India.

From this point on, Liberty grew from strength to strength. Though often in direct competition with Naaz,

Filmistan, Vivek and later Rachna, it carved out its own niche as a family cinema which avoided sleazy fare. That was the principal reason why the trend of morning shows, generally the time smutty films were shown, did not start here at all. Liberty preferred not to have morning shows rather than put up seedy posters which would be seen by family audiences coming in for the main movie later in the day. Similarly, inside the hall, not just in the balcony, even in the stalls, the staff created special sections for women and families by bunching them together. The principles were firm when it came to the 3D craze; Rajan Gupta arguing that a 3D film, watched for more than 40 minutes or so, left the viewers with a headache and a feeling of drowsiness. This principled opposition to new technology meant Liberty never showed films like *Shiva ka Insaaf* (1985), *Maha Shaktimaan* (1985) and the rest.

Liberty rapidly became a preferred destination for film distributors as well. *Sholay* and *Jai Santoshi Maa* did good business in 1975 as did *Dharamveer* in 1977, the film that sent black-marketeers into overdrive. Before that, *Aarzoo* (1965) had kept the cash registers ringing, much like *Sacha Jhutha* (1970). Then there was *Bobby* (1973), for whose premiere Raj Kapoor himself turned up. He arrived from the main gate with fans extending their hands to touch him, and had to leave from the rear gate to avoid a repeat. A maddening rush announced the arrival of Manmohan Desai's *Coolie* (1983) too. However, the craze that accompanied the run of Sooraj Barjatya's *Maine Pyar Kiya* (1989) was unparalleled. The film went on to do a silver jubilee. The cinema, unfortunately, blotted its copybook a shade when it showed films like *Yamraaj* (1998), a Mithun Chakraborty-Jackie Shroff starrer, and *Jallad* (1995) in the mid-'90s.

In 1996, in the midst of a fast-approaching winter and festive season, Gulzar's *Maachis* (1996) was making headlines as much for its topicality as its earthy music. Chandrachur Singh was being hailed as a bright new find, Tabu could scarcely disappoint, and all over the city, one could hear, 'Chappa Chappa Charkha Chale'. One evening, Gulzar decided to visit a cinema hall playing his movie, choosing Liberty as his destination to show up with the cast of the film, minus the heroine. A 'housefull' board greeted them. Too often, critics had panned him as appealing only to a discerning few and on that day, Gulzar happily soaked in the adulation. As he was led inside the hall by the proprietor, Rajan Gupta, he stopped for a bit and said, *'Iss mauqe par to ek photo ho jaye'* (This occasion calls for a photo). A photographer was promptly arranged, and Gulzar, beaming from ear to ear, posed for the picture along with Gupta and Kirit Desai, the distributor, and the cast of the film.

Maachis indeed raked in the riches at Liberty, just as *Raja Jani* (1972) had done at the time of its release. The film which brought Hema Malini to the hall was a great crowd puller. A burqa was arranged for the actress so she could enter incognito and when she did so, the 'dream girl' was delighted to soak in the warm applause. She was surrounded mostly by women as Liberty had made the unique arrangement of seating women in the last two rows of the balcony, helping them avoid the unnecessary attention of men. Hema played her part well, opting to stay completely quiet for the fear of her voice being recognised by cinegoers.

The release of the unsung *Rani Aur Lalpari* (1975) prevented the hall from being part of history; this was the film that delayed GP Sippy's historic *Sholay* (1975) being shown here owing to a prior commitment to the former. When it did show the film a few weeks after its release in mid-1975, *Sholay* collected good numbers at Liberty and the film also achieved a unique feat. Its first run here was of merely two weeks, while the repeat run some three years later, lasted 10, notching up a rare distinction of the second run being longer than the first one!

On another occasion, Liberty predictably played *Jai Santoshi Maa* (1975) more than once. Every time the film showed here, the faithful would turn up in large numbers and add to the collections. Some, like at many cinemas in the city, even took off their shoes in front of cut-outs placed in the lobby of the cinema, did a brief *puja* in front of the deity, before entering the hall.

All the films put together, however, only underscore fine offerings in the past and the present. Liberty continues to be an exhilarating affair—a hall for family audiences and a cinema for top banners.

V

Halls in Between

48 NAAZ, Cycle Market, Jhandewalan

Away from the heat and grime of politics, the winter of 1975 was a long and fruitful one. It came wrapped in layers of mist and answered the prayers of virtually all movie fans—those with a penchant for *paisa vasool* cinema, those who swore by the giant canvas and even those who preferred their fare soft and gentle. Cinema halls in the city did stupendous business with cash registers jingling almost everywhere—from the age-old A-graders of Connaught Place and the Walled City to relatively new entrants in north, west, south and east Delhi. Not to be left out in the gainful period were halls located on the periphery of the more elite ones, in Paharganj and Jhandewalan, for instance. There was business to be conducted, films to be shown, viewers to be pleased and profits to be made. Even the imposition of Emergency could not curtail cinema lovers. Winter offered viewers films as varied as *Mili* (1975) and *Khushboo* (1975) on the one hand and *Sholay* (1975) and *Deewar* (1975) on the other. Sandwiched in between were *Julie* (1975), *Geet Gata Chal* (1975), *Amanush* (1975) and Shyam Benegal's *Nishant* (1975), which surprised the pundits with its collections at Regal. Also surprising was the Muslim devotional *Dayar-e-Madina* (1975) which managed a screening at Eros, Filmistan and Chanakya. This paved the way for a film like *Quran ur Imaan* (1974) which had a belated show here. Then there was the ever-popular *Jai Santoshi Maa* (1975), *Roti Kapda aur Makaan* (1974) and *Pratiggya* (1975). The English-speaking audience had their choices too, with *Ben Hur* (1959) still doing the rounds, *Avanti* (1972), *Fear is the Key* (1972) and *Farewell Friend* (1968).

Naaz, though, was among a handful of halls that was left out of the rush. It had to wait its turn, brooding over missed opportunities as new strategies were formulated to take on competition. Even as *Sholay* was hailed as 'the biggest hit ever' and was attracting housefull shows at Plaza just a couple of kilometres away, Naaz failed to get a slice of the pie; the film was to come here weeks later. *Mili,* whose posters proclaimed that the film mirrored a man's mind and a woman's soul, did not show here. In a late decision, the film went to Regal and Milan and *Khushboo* was shown at Filmistan, which, along with Liberty and Naaz were the next choice of exhibitors after the Connaught Place and Old Delhi cinemas. However, Naaz restored a semblance of balance to the competition by showing *Amanush*, the weepy saga that garnered decent collections at most places. But this was a not good enough to take on the avalanche of simultaneous blockbusters running elsewhere. Soon, Naaz reverted to screening either yesteryear hits or appealing to the baser instincts of the audience to stay in business. A film like *Awara* (1951) arrived here more than 20 years after it first released. Then a sleazy new release like *Kaam Shastra* (1975) also got two shots at popularity.

Business was meagre and soon, Naaz, located at a stone's throw from the Connaught Place quartet of Rivoli, Regal, Plaza and Odeon, seemed a stunted tree in comparison. It struggled to shake off this image in subsequent years, though it even screened films like *Eye Witness* (1981), *Neel Kamal*

(1968) and *Waqt* (1965). It also showed Mithun Chakraborty films like *Surakshaa* (1979) and *Unnees Bees (1980)*, a handful of Amitabh Bachchan-starrers like *Don* (1978) and *Kaalia* (1981) and a few Dev Anand-Raj Kapoor films on a re-run.

Naaz attempted to get into the viewers' good books by playing the choicest regional films at rates as low as 10 *anna*s. A festival of Bengali films was once held here. Often, Marathi films were screened in the morning shows and were lapped up by RSS volunteers staying nearby. *Pahu Re Kitti Vaat* (1963) stayed on for eight weeks. Much the same happened with the morning shows of Punjabi films welcomed by Punjabi immigrants settled in and around Karol Bagh, Patel Nagar and Rajendra Nagar. Naaz also played Bhojpuri films in the morning slots much before the genre drummed up enormous business in the early 2000s.

The hall had its bitter moments, too, when films originally scheduled to be released here went elsewhere at the last moment. In 1960, *Mehlon Ka Khwab* (1960) did not show here even though the film was meant to be released only at Naaz and Golcha, leading to a protracted legal battle. Later, *Aandhi* (1975), often the topic of discussion in a city of the politically aware, was also slated to have a screening and after being initially withheld, found a release post-Emergency. It did notch up the numbers but this did not change the fate of the cinema.

The moment distributors had to decide on theatres for big banners and daily four shows, Naaz invariably lost out to the Big Four of Connaught Place on the one side and Liberty and Vivek on the other. Even Imperial in Paharganj stayed ahead of it for a film like *Bhakti Mein Shakti* (1978), while Shiela got a first look at *Deewaar, Shalimar* (1978) and *Tarzan* (1985). Naaz never reached the big league. On the rare occasion, it screened searing movies like *Ardh Satya* (1983). Once the going got tough, and it had to play films like *Doosri Sita* (1974), *Gaai Aur Gori* (1973) and *Jalte Badan* (1973), Naaz came up with an innovative method to attract patrons. It played two reels of the song, 'Dum Maro Dum' from *Hare Rama Hare Krishna* (1971) before these average films, the idea being to appeal to cinegoers with the promise of better things.

These desperate measures were a far cry from the 1950s and '60s when Naaz was a popular destination. Beginning with *Sarhad* in 1960, it showed films like *Biradari* (1966), *Navrang* (1959) and *Haqeeqat* (1964), the last of these actually playing to live performances of songs by a local troupe near the hall's entrance. But these moments of pride were few and far between to make running Naaz a viable proposition. About 20 years ago, it shut permanently after playing *Laadla* (1994).

49 FILMISTAN, Rani Jhansi Road

Soon after Independence, Delhi had a proliferation of corridor cinemas—halls that were established on busy trade and traffic routes. New show-houses were established on the outskirts of Old Delhi and the peripheries of Connaught Place. Cinema halls like Golcha in Daryaganj, Delite on Asaf Ali Road and Shiela in Paharganj were strategically located to cater to audiences from both Old and New Delhi. They were close enough for Old Dilliwalahs to reach after a cycle-rickshaw or a tonga ride, and at the same time removed from the hustle-bustle of the old city so people from other parts could watch movies here.

Similar to Golcha, Delite and Shiela were Filmistan on Rani Jhansi Road and, to a lesser extent, Naaz in Jhandewalan. In some ways, these two went beyond the concept of neighbourhood cinemas but also suffered because of their proximity to better known historic halls. Drawing an audience from beyond the immediate neighbourhood, their clientele was much more heterogeneous with Filmistan in particular doing a fine tightrope walk. Located between New and Old Delhi, its audiences included new immigrants from Pakistan and long-time residents of Tis Hazari and surrounding areas. They were a neat mix of Hindu and Muslim middle-class families and those from the working class. If at one time,

Filmistan seemed to be catering to the kind of audience one usually saw at Jagat—seasoned men with grey beards, women in burqas and younger men in sweat-drenched vests and trousers after a hard day spent pushing carts or lifting loads—and at other times it seemed more like Golcha's audience with fancy cars and well-off patrons heading to the higher priced-sections. Filmistan did cater to them too but ensured that its services remained affordable, its ambience neat and tidy and its nose above troubled waters. Though it was seldom the first choice of any banner or distributor, the hall was satisfied with playing second fiddle.

In 1975, it showed *Khushboo* (1975), but the film had a limited run and Filmistan had to hunt for more films to stay in business. The hall turned out to be right on the money when it decided to cater to children instead of following other cinema halls, which regularly displayed 'housefull' signs courtesy *Sholay* (1975), *Deewaar* (1975) or *Jai Santoshi Maa* (1975). Instead of going in for low-brow or middle of the road films, it screened the re-run of director Satyen Bose's 1954 film *Jagriti*, a Nehru Award-winning saga for children and this was no stop-gap or knee-jerk reaction. It was a well-planned and promoted venture, with schoolchildren being invited for special screenings in the noon shows. This ability to revamp itself according to emerging challenges had manifested itself in the 1960s too, with a screening of LV Prasad's *Daadi Maa* (1966), when the mood all over the country was sombre due to the Hanoi bombing incidents. It was during this period that Filmistan really proved its mettle, playing host to many hit films through a wonderful daily-change festival in 1966. As part of the festival, films like *Shaheed* (1965), *Tumsa Nahin Dekha* (1957) and *Munimji* (1955) played to a great response, prompting the management to host a similar festival a couple of years later. On that occasion, the focus was strictly on Dilip Kumar. *Devdas* (1955), *Deedar* (1951), *Leader* (1964) and *Gunga-Jumna* (1961) played to packed audiences, leading trade pundits to call Filmistan 'Dilip Kumar *ki purani filmon ka* hall' (the hall of Dilip Kumar's old films). This ability to think out of the box and take on competition head-on stood it in good stead.

The same ability came to the fore when the hall showed Hindu and Muslim devotional films by turns. *Shiv Bhakt Baba Balak Nath* (1972) and *Dayar-e-Madina* (1975) were screened one after the other. There were also rare occasions when Filmistan was not forced to play catch-up. Sunil Dutt's historic *Yaadein* (1964) played here and the management went out of its way to promote it as the 'world's first solo actor' film. A few critics sneered, '*Ek* actor *ki film hai, ek-do log hi dekhenge*' (The film has only one actor, only one or two persons will watch it). Though *Yaadein* did not set any box-office records, it registered a decent footfall. It was much the same story with the critically acclaimed *Ek Gaon ki Kahani* (1957) The response of viewers was much better to *Anarkali* (1953). When the much-talked about film reached here, it was promoted in a unique way: a van was hired and special lights were installed behind the film's set-ups placed on the vehicle. It used to move around with people looking at it in awe. Hand-pushed carts which moved around playing music from the film, with the film's set-ups were also hired,.

There were slip-ups in its history too. In a move to make quick money, Filmistan showed films like *Daku Mangal Singh* (1966), *Jangal Mein Mangal* (1972) and *Kisan aur Bhagwan* (1974). The frontbenchers turned up and these films garnered good money but for Filmistan the gain was temporary and the loss long lasting. The image of low-brow action quickie proved difficult to shake off and the hall gained a reputation of playing any kind of film, from the internationally acclaimed *Aan* (1952) and National Award-winning *Ankur* (1974) to *Sasta Khoon, Mehnga Pyar* (1970) and *Ranga Khush* (1975). The high-brow started keeping away because of the latter kind of movies, not returning even when the hall was refurbished in the mid-2000s. The stalls' crowd kept the business going but as it became more and more difficult to get top banners, Filmistan ceased to matter. Towards the end, it became the release address for many C-grade or much-delayed flicks that failed to find takers anywhere else. It was not much of a surprise when the hall closed down soon after the construction of a flyover began right next to it towards the end of the first decade of the new millennium.

The cinema that shared its name with the much loftier studio in Bombay deserved better.

VI

Cinemascape South

50 CHANAKYA, Chanakyapuri

When Chanakya began screening films in 1971, the much talked-about *Mera Naam Joker* (1970) was its first offering. But it was the name of the last film released here that summed up Chanakya's status in the eyes of movie-lovers in the capital—*Taare Zameen Par* (2007). A genuine article amid many camouflaged losers, Chanakya had great panache, serving up grace and class in an environment to die for—the vast greens of Chanakyapuri's diplomatic arena with its wide and well-lined roads and disciplined traffic. On a good day, you could hear the mynah and the koel sing, on a bad one, you could hear the engine of a noisy car whirring in the distance.

With an enviable selection of movies, Chanakya had the goods and the gumption to toot its own horn. An outing at Chanakya meant much more than just going for a movie; it was a place where hours could be spent. You could take in a movie at Chanakya, dine at any of the eateries around it and then drive or stroll down Shanti Path. Over the next 37 years or so after its inception, it continued to be a proud theatre, fully equipped to take on the competition. Unlike some of the competitors, it never masqueraded as two theatres rolled into one but merely catered to the different sensibilities of different viewers, each of whom were treasured and pampered.

Much before multiplexes tom-tommed flexi-timings and multiple choice for viewers, Chanakya had done as much with the understatement befitting a seasoned poet. For much of the 1970s and '80s, Chanakya played the best of Hollywood, thrice, at times four times a day—like Priya and Archana in south Delhi around the same time, and the Connaught Place cinemas a little earlier. Yet, it kept a window for Hindi cinema. A film that worked for its viewers worked for Chanakya—it was the same hall that had space for Shyam Benegal's *Nishant* (1975) as well as devotionals like *Deen aur Iman* (1975) and *Jai Santoshi Maa* (1975). Without adopting an arrogant stand, the hall showed these films after much lesser cinemas had had a happy experience screening them.

Apart from that, Chanakya chose its own subjects. And then the fans chose to accept them. In 1980, screening *The Blue Lagoon* (1980) made the cinema look like a free spirit. Youngsters from Delhi University, Jawaharlal Nehru University and Jamia Millia Islamia boarded the 'U-special' DTC buses to show up at the theatre. In an age when prudery reigned, young college-goers had their moments of satisfaction while watching the film at Chanakya without the fear of a chaperon standing behind them. It was the absence of such condescension at Chanakya that endeared it to the masses, particularly the youngsters. It was not so much about the movies but about being seen at Chanakya that mattered, with a packet of popcorn in one hand, a cola in the other and a half-torn movie ticket in the pocket—the other half was with the usher who tore the ticket at the entry and purposefully guided you to your seat.

The hall had a beautiful staircase wide enough for four people to climb towards its elegant and stately interiors. The carpets were thick and velvety, the push-back seats had enough foam for comfort and ample leg space. First-row patrons in the balcony had the added advantage of having a foot wide and a little under two-feet high wall with wooden panel in front of them. The wall which was a foot from the front of the chairs was at the same height as the armrest of the seat. It was gladly used as a little improvised dining table by many. There were three wings in this section with generous space between them as the management resisted the temptation to add a row of seats to each wing. It meant at least 40-odd less seats but at the 1080-seater hall, nobody had cause for complaint. Unless, of course, you were found speaking on your mobile. That was the moment which tested the patience of others, particularly in a city where other halls reverberated with the sound of vendors selling their wares. At this cinema, nobody brooked any disturbance whatsoever.

Despite being favoured by the young, Chanakya was a prim and proper cinema that laid stock on discipline, be it the behaviour of patrons or the timings of shows. There are hardly instances of audiences dancing in the aisles or film screenings being delayed.

Interestingly, Chanakya was not always Chanakya. Before it was given its more popular name, the hall was called Chanakyarama for a little under a decade since its inception. Under that name, it made big collections with *Gone With the Wind* (1939), *Break Out* (1975) and *The Last Run* (1971) like it did with *The Odessa File* (1974) and *Skyjacked* (1972). Back in the early '70s, Chanakyarama proudly promoted itself as a '70 mm cinema with stereophonic sound'. Under its well-decorated belt were also memorable Hindi titles like *Satyakam* (1969), *Sagina* (1974), *Daag* (1973), *Pati, Patni Aur Woh* (1978), *Bobby* (1973) and *Khushboo* (1975)—noon show specials. It wasn't till well into the '90s that Hindi films were shown in four regular shows here—then, films like *Hum Tum* (2004), *Fida* (2004), *Maqbool* (2004), *Andaaz* (2003), *Bhoot* (2003) and the rest collected good numbers though the likes of *Kasoor* (2001) and *Paap* (2004) flopped at the box office. At times though the hall had the embarrassing experience of not playing a film even after putting up its hoardings on its premises and its posters in the 'next change' section. For instance, director S Ramanathan's long delayed *Zamaanat* that was announced in 1986, shelved soon after, revived almost 10 years later. The film was scheduled to be released in three daily shows here in 2004 but ultimately it was cancelled at the last minute due to legal hassles. That was a rare dampener for the hall which otherwise managed to play more than a single film most of the time by keeping the noon show for one film and the matinee, evening and night shows for the other. For instance, *Farewell Friend* (1968) did the rounds here in the mornings. A film that made headlines was Richard Attenborough's *Gandhi* (1982), whose English version played at Chanakya to packed houses. South Delhi schools brought in students by busloads and it was one of those rare occasions when marigold garlands greeted the viewers and little booklets on the Father of the Nation were distributed free of cost.

A similarly enlightening atmosphere prevailed when Chanakya showed *To Sir, With Love* (1967), the film that consistently finds a place in must-watch lists. The hall's initial commitment to two weeks in 1983 was extended to six, then two more. Eventually, the film celebrated 100 days. Such was the rush at the hall that many patrons played it safe by booking tickets at the counter near Odeon in Connaught Place, which did brisk business as cinegoers booked a ticket in the busy market and headed to the cinema on the weekend. Chanakya attracted good footfall, business was seldom sluggish and films never plodded on and on. Their run was either short and sweet or slightly longer and enjoyable; fans were always left wanting more. Cinema was celebrated here, epitomised in the proliferation of Hitchcock films that attracted huge crowds at the hall more than a decade after their release. *Dial M for Murder* (1954) and *Psycho* (1960) drew endless crowds. The best, though, was reserved for Gregory Peck's *The Omen* (1976), during which ambulances had to be kept ready outside the hall in case some viewers fainted.

The sands of time ran out too soon as the hall had been given out only on lease by the New Delhi Municipal Council in 1971. Chanakya wasn't around for long compared to other cinemas, but the memories it provided viewers were imperishable. Bollywood biggies and the who's who of the world of English film patrons in Delhi came to the hall and enjoyed its hospitality. It was also a hub for youngsters, much more than an amusing diversion.

And then the NDMC decided to raze the theatre complex and build a multiplex-cum-mall on a build-operate-transfer basis. Thus, Chanakya, the much-loved single screen theatre, passed into the pages of history. None could have been more dignified at the final hour.

51 ARCHANA, Greater Kailash I

The 1970s was probably the golden era for Hollywood films in the capital, just as Muslim socials had reigned supreme in the Walled City in the 1950s. Cinema halls, as wide-ranging in location and audience as Amba and Archana, Naaz and Priya, Shiela and Chanakya, Odeon and Sapna, caught on to this craze. A few of them, like Archana, Chanakya and Shiela, screened films in three daily shows, while others did a show a day. As a result, it was not rare to find many Hollywood films competing for attention at the same time. For instance, in September, 1973, films like *The Last Run* (1971), *An Affair to Remember* (1957), *A Candidate for a Killing* (1969), *The Sultans,* (1966) *Man Hunter* (1973), *Eye Witness* (1970) and *The Crown of the Russian Empire* (1971), all played at the same time. In a rare occurrence, Plaza showed *Battle of Berlin* (1973) while Archana screened *Battle of Britain* (1969). Such was the appeal of Hollywood films that it was not unusual to find three of the four theatres in Connaught Place—Rivoli, Odeon and Plaza—playing English films with Shiela, located just a couple of kilometres away, doing likewise. For a while, the Connaught Place halls were to English cinema what Moti, Kumar, Majestic, Jubilee, Ritz, Novelty and Jagat were to Hindi films.

Yet no hall played English films with the regularity and panache of Archana, the south Delhi hall that came up more than two decades after Independence but soon became the favourite of discerning cinegoers as well as a popular haunt of the young. Chanakya and Priya too played Hollywood films but made exceptions every now and then, showing films like *Jai Santoshi Maa* (1975), *Dayar-e-Madina* (1975), *Dulhan Wohi Jo Piya Mann Bhaye* (1977) and so on. Archana stayed honest to English films, reserving only the noon slot for Hindi ones, where films like *Avishkaar* (1974), *Caravan* (1971) and *Kora Kaagaz* (1974) found a steady audience. The morning slot was reserved for English films that had run their course but still had a niche audience. Then, from the matinee slots to the night shows, Archana, established by Atma Ram Chaddha, played mainstream Hollywood fare. If a film played at Archana, that was enough to deem it worth watching. At other cinemas, fans of English movies had to hurry because often, a film played Friday to Sunday and another came in for the Monday-to-Thursday slot. At Archana, though, this was usually not the case.

The cinema had an interesting seating arrangement. There was a long and steep front stall, with tickets priced only at 65 paise in the '70s; this section used to register a great footfall. It meant that for Rs 1.30 you could go on a date and watch an Academy Award winner like *Julia* (1977) or the hugely popular *Avanti* (1972) starring Jack Lemmon. When John Travolta's *Saturday Night Fever* (1977) played, college students from all around used to come in only to watch the title song and would leave once it ended. A little before that, when Archana played a re-run of *Wedding Night* (released initially in 1970), the youngsters came in hordes. They populated the stalls, while the older viewers filled the balcony. It was a surprise hit.

The students would make a beeline for the cheapest tickets because the ticket price used to go up to Rs 2.25 after the first 13 rows, not an easy sum to procure for many of them. If they were lucky, they could find themselves seated in the last row before the expensive seats began, where viewers would have shelled out almost four times the price! Others who were better off would bring along their girlfriends on a bike, spending another 50 paise on parking. Yet, even with all this extravagance, they would still spend less than Rs 2.

Despite *Saturday Night Fever* or *Julia* being huge hits, their popularity faded when compared to the heady craze generated by Bruce Lee films. For weeks on end in the late '70s and early '80s, Lee's films reigned supreme. He became a cult figure here, like elsewhere in the world, and Archana soaked it in. The fans came in droves, ensuring that his movies did not have a run of just one weekend or a week. Young men stepping out of the hall after watching the film would often be found swinging their arms in martial arts fashion. While *The Exorcist* (1973) showed no signs of ending its run at Priya and *The Body* (1974) did likewise at Chanakya, there was nothing to beat the *Dragon* series—*Return of the Dragon* (1972) and *Enter the Dragon* (1973) at Archana. Over the years, it hosted many International Film Festival of Indian movies too. During IFFI, usual film screenings were curtailed to accommodate festival films. At times, morning and evening shows were reserved for IFFI while noon, matinee and night slots took care of the films then running on the circuit.

The hall folded up in the late 1980s following a series of less than clean films picked by a management that was not always aware of the latest in the trade circle. A film like *Bedroom Eyes* (1984) cast a shadow over its operations and it failed to emerge from this dampener despite playings films like *Kiss Me Goodbye* (1982) and *An Officer and a Gentleman* (1982). Towards the end, it did the unthinkable, dabbling in

Hindi films. Keshu Ramsay's *Mera Shikaar* (1988) played to almost empty hall in the late '80s. Like a star trying for one last hurrah, it made a brief comeback as a mini-theatre in the late '80s. But it just wasn't the same anymore. The charm had gone. Archana quietly exited.

52 SUDERSHAN, Gautam Nagar

Arguably the first cinema in south Delhi—long before Uphaar, Anupam, Archana, Priya, Paras, Savitri, Sangam and Alankar came up—Sudershan was also among the first cinema halls to be established after Independence. Though the government gave prime land for setting up cinema halls in community spaces, it took more than a while for cinema houses like Eros, owned by the Soods and Uphaar, owned by the Ansals, to be founded.

Sudershan was built in 1952 by Rai Sahib Gautam, after whom the area is named and was initially named Mohini after his daughter. But she died very young and an emotionally distraught Rai Sahib sold the cinema to Brij Lal Chawla, an immigrant from Pakistan. Minor changes were made to the hall and it was renamed Sudershan.

Old-timers recall that the hall, with its big-screen logo, was a favourite destination of cinegoers in this part of the city. Not only did films like *Mahal* (released elsewhere in the city in 1949) and *Anarkali* (1953) show here, the cinema went on to carve out a reputation as everybody's very own neighbourhood theatre. People would say, *'Apne* Sudershan *par aayegi to dekhenge'* (We will watch the film when it comes to our Sudershan).

It was embraced by the elite too. Back in the early '50s, when it was still called Mohini, Prime Minister Jawaharlal

Nehru, came here along with a couple of ministerial colleagues to watch *Baiju Bawra* (1952), a film that had attracted a huge crowd.

This cinema did not have the history of the Old Delhi halls or the aesthetics of the Connaught Place cinema houses but its simple and elegant interiors were much appreciated. Movies were changed swiftly here, with patrons staying updated with the latest. For the first few years after its inception, it had Eros and Shalimar close by for company and competition, later followed by Kamal.

The hall also played many low-grade films and frequently took to showing films which had done the rounds of other cinema houses in the city. But on occasion, it did manage to upstage its fancier rivals. In 1975, Priya screened the Independence Day bonanza *Jai Santoshi Maa* (1975) three months after the film had arrived at Sudershan and was one of many halls which could show it only after it had been screened at Sudershan. Hoping to follow up its success with more of the same, the management also released *Ganga Sagar* (1978) and wooed prospective viewers with a catchy phrase, *'Char dham baar baar, Ganga Sagar ek baar'* (Visit the four holy places many times over, visit Ganga Sagar once). Special radio programmes were broadcast on the film and Sudershan, like Kumar in the Walled City and Milan in Karampura, raked in the profits. Over the years, it cultivated a steady audience for devotionals, playing *Vishnu Puran* (1973) a couple of years before *Jai Santoshi Maa. Har Har Mahadev* (1974), touted as 'Shiv Purana on screen', also ran here to packed houses. Its success was at least partially due to the presence of Dara Singh in the cast.

Especially memorable was the Mahipal-starrer *Jahan Sati Wahan Bhagwan* (1965), a film that ran in most smaller and far-flung theatres in the city in 1966 and was promoted as a 'musical entertainer for families' so viewers were urged thus: *'Biwi, behen, beti aur bahu ko saath layein'* (Bring along your wife, sister, daughter and daughter-in-law). This film also showed at Imperial, Laxmi, Kumar and Shalimar. The film's good performance at the box office meant that the much-hailed *Mera Saaya* (1966) had to be taken off at some cinemas after a limited run.

However, Sudershan was not all about period films or devotionals. In the 1960s, it played films with a strong social mooring, for instance, *Nai Umar Ki Nai Fasal* (1965), director R Chandra's film which talked about the aspirations of youth. It came soon after India fought two wars in 1962 and 1965. There was also a film like *Devar* (1966) which was promoted with a literary flourish. The posters at Sudershan informed the viewers that the film was based on Tara Shankar Bandyopadhyay's short novel, *Naa*. Similarly, for *Bahare Phir Bhi Aayengi* (1966), viewers were wooed with the catchline: 'a soul-stirring story of the spring and autumn in a woman's life'. The film attracted tremendous crowds, as did *Kohinoor* (1960), *Raja Jani* (1972) and later, *Johny Mera Naam* which originally released in 1970 but had its first outing here after a couple of years. Sudershan came to be identified as an address for playing popular films, many of which were screened on the demand of the local public.

However, as south Delhi became the residential area of the upper middle class, Sudershan ceased to be *'apna'* cinema, as it was once fondly referred to. The audiences began craving for more Hollywood films and top-notch Hindi movies in air-conditioned comfort. Pirated video cassettes and VCRs available on rent also affected business. For Rs 50, people could watch up to four films in one night at home.

As middle-class viewers opted for films at home or at high-brow theatres, Sudershan took to playing re-runs in the early 1980s but this could only postpone the inevitable. The poorer section of the audiences, who made up a good chunk of the stalls' crowd in the latter years, moved to more affordable areas like Ashram, Badarpur and Faridabad.

Sudershan's loss was the gain of Shalimar and Seble.

53 UPHAAR, Green Park

A few years after a cinema culture had been established in south Delhi, the government decided to allot land for building movie halls in the area. New cinemas were established as part of community development centres, the idea being to blend their operations with market and commerce. It was different from the cinemas in Old Delhi, which had both commercial establishments and private residences around them. These new structures were planned undertakings, located close enough to middle-class residential colonies and well-connected with public transport to encourage viewers from beyond the immediate vicinity. Alankar, Sapna, Paras, Savitri, all came up in south Delhi one after the other as part of this new trend, as did Uphaar. Though the cinema cut a sorry figure following the fire tragedy on 13th June, 1997, it had been much visited over the years.

My first brush with Uphaar was in the summer of 1984 when the cinema was showing *Sharaabi* (1984), seasoned director Prakash Mehra's sixth hit with Amitabh Bachchan. Uphaar had shown each of the earlier five—*Zanjeer* (1973), *Hera Pheri* (1976), *Muqaddar ka Sikandar* (1978), *Lawaaris* (1981) and *Namak Halaal* (1982)—and was attracting the audience in droves for this one too. It ran for weeks and weeks with black-marketeers lapping up their profits as well. Bappi

Lahiri had composed the film's music, a roaring hit with songs like 'De De Pyar De', 'Mujhe Nau Lakha Manga De Re' and 'Inteha Ho Gayee Intezar Ki' blaring from every corner shop. Posters announcing the film covered the *paanwala*'s stall on three sides and at the tea stall outside the cinema, you found Amitabh Bachchan with either his trademark '*sharaabi*' shot or the final sequence of the song, 'Mujhe Nau Lakha Manga De Re' where he had a bleeding hand. In many other posters, Jaya Prada, was seen embracing Bachchan. In some, she was alone with a microphone in her hand, doing a little jig with her bare left shoulder visible. The balcony viewers confined themselves to wide smiles in appreciation but those in the stalls were much more expressive, throwing *aath aana* coins at the screen. This response was not unexpected; when Bachchan's *Lawaaris* and *Namak Halaal* played here earlier, the stalls again got into the action, clapping, whistling and dancing to songs like 'Apni To Kat Jayegi' and 'Aaj Rapat Jayein To Humein Na Utthaiyo'.

Sharaabi went on to complete a silver jubilee in the city, returning to Uphaar a second time on popular demand. Though Uphaar cultivated an image for playing all films of the Prakash Mehra-Amitabh Bachchan combination, it had space for family entertainers as well. In the early '70s, *Jeevan Sangram* (1974) drew such a terrific response from family audiences that it was given tax-free status which further fuelled its fine run. Films like director S Ramanathan's *Devta* (1978), Arvind Sen's *Atithi* (1978), T Prakash Rao's *Hamara Sansar* (1978) and Raj Khosla's *Main Tulsi Tere Aangan Ki* (1978) also reinforced Uphaar's image as a family cinema in the first decade or so of its existence. Even devotionals like *Har Har Mahadev* (1974) and *Ganga Sagar* (1978) found their way here though, for some reason, the much talked-about *Jai*

Santoshi Maa (1975) went first to Sudershan close by, then to Priya a short distance away.

In the mid-'80s came *Sanjog* (1985), director K Viswanath's weepy saga whose lullaby 'Zu Zu Zu...Yashoda Ka Nandlala' swept all popularity charts. The film's box office release had been slightly delayed but this only worked in its favour as Laxmikant-Pyarelal's music had created a buzz around the movie. When it finally released, the *paanwala* at the hall found an ingenious way of making a quick buck by selling music cassettes of the film's songs. He must have done good business considering the film attracted good crowds and ran for more than a month.

Ghulami (1985), *Mera Saathi* (1985) and *Hum* (1991) also struck it rich at the box office. Uphaar, by then well renovated with a deep brown façade complementing the pale white interiors, rose in popularity.

On 13th June, 1997 the film being screened was *Border* (1997), which recounted the Battle of Longewala with cinematic liberties. The movie had created a stir before its release and the masses were eager to take it in, resulting in huge crowds. Some probably came out of hero worship—the film had Sunny Deol, Jackie Shroff and Sunil Shetty—while others were moved by patriotic feelings. Still others came for the music by Anu Malik and the all-time hit song 'Sandese Aate Hain'. But regardless of such happy details, calamity struck.

As the film played inside the hall, Uphaar recorded one of the worst fire tragedies in the history of Indian cinema. The flame was said to have started from a transformer kept in the basement of the hall, which was also used as a car parking. More than a hundred people were seriously injured in the stampede as they ran for their lives; 59 people died, mostly due to suffocation. While the occupants of the stalls downstairs were able to rush out in the nick of time, many in the balcony could not find their way to safety. Fire tenders were employed to control the flames which blazed across five storeys but it took more than an hour to bring the situation under control. Many succumbed to their injuries while being rushed to nearby hospitals.

Still reeling from the shock, the relatives of the victims and the deceased came together to form The Association of Victims of the Uphaar Tragedy and filed a case against the cinema authorities. Following a prolonged legal battle, they did get some compensation but the Supreme Court, while upholding the judgement of the Delhi High Court, slashed the damages to be paid by the Ansals from the earlier Rs 2.5 crores to Rs 25 lakhs. The kin of the victims have set up a Smriti Upvan, a little memorial outside Uphaar where prayer meetings are held every year in June. The prayers provide balm to the wounds of the families of some who had come to watch *Border*, got hooked on to the Javed Akhtar's lyrics. 'Ghar kab aaoge, likho kab aaoge…ke tum bin ye ghar soona soona hai', wrote the poet. But the dead will never return home.

Uphaar proved a misnomer. The hall stays shut.

54 SAPNA, East of Kailash

Cinema came to south Delhi after central, north and even east Delhi. The cinema halls there date back more than 70 years but in south Delhi, they came into their own only in the 1970s. Among the better-known ones, Paras, in Nehru Place, and Savitri, near Masjid Moth, came up in the early 1970s. These were followed by Anupam which about a decade after it opened, became a milestone in the history of Indian cinema when it turned into the first ever multi-screen hall in the city. Before these landmark establishments, though, lies Sapna's story. But its early-bird advantage was short-lived as competition proved quite a handful.

The pet project of the Kukreja family, Sapna came up in 1970 with *Holi Ayee Re* (1970), a film that was to grace its screen for the next six months and complete a glorious silver jubilee. Starring Shatrughan Sinha and Mala Sinha, the film's songs, including Mukesh's memorable number, 'Meri Tamannao Ki Taqdeer Tum Sanwar Do', helped get repeat viewers. For the first month, the 1,102-seater hall had no unoccupied quarters as the front, middle and real stalls and the balcony reported housefull business. There was a box too, but, unlike other halls in Delhi, it was made for non-commercial reasons—to accommodate the guests and family members of the proprietors.

Ever since its launch, Sapna has gone about its business in a quiet, discrete and no-nonsense manner. It has seldom made headlines and hardly ever reported crowd trouble. There have been exceptions like the radical elements who 'advised' the management to stop showing *Jo Bole So Nihaal* (2005), the Sunny Deol-starrer that ran into trouble on the day of its release. But such incidents have been very rare at a hall that has for the longest time been quiet and tranquil.

When Rajshri Film's *Hum Aapke Hain Koun...!* was released in 1994, Sapna was one of two halls where the film was first shown, a marked departure from the practice of every film opening at about a dozen halls in Delhi and Ghaziabad. With such a low-key beginning and limited prints available, the astounding audience response was unprecedented. Not only was every show housefull, but the crowd that waited outside to purchase a ticket grew with each passing day. On looking down from the first floor of the cinema, you could see people tripping over each other trying to get in. Even black-marketeers—otherwise not conspicuous at Sapna—made hay while the sun shone; people standing 100 metres away near departmental stores in the East of Kailash market preferred to lay their hands on a ticket rather than make it to the turnstiles and find that all the tickets were taken! The hall had a capacity of 1,042 then—the seats had been reduced after a renovation—and there were about 5,000 clamouring for tickets before each show. The film ran for almost 40 weeks at a stretch, the longest run here. While the lesser mortals sweated it out, India cricketers Kapil Dev and Bishen Singh Bedi were lucky, as was the BJP leader Sushma Swaraj. For them, the management kept the doors of the private box open.

There were even more dramatic scenes when Subhash Ghai's *Khalnayak* (1993) was released. The showman arrived at Sapna with Sanjay Dutt, Jackie Shroff, Madhuri Dixit and other actors. The film's music was already talked about for its song, 'Choli Ke Peeche Kya Hai' and there were media reports of *Khalnayak* being Dutt's 'comeback' film, one where he would blur the line between being a hero and a villain. Such was the craze that when Mohan Kukreja's secretary, Suraj Singh Rawat, went back home in a chartered bus, he would carry a couple of ticket booklets. The next morning when he came back to work, all the tickets would have been sold to fellow travellers.

The *Khalnayak* experience was repeated more recently at Sapna after the release of *Dabangg* (2010), which had a hit item song, 'Munni Badnaam Hui'. When the song played, many men danced in the aisles, some moving to the stage, others throwing coins at Malaika Arora on the screen. Once it ended, there were wolf whistles and loud calls for an encore. That particular request wasn't granted but there were occasions when the Sapna management accommodated public pleas, including the special letters on student union letter heads sent from colleges in the vicinity. The request would be to keep balcony seats for a bunch of students, and the cinema was generous enough to take them all in. The pleas made by the students unions of PG-DAV and Deshbandhu colleges were usually taken up, as were requests from corporate houses to book the entire balcony section for their dealers, distributors and officials. Mass bookings of this kind were done only from Monday to Thursday.

But that was in another age that included super hits like *Pyar Jhukta Nahin* (1985), *Insaaf Kaun Karega* (1984), *Aashiqui* (1990), *Border* (1997), *Gadar* (2001), *Lagaan* (2001) and *Taare Zameen Par* (2007). Before them all, *Geet Gaata Chal* (1975) was screened here; it was also playing at Kamal, among a handful of instances of the same film playing at two south Delhi cinemas simultaneously. The other one, of course, was *Sholay* (1975), which, again, played at Kamal at the same time. The competition for attracting viewers to *Sholay* was fiercer; Sapna wooed them by informing them through print advertisements that it was showing the film with an 'additional reel of Asrani and Keshto Mukherjee'. Then came *Akhiyon ke Jharokhon Se* (1978), for which the craze showed no signs of abating for months. It ran for 30 weeks, 26 of them housefull. At that time, Sapna even felt emboldened to play English films, one of which, *Ben Hur* (1959), had record attendance here more than a decade after its international release. Regional films, played on Sunday mornings, did not do badly either with tickets often booked in advance.

Around 2012, business was conspicuously down at Sapna. With most films struggling to stay afloat after the first week, the night shows were often cancelled for want of viewers. Films like Ketan Mehta's *Mangal Pandey* (2005) came a cropper at the box office and *Race-2* (2013) also failed to enthuse cinegoers after the first weekend. Those trying to delve into fond memories associated with Sapna will have to be content with movies like Rajkumar Santoshi's *Ghayal* (1990), Mahesh Manjrekar's *Astitva* (2000), and others from recent times.

Competition from Paras kept Sapna on its toes but when the former was replaced with a multiplex (Satyam in Nehru Place), Sapna had to try even harder to attract customers. Now, it is also poised to go the multiplex way.

55 PARAS, Nehru Place

The oft-expressed sentiment of cinema cutting across religious boundaries comes to mind in a discussion on Paras, the aesthetically grand hall that was as accommodating as it was intimidating. When it came up in Nehru Place in 1971, the area was better known for the Kalkaji temple. In its vicinity, Sapna was quite new and Savitri yet to be built. Paras sneaked in unannounced. There it was in all its glory—it had a well-ventilated front with a crisscross pattern of red and lemon, an elegant foyer, and 1,200 seats which were later increased to 1,300. Passersby watched in admiration and the industry took note as well.

It opened with *Purab Aur Pachhim* (1970) on 21st January, 1971, for which several celebrities jetted down here, among them Manoj Kumar, Saira Banu, Ashok Kumar, Pran, Kalyanji, Anandji. It was probably the first time a host of stars of Hindi cinema visited a hall in south Delhi. In the past, they had graced premieres in Connaught Place and Old Delhi but the south Delhi halls did not have a similar evocative ring. Paras broke the trend. This film on the east-west divide pushed the owners of Paras, the Malhotra, the exhibitors and distributors to get the cinema up and running for the release. The hall was made ready in a record 13 months, the owners having obtained permission from the concerned government departments only towards the end of December 1969. The hall was not supposed to be limited to either the middle class or the working class and the initial affordable admission rates meant Paras was never short of patrons in any category. A little later, *Kora Kaagaz* (1974) had a long stint here, proving that family audiences could make a film tick at the box office and keep a cinema in business. In fact, it was on family audiences that Paras thrived. While Sapna was often preferred by youngsters, particularly students from the neighbouring Delhi University colleges, Paras hosted a lot of families, many of whom didn't book in advance, yet managed to procure tickets at the last moment because of its seating capacity, the highest in south Delhi. It was the second highest across the city, after Vishal.

The same family crowd made the cash registers ring loud and clear in two instances separated by almost a decade. The first time was with the screening of *Jai Santoshi Maa* (1975), a low-budget devotional that arrived without great expectations but went on to do thundering business across the country. It had a great run at Paras. Most of the viewers would reach the hall after a *darshan* at the temple nearby and regarded the film to be nothing but an extension of their belief. The 1975 mythological, starring Bharat Bhushan and Anita Guha, evoked religious fervour with its *bhajans* by Usha Mangeshkar and Mahendra Kapoor. From every *jagran* at every street corner, you could hear them playing, 'Main Toh Aarti Utarun Re' and 'Yahan Wahan Dekhun Jahan'. The audience came with joss sticks and prayer *thalis* and groups of women chanted along with Usha Mangeshkar. Some went a step further and placed a *diya* at the entrance of the cinema complex, distributed *prasad* and sought blessings from the goddess. For a few weeks, Paras was almost a temple.

The fervour was repeated a decade later with Manmohan Desai's *Coolie*. It was during the shooting of this film that Amitabh Bachchan had a near-fatal accident. The 1984 film had a Muslim devotional song, 'Madeenewale Se Mera Salaam Kehna'. Once again, the audiences loved it, clapping when Bachchan arrived on the screen and many standing up in reverence when the song played late in the second half. Paras, unwittingly, united the audience beyond the differences of faith. It also brought together people from other parts of the world. Realising that playing fade-outs of Hollywood cinema wouldn't work in the morning show slot—Archana specialised in playing English films and was located nearby—Paras chose to play Nepalese films in the morning slot, becoming the only theatre to do so. There was a significant Nepali population in the vicinity.

Families from Kalkaji, Kailash Colony and Garhi regarded Paras as their cinema, the place where they could go and land a ticket even if they went at the last minute. Distributors of big-budget films opted for Paras by choice. Its air-conditioned comfort, big screen and prime location, all combined to make it a viable venture.

The show went on smoothly for a little under three decades, till the first multiplex in the city, PVR Anupam, opened in 1997. Paras, located not too far away, was among the first to suffer, followed by Savitri and Sapna.

As more and more corporate offices and new posh hotels sprung up all around, Paras stood dwarfed before shutting down for good in 2007.

56 CHANDERLOK, Chittaranjan Park

Urbanisation was a reality in India of 1970s. More and more skilled and unskilled men left the villages in search of better livelihood in the cities. Over time, they came to live in clusters in metropolises. Often bereft of even the basic amenities, the men, in the age group of 20 to 40 lived together, in accommodations close to their place of work. Many were married but stayed as bachelors, sharing the space with other men similarly placed. While their families stayed behind in eastern Uttar Pradesh, Bihar or Bengal, the men toiled away in Delhi. Their earnings were meagre, many not making more than Rs 20 a day, with the skilled ones getting perhaps Rs 40. Delhi, for them, was an alienating city; people earned their livelihood here but their hearts lay elsewhere.

Cinema, under the circumstances, played an edifying role, giving patrons moments of rest and leisure. Little wonder then that Amitabh Bachchan's films with the larger-than-life Angry Young Man portrayals became a hit with the masses in 1970s. Guru Dutt's stark reality found few takers even in re-runs and Shyam Benegal's new wave cinema appealed only to the well heeled. Bachchan was the common man's hero. With him, for a few fleeting moments, the men away from home could forget the tensions of everyday life and escape to a world of love and prosperity.

At such a time, the concept of neighbourhood cinema took root. If in the 1950s and a good part of the '60s, there were temporary, almost nomadic cinemas with permits for two months which operated in areas like Model Town, Zakhira, Subhash Nagar and Ganesh Nagar, in the 1970s, many cinema houses came up in areas with either traditional inhabitants in select pockets or those with a large number of migrant workers. Hence, Kisan, Swarn and Kalyan made their presence felt in east Delhi, Suraj came up in Najafgarh, Apsara, Aradhana, Jyoti had a fine run on the Delhi-UP border in district Ghaziabad and Seble catered to the population living on the edge of the city in Badarpur, which then seemed a godforsaken place.

Chanderlok, which started in the '70s and did business for a little more than 30 years near Chittaranjan Park, catering to the requirement of migrant workers living in and around Govindpuri, Kalkaji and Nehru Place. For the middle class, there were halls like Sapna, Paras, Alankar and Savitri; for the immigrant crowd there was Chanderlok. Sapna and others also had front stall tickets which were not very expensive but they often played films which did not make sense to the unlettered audience. Or, as in the case of Alankar, they were not within walking distance. A to-and-fro bus ticket cost almost a rupee, something which many struggled to save. With Chanderlok, everything was perfect: it was close by, not more than a few minutes brisk walk from Govindpuri, its tickets rates were affordable, its films, even if delayed in release, often struck a chord with the viewers. Off and on, Chanderlok also played Bengali films on Sundays, watched by the formerly East Pakistani inhabitants of the area.

Inside, the cinema was nothing out of the ordinary: a long shed with slanting asbestos sheets, passable seats, a 35 mm screen and only air-cooled comfort. For some patrons, even its two-blade fans were a luxury. The hall had a seating capacity of 850 which meant it was easier to procure a ticket at the current booking window. Even as late as the mid-1980s, its basic admission rate did not go beyond Rs 5.50.

However, where Chanderlok really scored was in recreating the ambience of a village or a small town *mandva* in the city. Viewers were removed from their families by hundreds of kilometres but these movies took them back to their roots. Often, there were loud calls, whistles, claps and even instant dances by the audience while special songs elicited calls like '*Bhai, phir se chala de*' (Brother, please play it again) or 'Action replay *kar de*' (Please replay the action). Of course, the projector room guy did not oblige often but once in a while, when he did, it was much appreciated.

The actual running time of the films was not always smooth. If a film was meant to be over in less than three hours with an interval of 15 minutes, it often took three and a half hours, sometimes even four, delayed by the frequent interludes for eatables. Every now and then, vendors used to enter the hall, calling out aloud for *moongfali, chai, biscut* and *pakoda*.

Chanderlok, like Lokesh, Suraj and Raaj, was for long a temporary hall. It kept a low profile and was satisfied with films like *Dharma* (1973), *Azaad* (1978), *Haath Ki Safai* (1974). In the early and mid-'80s, it took to playing Haryanvi films like *Chandrawal* (1984) and *Sasural* (1984) to a great response. Though hardly any Hindi film lasted for even three weeks here, Haryanvi films stayed on for up to six weeks.

The beginning and end of this hall was high profile. It opened with *Jai Santoshi Maa* (1975) and ended with *Gadar* (2001), much appreciated by all. In between, it also played Rajshri's mega hit, *Dulhan Wohi Jo Piya Mann Bhaye* (originally released in 1977). It, however, had to wait till the 49th week for the golden jubilee film to play here.

Gradually, though, Chanderlok was eclipsed by larger ventures in the capital. As the purchasing power of the masses increased and satellite television found its way into almost every home, Chanderlok struggled to find takers for the re-runs it played under an asbestos sheet. It has not functioned since 2002.

57 ANUPAM, Saket

For quite a while in the early 1980s, Saket was a sleepy outpost of south Delhi. It had plenty of DDA flats, most of them unoccupied, along with private residential units and lots of empty spaces as houses had not yet been built. All around the colony lay vast stretches of green—Said ul Ajaib was not even a speck in the distance—and one could see peacocks dancing in the rain near Gyan Bharti School. There was only one small neighbourhood market close by. Over the years, as apartments started filling up, plots yielded space to houses, a government senior secondary school came up and the Delhi Transport Corporation increased the frequency of its bus service to this area. After the opening of a couple of restaurants in the local community market, Anupam cinema was established under the ownership of the Ansal group which also owned the ill-fated Uphaar cinema in Green Park.

Though there was no immediate competition for Anupam—the closest halls were in Nehru Place, about five kilometres away—it took some time to get going as only a handful of local residents patronised it. Opening with Harmesh Malhotra's *Choron Ki Baraat* (1980), a Shatrughan Sinha-Neetu Singh starrer, the hall took its time to find success. For those staying even three or four kilometres away, Anupam seemed a cinema too far. The hall showed *Razia*

Sultan (1983) and got a tepid response—like most cinemas in Delhi—and even played re-runs of *Sholay* (1975), *Naseeb* (1981) and *Kaalia* (1981) to stay afloat.

However, things got better when the southern brigade invaded cinema: the Padmalaya films and those of D Rama Naidu, K Raghavendra Rao and K Bappiah often opened here and found a steady audience. The hall also got a fine response with films like *Muddat* (1986), *Bhagwan Dada* (1986), *Majaal* (1987), *Chaalbaaz* (1989) and *Naakabandi* (1990). These were all entertainers and found ready takers at the box office here at least in part because it was very difficult to lay one's hands on a ticket elsewhere. Thanks to the movies, even nondescript restaurants with nothing more than Indian versions of Chinese and continental fare, and plastic tables and chairs, started registering better business as youngsters started trickling in.

Even though Anupam attracted big banners and often played films in the week of their release, it did not necessarily translate into a significantly higher footfall on weekdays. The Ansals were not too keen to pump in more money to give it a facelift, unlike Uphaar which had undergone a completed transformation about a decade after Anupam was inaugurated. The latter continued with its sleepy ambience; it was a steady hall that offered new movies and little else.

Then came the moment which was to redefine the way India would watch films in future. For the first time, a cinema hall had more than one screen and with this swift stroke, the past was cast aside for good. The Ansals handed over Anupam to the Bijlis, who owned Priya. They had intended to turn Priya into a multiplex but refrained from doing so because that single-screen cinema was registering good business. For the first time ever, a cinema showed more than one film simultaneously. As for Anupam, seldom the first choice, it started attracting fans in hordes. Until now, cinemas had at best offered a mix of different films on the same day but viewers had never been given the option of choosing which movie to watch in shows that ran almost parallel to each other.

Times had changed. The Bijlis, with Ajay at the helm, got in touch with Australia's Village Roadshow which was considering setting up shop in India. In 1995, the two joined hands, with the Bijlis getting the major share in the new concern. Thus, Priya Village Roadshow was formed—named so because the concept was initially mooted for Priya. In 1997, Anupam was converted into a four-screen multiplex, the first in the country. At Anupam-4, rechristened to denote the number of screens, watching films ceased to be only about leisure, it became a lifestyle. They were no longer movies that were to be watched on weekends with the family; the area became a hangout zone and the days of air-cooled theatres, rickety chairs and blurred screens were soon to be relegated to memory. Anupam-4 also transformed Saket from a low-profile colony into a happening place. Where once all roads were deserted in the afternoon, traffic jams became a regular feature. The residential colonies became much sought-after and land prices shot up manifold. A single cinema had changed the landscape of the area forever.

Despite being the first of its kind, Anupam-4 has not always been a smooth business venture. Around a decade ago, ICICI Venture had to step in and bail out the cinema after the withdrawal of Village Roadshow due to security fears following the 9/11 attacks in New York. Of late, more multiplexes have come up around Anupam-4 and the footfall at the now nostalgia-laden hall is not as heady as it used to be. But nothing can change the fact that it was the establishment of Anupam-4 that started a trend many other cinemas were to follow.

58 SEBLE, Badarpur

On the morning of 1st November, 1984, Seble presented a ghastly sight. Nobody who saw the hall could make out that less than 24 hours earlier, it was a fully functioning cinema. Prime Minister Indira Gandhi's assassination was followed by mindless violence in the capital and hundreds of Sikh establishments were looted and burnt down. Like Palace and Swarn, Seble was owned by a Sikh family, the famous Sebles from Peshawar, whose scion, Ranjit Singh Seble, was the man behind the cinema hall. Its beginnings were in a tin shed in RK Puram before it became a semi-permanent structure in 1973 in Badarpur.

On 31st October, only the noon show ran at Seble, the others being cancelled as reports of violence from different parts of Delhi poured in. Late evening, a mob with cans of petrol, gas cylinders, shovels and sticks arrived at the hall and within half an hour, the hall was brought down, its seats burnt, its walls and ceiling broken and the screen torn to pieces. The film reels, posters and photographs were consigned to flames.

For a week, the Sebles could not muster up the courage to come to the hall. One day, a film producer prevailed upon them to visit the site, and staffers pleaded with them to revive the hall. This, however, was easier said than done because absolutely nothing could be salvaged. It would have to be rebuilt from scratch. This was the moment when a combination of wisdom and providence came into play. A scrap dealer happened to be passing by the ruins and offered to pay Rs 30,000 for all the iron he could retrieve from the ruins. A debris collector offered to clear the premises within 24 hours, charging Rs 3,000. He kept his word. Moments later, a painter, Mukhtar, came by. He had painted the hall when it was set up in 1973. The staffers put the nightmare behind them and put in whatever resources they had. Ranjit Singh Seble himself virtually stayed at the construction sight from dawn to well past dusk, eating meals with staffers and negotiating with banks. Three weeks after the renewal exercise, Seble was back, majestic as ever. The Seble story rapidly became the stuff of legend and Pranlal Mehta's Dharmendra-Rajesh Khanna starrer *Dharm Aur Qanoon* (1984) was screened to mark its fresh start.

Providence played an important role for the Sebles. While Indira Gandhi's assassination led to the violence the hall eventually fell prey to, it was also because of her that the cinema became a viable business to begin with. In 1970, her cavalcade was moving past a tin shed in RK Puram. This structure stood out like a sore thumb amid all the government buildings and sylvan surroundings and Mrs Gandhi ordered it to be shifted. For this, alternate land was provided in Badarpur. That led to the establishment of Seble, for long a temporary theatre.

Even though the area was considered far-flung then, labourers, rickshaw-pullers, shop attendants and others in the vicinity turned up in huge numbers to watch action movies from Bollywood at the all-new cinema in 1973. It opened with *Haridarshan* (1972) and a licence was granted for three years. But hardly anybody knew how to pronounce its name; some called it Seb-Lay, others opted for Sibal. Though Seble—pronounced simply, Sibal—came about relatively late in the day, the Sebles had been in the cinema business since pre-Partition days. In 1932, they used to own Landsdown cinema in Rawalpindi.

Unlike the halls in Old Delhi in the '70s, the 500-seater Seble has always been a hall the working class identifies with. Compared to the more centrally located halls of Connaught Place, it registered better numbers in the noon and matinee shows, and grew quietly. If in the early '70s, one could watch a film at Seble for as little as 60 paise, at the permanent hall the going rate was at least Rs 2.

While most halls in the city have photos of Sohrab Modi, Dilip Kumar, Raj Kapoor and Shammi Kapoor in their galleries and reception area, Seble's 'they were here' list is more humble. Danny Denzongpa and Mahendra Shah visited the hall in 1973, two decades before it acquired 'permanent' status with the screening of Rakesh Roshan's Shah Rukh Khan-Salman Khan-starrer *Karan Arjun* in 1995. Keeping in mind the profile of the area, the biggest grosser proved to be, rather predictably, Anil Sharma's *Gadar* (2001). The film completed 100 days in 2001, after first being screened on 15th June.

Today, Seble continues to show films, unobtrusively. No fancy launches, no premieres, just films for undemanding souls. It serves a purpose for those for whom cinema is still the most viable mode of entertainment.

59 SHALIMAR, Ashram, Mathura Road

The grey building with peeling plaster and broken glass scattered around is one of the most unlikely places to find a cinema hall. Children squat by the railway tracks nearby to answer nature's call and neat piles of bricks are stacked by the side of the road, lined with rows of shops of limestone and red sandstone. Sacks of cement can be seen, neatly arranged outside the shops and in no danger of being taken away. This is a market for construction raw material, and not a place offering celluloid fantasies.

Further down the road are multi-storeyed houses, almost all of which initially belonged to refugees from Pakistan who made Ashram their place of residence after spending a few years at Purana Quila. Some were given land in Lajpat Nagar close by while others came to Jangpura, Ashram and Bhogal. With the passage of time, the little houses, often not more than 50 metres, have turned into impressive pieces of architecture with marble flooring, niches and iron gateways. Shalimar, the cinema hall, is right here, a simple rectangular structure of brick and cement with a slanting tin roof, easily dwarfed by the taller buildings that surround it. It presents a picture of neglect; it relates a sad story.

It was not always like this. There was a time in the distant past when Shalimar, which means 'Abode of Love', was as good as its name. It stood for popular entertainment for locals who had been dispossessed and deprived during Partition. The meagre, affordable joys of Shalimar offered a little window away from everyday frustrations. Here was a cinema that did not burn a hole in their pocket with its admission rates and did not screen films that needed a workout for the grey cells—just simple escapist fare that elicited smiles and whistles.

Once it was a colourful hall with floral motifs on the glass panes. The view from the hall was a soothing one; back then, the Ashram flyover was not covered with soot and the fields around it had more than a touch of green. Shalimar showed films as illustrious as *Dil Ne Phir Yaad Kiya* (1966), *Kati Patang* (1970), *Hum Kahan Ja Rahein Hain* (1966) and *Daadi Maa* (1966), the latter was even praised by Babu Jagjivan Ram. With an admission rate of not more than two *anna*s in the early years, it played many packed shows. Over time, the seating capacity, which started at a little under 400, went up to 485. The fare went up gradually but was always less expensive than Eros, Alankar and Grandlay. While those halls attracted middle-class viewers, Shalimar played host to those for whom cinema was the only affordable means of entertainment. The difference in the earning capacity of viewers percolated down to the ticket prices as well. Even when it had to close, roughly seven years ago, the maximum price for a ticket was Rs 30 and the minimum, Rs 15.

Shalimar, almost always off the map for mainstream viewers, had its share of crises. It closed operations during the Emergency—besides Shiela, it became a rare hall to down its shutters in 1975—and had to face the wrath of rioters in 1984 after the assassination of Prime Minister Indira Gandhi. But the locals rose to the occasion and did not let their cherished hall be ruined. The owners, however, reopened it only in 1989.

In its second wind, Shalimar no longer played new movies, instead showing re-runs of recent hits and peddling old films. When fresh material did find a screening here, they were C-grade action flicks, the kind Dharmendra, Mithun Chakraborty, Hemant Birje, Satnam Kaur and Gautami dished out for a while in the 1990s. *Gundagardi* (1997), *Munnibai* (1999) and *Ganga ki Kasam* (1999) all worked at the box office but were a sad departure for the hall from the days of *Bairaag* (1976) and *Sagina* (1974) in the 1970s.

Today, the show is over at Shalimar. Its insides are as sad and forsaken as its exteriors. The carpet is long gone, the curtains are burnt and the screen is dust-laden. The chairs are missing and a handful of urchins have made it their temporary abode. They light their *bidis*, play their games and when tiredness overcomes them, they rest their weary bodies on its steps. Cinegoers in the area have lost the hall that provided a welcome distraction from life's strains. Today, as multiplexes boom across the city, Shalimar awaits a buyer, and a new lease of life.

60 RACE COURSE, STADIUM, PALAM, Race Course, National Stadium, Palam

The three halls—Race Course, Stadium and Palam—are a delectable footnote in the history of Delhi's cinema hall. Never first-choice halls for many but in their own unique, understated ways, they did play a vital role in bringing films to people otherwise deprived of movie fare. Meant especially for defence personnel, civilians were not prohibited from watching films at these cinemas, but allowed entry only if seats were left after the intended occupants had got their tickets.

Though each cinema was unique in its way, the three halls owned by the Sahnis of Odeon-Rivoli fame, used to be air-cooled at the best of times, and often naturally cooled to save on electricity costs. The rear stalls had to make do with used twin-blade fans fixed on the side walls—there was no balcony—from 1950s. The fans made plenty of noise but gave out only little air. The viewers in those sections, though, were a privileged lot—those in the front only had natural cooling comfort. During the day, there was no ventilation and at night, ushers would open the doors on both sides for cross ventilation. The breeze that blew in, brought with it flies and mosquitoes. The seats were all wooden and only a jute carpet was spread out on the cement floor below the seats. The screen was 35 mm and films graced these halls at least a month after showing elsewhere in the city. In film circles, they were called *'piti hui'* or flop films. A seasoned viewer knew that if a film was playing at any of these three, it meant it was on its way out of the city. Even in that delayed screening, an order was followed in these *'fauji'* halls. A new film would invariably come to Race Course first; after a week's run, it would be shifted to Stadium. After another week there, it would finally grace the Palam screen. Only in rare cases would Stadium get first preference, and Palam rarely did. Blockbusters like *Qurbani* (1980), *Daku aur Jawan* (1978) and *Trishul* (1978) were regularly screened here but mythologicals were mostly given a miss.

Tickets were priced on the lower side, keeping in mind the viewers. For the first weekend, only defence personnel would be present and from Mondays, civilians could get an entry. Even then, certain rows were reserved. Lore has it that some *jawan*s found a way to make easy money, buying tickets in advance and selling them to civilians.

Race Course lived up to its name. Minutes before each show, the barricade would be removed and cinegoers had to sprint across a vast stretch of land to reach the ticket counter. The clerk usually followed the first come-first served policy so this system favoured those who could run faster than others. At Stadium, young men would take help from a friendly 'uncle' who sold books of film songs at the hall. They would plead with him to 'arrange' some tickets and he would almost invariably manage without any extra charges. Over a period of time, he developed a special relationship with some young men for whom he kept tickets ready with his books.

For refreshments, the patrons did not have to step out; vendors would come into the auditorium, selling everything from bread *pakoras* and samosas to groundnuts! Though the halls offered tickets at abysmally low rates, some viewers decided that if they could not watch a film, they would 'hear' it! Those were the days of non-stereophonic halls, and Race Course, Stadium and Palam made no attempt to prevent sound from travelling out. Some young men would sit behind the screen and hear all the dialogues as though they were listening to a radio. Then there were youngsters who would all want to watch the film but wouldn't have sufficient money to purchase tickets. They devised an ingenious formula to watch films here, thanks to lax ushers. Some of them watched the film till the interval; others after the interval. The 10-minute break would be utilised to apprise the second half audience with the film's developments in the first half and also to pass on half-torn tickets.

About two decades ago, the three cinemas downed their shutters as it was no longer viable to show films at such low rates. The defence personnel too had other avenues of entertainment. With the closure of the halls, Delhi lost its most affordable cinemas.

61 ALANKAR, Lajpat Nagar

It could have been among south Delhi's first cinemas but a dispute among the partners meant Alankar's arrival was delayed by years. The plot for the cinema was allotted by the Ministry of Rehabilitation towards the end of the 1950s but the allottees got embroiled in a dispute which led to it being auctioned off. Ultimately, when Alankar did finally appear close to Lajpat Nagar Central Market, the area was well populated with refugees from Lahore, Peshawar and Rawalpindi and the demographic profile of the audience meant escapist fare was the order of the day. Alankar played A-grade banners with aplomb, running good business especially on weekends and Mondays, the local holiday. In contrast to many cinemas, its night shows registered a good footfall, owing partly to the cinema's location next to the local police station which probably instilled a greater sense of security among the cinegoers. First, Rajesh Khanna, and then, Amitabh Bachchan became the darling of the audiences here. Their films ran to packed houses, with *Aradhana* (1969), *Amar Prem* (1972), *Kaalia* (1981)and *Mard* (2005) doing so well that the black-marketeers could barely stop smiling.

The hall gave way to one of the earliest multiplexes of the city, 3CS in 2002.

62 DEFENCE, Delhi Cantonment

From the 1950s, there were three cinema halls catering to the armed forces, notably, Race Course, Stadium and Palam which lasted for around four decades. Then there were two others, Defence in Delhi Cantonment and Anand Parbat. Unlike these three, Defence played top class fare alongside the biggies of the city; it seldom picked from the leftovers. When director Narindra Suri's Sadhna starrer *Vandana* (1975) was mustering good numbers in the mid-'70s at Delite, it showed here too, to a similarly encouraging response. Manmohan Desai's *Roti* (1974) played here while it did at West End, Eros and Vishal. About a decade before that, Defence showed Nitin Bose's *Hum Kahan Ja Rahein Hain* (1966) while it played at the more celebrated Majestic, just as it showed *Do Badan* (1966), which played at Jagat at the same time.

Small, compact halls, they always gave first preference to the defence forces for tickets and generally showed classy fare in simple, clean, small-town halls. Unfortunately, they shut down a little over three decades ago—first the hall at Anand Parbat closed, followed by the one in Delhi Cantonment.

63 EROS, Jangpura

Eros was the earliest mainstream hall in south Delhi, having started operations in 1956, almost a decade and a half before Sapna, Alankar, Paras and the rest. Eros chose its fare smartly, striking a good balance between films with creative merits and those with mass appeal. It played some of the biggest films in the first week of their release but whenever the going got a bit dull, Eros got rid of the lull by churning out a festival of evergreen hits. Hence, it played Shakti Samanta's *Aradhana* (1969) to a great response as well as Raj Kapoor's timeless *Awara* (1951) and M Sadiq's *Taj Mahal* (1963). In fact, *Awara* played here more than once, having been a part of an evergreen hits' festival in 1971 when Eros showed *Gumraah* (1963), *Barsaat* (1949), *Sadhna* (1958) and *Ganwaar* (1970). It lost some of its sheen by showing films like *Ranga Khush* (1975) and *Guru Aur Chela* (1973) in the mid-'70s. As its proprietors owned Vishal too, Eros often showed the same film as the former.

A few years ago, Eros revamped itself, cutting down drastically on its seating capacity. Now a 317-seater, Eros, will, forever be known as the hall that brought films to south Delhi along with Shalimar and Sudershan.

64 GRANDLAY, New Friends Colony

Among the last cinemas to make an appearance in south Delhi, its arrival at the entrance to New Friends Colony was doubtless facilitated by the vast influx of population from Old Delhi to Okhla. In the late 1970s, a demographic shift began from the Walled City to Nizamuddin, Preet Vihar and Okhla, the highest density being witnessed in Okhla. As erstwhile Old Delhi residents, they were used to a thriving cinema culture and Grandlay sought to give them a semblance of similar fare from the early '80s. It was patronised both by the middle-class residents of Okhla and students of Jamia Millia Islamia, and a few relatively older residents of New Friends Colony.

The hall showed a number of family dramas like *Pyar Ke Do Pal* (1986) and action flicks like *Insaaf Kaun Karega* (1984), *Majaal* (1987) and *Jeene Nahin Doonga* (1984). They all garnered decent numbers at the box office. However, as the cinema business hit a lull in the 1990s, it temporarily closed down before making a comeback as Batra Glitz. The show goes on here and the screenings are at par with the best in business.

65 KAMAL, Green Park

Among the early entrants in that part of the city, Kamal was one of the preferred theatres in south Delhi for film exhibitors. In 1975, it recorded a housefull attendance for *Mera Gaon Mera Desh* (1971), as it did for *Roti Kapda Aur Makaan* (1974), when it advertised itself as 'a centrally air-conditioned hall with a 70 mm screen'. Rajshri's *Dulhan Wohi Jo Piya Mann Bhaye* (1977), on its way to a golden jubilee in the city, had a fine run here. From the beginning of the '70s till about five years later, Kamal catered to popular tastes when it showed Joginder's *Ranga Khush* (1975) but it also tried to strike a balance between the popular and the niche, showing both *Do Badan* (1966) and *Patton* (1970) with equal élan. Gulzar's *Mere Apne* (1971) played to housefull shows, the film holding its own at a time when the competition in the city included *Satyakam* (1969), *Hanste Zakhm* (1973), *Zanjeer* (1973) and *Bobby* (1973).

The hall downed its shutters more than 20 years ago. Today, there are smart car showrooms there.

66 PRIYA, Vasant Vihar

For years, Priya stood out as a place for well-heeled cinegoers, ladies and gentlemen for whom cinema meant the latest of Hollywood and an occasional date with middle-rung Hindi cinema. There were no commercial *masala* entertainers and no smut. Priya, along with Chanakya and Archana, stood out for showing English movies even in the mid-'80s when others like Shiela, Plaza, Odeon and Rivoli had switched over to Hindi cinema completely or left only an occasional window open for Hollywood. In the 1970s, *Mili* (1975) was screened here. The Jaya Bhaduri-starrer proved that women could carry a film on their shoulders without playing the role of a nautch girl or Mother India. The film ran for a month or so, a rarity at a hall that believed in showing films for a limited interval of a week or two. Priya's reservation about showing Hindi films meant that a blockbuster like *Jai Santoshi Maa* (1975) finally graced its screen after running for more than three months at about two dozen halls in the city. But lagging behind the competition was mostly an unusual occurrence as far as Priya was concerned. Otherwise, the hall that showed many of the *Dragon* series movies and even *The Exorcist* (1973) largely scored brownie points. The hall was among the first to embrace the multiplex phenomenon, turning into PVR Priya in 2000.

67 SANGAM, RK Puram

Established in the mid-'70s, Sangam was always known as the hall frequented by government servants and others living close by. Despite being relatively low profile, the movies it screened kept it at par with other well-known halls. It showed everything—from family dramas to action films and devotionals. Sangam had space for regional fare as well, first playing Malayalam films on weekends, then Bengali and even Garhwali films till recently.

With a seating capacity of over 1,000, running housefull shows was never easy and business dwindled over the past decade or so.

68 SAVITRI, Greater Kailash II

The hall that showed an all-time hit like *Dilwale Dulhaniya Le Jayenge* (1995) deserved better than the fate with which it eventually met. It came up close on the heels of Sapna and Paras but managed to carve out a niche of its own as residents of south Delhi suddenly got a range of cinema halls to choose from. From its early days, Savitri played a mix and match of Hindi and English films. Chandra Barot's *Don* (1978) graced its screen in the silver jubilee week and then came re-runs of timeless hits like *Too Bad, She's Bad!* (1955), *Tender Scoundrel* (1966) and *The Old Testament* (1962). A variety in content was the cinema's hallmark. While it showed Hindi films in three or even four shows daily, English films got either a noon or morning slot. The strategy was the exact opposite of what Archana—a stone's throw from Savitri—was doing.

Though the cinema came up in a commercial hub as part of the community development programme, its location went against it. It was too close to a busy traffic intersection, parking was an issue and the local residents did not always look favourably at the hall attracting people from far and wide. Screening films like *Rangeela* (1995) and *Satya* (1998), Savitri managed to prove that given a slightly better roll of the dice, it could have had as flourishing an innings as Sapna close by.

69 VIRAT, Deoli

Among the late entrants in south Delhi, Virat, in Deoli, concentrated on playing formula films with an emphasis on action. The films usually ran for two-three weeks here. To its credit, Virat often played the films in the week of their release and kept ticket prices on the lower side to make it attractive for the largely lesser privileged constituency. Its mode of publicity was the old-school style: sticking posters of the current film at vantage points around the hall. All posters had one crucial value addition: a strip pasted at the top of the poster which announced that the film was showing at Virat. However, when quality films became more and more expensive, Virat found itself losing out to Savitri, Paras and Anupam. It was no longer possible to buy new films at the rates quoted by the market. At the same time, it was not possible to increase the admission fare. Caught in a no-win situation, the hall downed its shutters more than a decade-and-half ago.

VII

Movie Waves Along the Yamuna

70 SWARN CINEMA, Vishwas Nagar

In the early years of the new millennium, it was common for new cinema halls to spring up in newer parts of Delhi. One fine morning, when the ever enthusiastic OP Katyal, widely popular as Chacha in the film business circles in Bhagirath Place, asked me to visit Supreme cinema, I thought I knew what to expect. 'Is there a new cinema in Kanti Nagar?' I asked. *'Nahin, jo purana Swarn thha, jisko dango mein jala diya thha, woh ab Supreme ke naam se khul gaya hai. Poora hall renovate ho gaya hai'* (No, the erstwhile Swarn cinema which was burnt down during the 1984 riots has opened as Supreme. The complete hall has been renovated). You must come. It has a wide screen,' said Chacha.

I did not accept his invitation that day but his words took me back to the gory aftermath of the assassination of Prime Minister Indira Gandhi in 1984. Swarn Cinema, along with Seble and Janak, bore the brunt of the attacks on cinema halls. Owned by prominent Sikh families of the city, the cinemas were reduced to ashes. Named after owner Swarn Singh Kamal, the cinema was attacked by a mob as it played Rajkumar Kohli's multi-starrer *Jeene Nahin Doonga* (1984). On 31st October, 1984, the hall closed down after the matinee show as news of violence from many parts of the city poured in. Just as well. Soon, Swarn too was to be the site of unprovoked mob fury. The masses came armed with petrol and gas cylinders, threatening to burn everything and everyone in sight. Fortunately, there were no viewers inside as the hall was closed and within no time, the ceiling was burnt and the furniture reduced to ashes. The projector too was completely burnt. The mob's fury abated only after the hall was reduced to a shadow of its original self. The owners paid with their life at their house in Krishna Nagar close by.

The hall was closed for 18 days but darkness was soon to be followed by dawn. While it was shut, reconstruction started in full swing and the staff worked day and night. The Rajshris, famous for their family films, came forward to help Singh's family. The show resumed, in less than three weeks, with the screening of *Dharam-Veer* (1977), Manmohan Desai's mega hit. The riches-to-ashes-to-riches story had come full circle.

Much before the 1984 tragedy, Swarn took cinema to the masses in a language they understood, filling a vacuum on the cinema map of east Delhi where choices were few and far between. There was good old Radhu in Shahdara and Laxmi in Gandhi Nagar but precious little else. For years before Radhu Palace came up in the early '80s, Swarn provided middle-class viewers in this part of the city with a neighbourhood cinema that showed the latest films, most of them family-oriented and neat and clean romantic entertainers. Occasionally, it catered to the working classes too, with a few action-packed thrillers thrown in. These viewers packed the stalls, whistled, clapped and often requested the guys in the projector room to rewind a sequence or two. Films like *Changez Khan* (1957) and *Azaad* (1978) did well in repeat run, as did Vinod Mehra-Yogeeta Bali's *Parde Ke Peechhey* (1971) that attracted hordes for its subject—ghosts, superstition and crime.

Swarn Singh Kamal had learnt wise lessons about the craft from prior experience. He used to run a touring cinema in Palam in the early '60s until he acquired a plot of land in Vishwas Nagar trans-Yamuna, paving the way for a full-fledged cinema. However, it got permanent status years after it was established. Initially, a tin-shed structure with no air-conditioning and only two-blade fans for ventilation, it claimed to be the second largest hall in the city, its 1,204 seats second only to the numbers touted by Vishal in Rajouri Garden. The initial admission rates were a mere 5 and 10 paise. In the beginning, there was no balcony section, the section for the so-called 'gentry' being added only in 1981 with a princely admission fare of Rs 3.

Like almost all halls, it used to fill the morning show slot with re-runs of Hindi and English films. A special niche, however, was reserved for Assamese and Nepalese films as a large number of people from both places lived in the vicinity. What Paras did in the 1980s and '90s—playing films from Assam as well as Nepal—Swarn did about a decade earlier. These films arrived without too much publicity but were eagerly lapped up. And in its own understated way, Swarn filled a little blank of the city's cine map—until then there was no outlet for Assamese cinema in Delhi.

The hall's management also found ingenious and familiar ways to draw wider audiences. A cycle-rickshaw used to move around the locality with the posters of the film then showing at Swarn in daily four shows. Four sides of the vehicle were covered with posters. A fifth poster—of the film playing in the morning slot—used to hang in front of the rickshaw's handle, or at times, trail below the poster at the back, like a mudguard in a car. When the film *Badla aur Balidan* released here in 1980, it was promoted with hoardings and banners put up on a tempo and a tonga strategically placed to ensure maximum viewership.

After a little over two and a half decades of an unchallenged run in the area, Swarn encountered competition in Radhu Palace. Peace was bought with a tacit agreement that the two halls would not play the same film to avoid cutting into each other's business. Of course, this did not prevent Swarn from vying for the best movies east of Delhi, its competitive streak fuelled by the experience of notching up mega hits in this part of the city. Usually, movies ran for a couple of weeks or a little more but Swarn recorded silver jubilees as well with *Mera Gaon Mera Desh* (1971) and *Roti Kapda Aur Makaan* (1974).

In the late 1980s and early '90s, Swarn registered many hits. When it played Amitabh Bachchan's *Shahenshah* (1988), students from the neighbouring Shyamlal College came in hundreds as indeed they did when Yash Chopra's *Chandni* (1989) was released here. Then there was the raging hit *Bandit Queen* (1994) that ran for 10 weeks too. Special shows had to be held to cater to the demands of the local population. The hall's last silver jubilee hit was Sooraj Barjatya's *Hum Aapke Hain Koun...! (1994)*. In fact, separate shows were organised for women from neighbouring middle-class colonies who would call up to book entire shows.

A few years after Rajshri's mega hit, Swarn's ownership passed on from the Singhs to the Bansals. The hall did not die. It was merely rechristened. The show went on.

71 GAGAN, Nand Nagri

There are few better joys for a mainstream cinema fan than to watch a Sunny Deol or Salman Khan starrer in the first show on the first day with a single-screen audience. The loud comments, cryptic remarks and passionate calls identifying the stars is an experience that multiplexes, with their limited seating capacity and high-brow viewers, can never hope to replicate. Gagan, a seldom talked-about cinema hall in east Delhi, has the rare distinction of being the preferred venue for screening the films of Sunny Deol earlier and, more recently, Salman Khan. Back in June 2001, the masses whistled and screamed when Sunny entered Pakistani territory in Anil Sharma's *Gadar* (2001). It seemed he was answering the collective prayer of the audience who believed he must beat the enemy in his own den. When Salman Khan went on an action-packed, punch-throwing, kick-boxing spree in *Dabangg* (2010), the reaction in the audience was such that it couldn't even be replicated by the raunchy 'Munni Badnaam Hui' number. His fans faithfully turn up at Gagan to watch his action-packed entertainers. And considering many of them are working-class Muslim men, the distributors have been smart enough to show a Salman Khan film every Eid! Business is never slack at that time.

The biggest hall on the other side of the Yamuna, Gagan is among a handful to report steady business in the face of multiplex challenges. A hall for people whose pockets allow few liberties but whose hearts know no bounds, Gagan has played the best of Bollywood for the faceless multitudes who queue up faithfully before the release of a new film to procure a ticket for the following Friday. First day-first show has an enduring charm, and Gagan has encapsulated it like few others. And it has done so at rates which have never affected the budget of the faithful. With a seating capacity of 982, it continues to be among the biggest in the capital, yet has rarely found itself in the limelight.

Starting out relatively late, in 1982, Gagan has grown to be the most preferred single-screen theatre in east Delhi. Back then, its front stall ticket cost 70 paise and the elite balcony seat came for Rs 2.40; today, prices have gone up to Rs 20 and Rs 50, respectively. When it opened with *Dharam Kanta* (1982), a multi-starrer with Raaj Kumar, Rajesh Khanna, Jeetendra and Waheeda Rehman, Gagan was the proverbial common man's cinema, with few ladies gracing its precincts. Most viewers were from the neighbouring Loni district and others from places along the Delhi-Ghaziabad border. Gradually, as word spread that Gagan offered air-cooled comfort with plush push-back seats and a clean atmosphere, families started trickling in and Gagan notched up the numbers with daily four shows and a special morning show at reduced rates. The turnout was brisk in the front, middle and rear stalls while the balcony was comparatively sedate. But when a more educated category of people started visiting and men started bringing their spouses along, Gagan created a new classification—the 'noble' category! The first two rows of the balcony, which offered a better view and more leg space, were reserved for this section of the audience. The viewers had to shell out Rs 10 extra to avail of the honour and comfort.

The screen here was always among the biggest, probably bigger than the halls in Old Delhi or Connaught Place, the prime centres for movie screenings until about two decades ago. For a hall in a resettlement area, it did terrific business, its noon show in particular registering a higher density. To pull in crowds by the hundreds, Gagan today, like in the past, regularly relies on action movies. The audiences are still brought up largely by men with the women's percentage being usually confined to single digits. While Salman Khan and Akshay Kumar are popular heroes here, one does not see a similar fascination for Shah Rukh Khan films which do better in the multiplexes in the vicinity. Most men here find him too artificial, too removed from their everyday life to identify with him. Some offerings from Hollywood were also much appreciated here, the hall being among the earliest in the city to show dubbed English films on a regular basis. *Godzilla* (1998) for one notched up magnificent numbers, thanks largely to its technical sheen and fine dubbing. Hollywood films are still shown in their dubbed Hindi version and collect good numbers due to their superior action.

A star never deigned to visit here, though, and neither has the hall recorded any silver jubilee, even when the crowds' favoured heroes are shown. It is seldom in the cinema listings of newspapers in the capital, but for the toiling masses in east Delhi, Gagan has always been a bright spot. Today, amid all the traffic snarls and dust and grime of ill-paved streets, Gagan continues to be a rare success model.

72 RADHU, Shahdara

Not a trace remains of Radhu cinema, the first hall to come up across the Yamuna. Driving on GT Road, the elegant Gianand can be seen. Just a little ahead is the swanky new Movie Palace. The erstwhile Swarn, now in a new avatar as Supreme, is also close by. But Radhu, which was located next to Gianand, has given way to V3S Mall, the new building, completely obliterating all traces of the earlier cinema.

For years, the two halls in Shahdara were complementary: you could try watching a film at Radhu but if procuring a ticket proved problematic, which was often the case, you could simply move to Gianand next door. In tandem, these cinemas gave the audience almost a kind of multiplex experience 30 years ago. Though Gianand came up later and stayed on longer, it was Radhu that set the trend of watching films across the Yamuna. It catered to many families staying in and around Shahdara and many workers from the industrial belt around it.

Radhu came up in the first years after Independence, sometime in the 1950s. A little hall, it dared to show films in east Delhi when it was considered an act of social defiance. Movies were looked down upon; only those gone astray or the dregs of society were said to spend their money on films. For women, it was nothing less than ignominy to be seen in a queue for a film ticket.

As a result, connoisseurs of cinema hardly stayed in this area. Most of the population was made up of either government servants, mostly clerical staff or migrant workers from Bihar and Uttar Pradesh who found a foothold in Delhi after Independence. The city with its upcoming factories, offered better avenues for earning for the largely illiterate sections of the migrant population. Government officers had no time or inclination for movies. For the migrant working class though, cinema was a rare and affordable entertainment. They could not always afford to pay for a ticket and they didn't possess the means to go to Old Delhi to watch a film, while the thought of watching one in Connaught Place did not even cross their mind. Radhu proved invaluable for them, providing both, the latest and old-time hits, in a tin shed. Viewers lined up for more than a 100 metres to procure a ticket for a Raj Kapoor or Dev Anand film, each of which had multiple hits at Radhu. Gradually, it came to be regarded as the go-to cinema in east Delhi for exhibitors and distributors. Its rising popularity also led to an increase in admission rates. Over the years, the highest rate of admission went up from '*aath anna*' to Rs 1.25 and then to Rs 40 at the 614-seater hall. The audience was only bothered about the film; the initial tin shed, wooden seats with little upholstery, bare concrete floor and the air-cooled ambience did not matter. As workers turned loyal patrons, Radhu had a long run. For more than a couple of decades, it was the solitary voice of cinema in this part of the city until it found a companion in Gianand, and later a competitor in Gagan. For men living in single-room tenements and *jhuggie*s of Shahdara and later Seelampur and Seemapuri, Radhu was a cinema that offered them films they could identify with. Some were action films with Dara Singh and Mumtaz and others were family entertainers like *Phool*

Aur Patthar (1966), *Mera Saaya* (1966), *Jeevan Sangram* (1974) and *Zameer* (1975).

The hall did not have a separate balcony. In a very egalitarian manner, viewers of the front, middle and rear stalls, all had similar seats. The cinema had a slanting floor, so the viewers in front were at a lower level and those in the rear at a higher level, so that everyone could comfortably watch the film.

Radhu played films on a limited engagement basis but stuck to top-drawer stuff from Bollywood for its regular four shows. In the weeks when there were no new releases, or films that released did not appeal to its clientele, Radhu showed the classics. Black-marketeers found plenty to do here, often booking tickets in bulk and selling them at many times their printed price. Deals were struck not at the hall but at a petrol pump nearby, or at the *chai* stalls in Bhola Nath Nagar. When films of Sanjay Dutt, Govinda and Amitabh Bachchan were released, the *chaiwala*s did good business.

With the passing years, more halls dotted the landscape of east Delhi. Gianand, Gagan and then Radhu Palace came into existence. Radhu, however, proved equal to the competition. It understood its limitations but worked within them to keep the business steady. It reinvented itself in the morning shows by focusing on Nepali films. Incidentally, Nepali films continued to be popular fare at many halls from the late 1980s. Radhu, Swarn and Paras all showed these films in the morning slot. Pertinently, the move stemmed from economics. Radhu, like others, had a sizeable popular of people of Nepalese origin or those who had temporarily migrated in search of livelihood.

This, however, was not enough to sustain it and with travel around the city facilitated with the Delhi Metro, it became easier to find new avenues for movie-watching.

Owner KK Radhu tried to improve fortunes by playing re-runs of films like *Maha Shaktimaan* (1985) and *Vijaypath* (1994). Family movies were cast aside, giving way to action flicks appealing to single men.

However, when even this niche segment of viewers opted for other cinemas, Radhu, the first single screen in east Delhi, bowed out.

73 GIANAND, Shahdara

About 40 years ago, east Delhi was simply Jamuna *paar* for the common man. Nothing more. Anything that happened there seemed to belong to another world altogether. It was not a preferred address for residence nor a convenient place to do business. Only little Radhu kept the flame for cinema burning in and around Shahdara until Swarn came up in Kanti Nagar in the 1970s. Laxmi did likewise in and around Gandhi Nagar, preceding all cinemas on the other side of the Yamuna. These halls initially played only re-runs or devotionals, which they got at cheap rates. All that changed when Gianand announced its arrival in the early '70s, followed by Gagan and Radhu Palace. And cinema viewing changed for good in east Delhi.

One look at Gianand and you are reminded of those innumerable cinema halls in the small towns of north India. Its yellow wash is an eyesore and the brick-lined floor brings to mind age-old *havelis* of Uttar Pradesh, those once majestic structures now in shambles but still preserved for the emotions associated with them. There is no sign of the gleaming marble or magnificent chandeliers which dot the central Delhi cinemas. Yet Gianand, which for long stood adjacent to Radhu, has been a unique and wonderful cinema. Judging the hall by its exteriors will not do. Located right next to a vegetable market, today it is close to the temporary dwellings of migrant labourers from Rajasthan. A cobbler does business here, sitting next to a man with a weighing machine and another who offers to pick wax from the ears of every passerby. The ground is rain-soaked and muddy and the surroundings make me feel like I am in a small town.

A couple of tentative steps forward and I find myself right in the precincts of Gianand. What a step or two can do! Everything is transformed. Seldom can a wall mean so much. The din outside seems distant; the ugliness of the surroundings seems a blur. The hall which appears nothing more than a square structure from the front and a series of blocks from the side is such a wonderful semi-circular piece of architecture from inside. Absolutely unique. The roof above reveals a series of neatly lined beams, each guarded by niches. The ceiling takes you back to post-medieval times when architecture had begun to incorporate Victorian influences into the predominantly Persian method of construction. A curving staircase is visible, leading to an even more aesthetically pleasing first floor, which appears to be like a semi circle leading to the balcony. The seats in the viewing area converge from two flanks.

Considering the hall was in a semi-industrial area with factories and small scale industries close by, it was commendable that families would still frequent this place. The hall always had a neat demarcation: the balcony was almost entirely filled with families while the working class occupied the stalls. The cheapest tickets were for 90 paise while the most expensive ones were a little over Rs 3.

Though the hall lacked a canteen on the ground floor, it had one on the first floor—this was perhaps a comment on the purchasing power of the different segments of the audiences. The canteen had at least a dozen garlanded deities—Ram, Shiv, Mahavir and Guru Nanak—all in happy co-existence.

In the middle of all these portraits, was one of Ajay Devgn from his first film, *Phool aur Kaante* (1991). It had been put up to commemorate the film's 50-day run here about 20 years ago. That was a rare instance of a film enjoying a long run here. In sharp contrast to the halls of Old Delhi, Gianand lived by the week, changing its fare for fans every Friday. A relatively late entrant in the mid-'70s, Gianand was also the preferred one for Manoj Kumar's films. His hits like *Roti Kapda Aur Makaan* (1974) and later *Kranti* (1981) ran to packed houses, with the former enjoying a re-run. Amitabh Bachchan's *Dostana* (1980) also attracted such a large crowd that queues for tickets extended up to the vegetable market.

An even better reception awaited *Avtaar* (1983), Rajesh Khanna's mega hit that brought cinegoers to halls in the thousands; its *bhajan*, 'Chalo Bulawa Aaya Hai' playing everywhere. This time, families came down to stalls from the relative privacy of balcony as the tickets in the section were almost always sold out within minutes of the plans opening. That was not the only change observed during the screening of *Avtaar* here. A local band often came down to play the song every day at the hall. So, viewers watched the song inside the hall, and heard it outside at the end of the show.

Bhakti Mein Shakti (1978) also attracted so many faithful that the film's original booking was extended by another week. Not as heady but still delightful was the performance of films like *Naseeb* (1981) and *Sone Ka Dil Lohe Ke Haath* (1978).

However, quite a different feat was accomplished by *Bin Maa Ke Bachche* (1980), an emotional saga that did so well in daily four shows that it had to be kept running in the morning shows because the hall had prior commitment to other films. Though *Bin Maa Ke Bachche* did very well, morning shows were not Gianand's forte. Little thought was spent on choosing films as often C-grade flicks from Hindi cinema and those from Hollywood were shown in this segment to viewers who often had only sleaze on their minds. Often many came to watch the explicit content only and walked out after that part of the film was over.

The morning show saga came to an end around five years ago, as it did at most halls in the city. With business dwindling due to multiplexes, Gianand ceased to be the first choice for exhibitors in east Delhi. First, the morning shows stopped, then the night shows and finally, everything came to an end.

Ironically enough, Gianand was closed after a poor run of Ajay Devgn's *Jigar* (1992). He was the man who had given the hall its biggest hit, *Phool Aur Kaante*. Today, the cinema that gave east Delhi its first cinemascope screen with air-cooled comfort, that was synonymous at its peak, with A-grade banners, has been reduced to a signpost of a forgotten past.

74 CHAND, Trilokpuri

In 1975, during the Emergency, many had to move from traditional living spaces into newer surroundings and start their life from scratch. Out went old neighbours and the comforts of shared joys and sorrows. Instead, people from Old Delhi's Turkman Gate area and some from Jama Masjid were relocated to Trilokpuri, a resettlement colony established with the prime objective of giving basic living space to the dispossessed and the displaced. After hundreds of houses were destroyed in Old Delhi, a large number of people had to settle in Trilokpuri which was nothing more than a stretch of wild greens on the Delhi border.

The new houses were cramped at not more than 22 square metres, with public toilets and erratic electricity. There was no running tap water. It would take a while before they could call Trilokpuri, now a congested working-class habitat near Mayur Vihar in east Delhi, their home. The process began with readily available public transport to their previous homes via a new bus service. The second facilitator was Chand cinema, which was established in 1980. It was expected to do great business. The new residents had been patrons of Delite cinema, whose front stalls were near empty in the immediate aftermath of the displacement from Turkman Gate, not to forget New Amar cinema in Old Delhi where a chunk of the audience was made up of the working-class men of the locality. It made business sense to open a cinema hall in the new settlement. By then, the people had basic amenities and had come to accept Trilokpuri and the neighbouring colonies of Kalyanpuri and Khichripuri as their new abode.

The launch of the cinema was a fancy affair, with marigold garlands, sweets and *agarbattis*. *Hukumat* (1987), *Zulm Ko Jalakar Raakh Kar Doonga* (1988), *Trinetra* (1991) and action-packed dramas like *Maati Maangey Khoon* (1984) whipped up magic at the box office. In between, there were top-drawer films as well, like Feroz Khan's *Qurbani* (1980) and Raj Kapoor's *Prem Rog* (1982).

With their success, Chand came to be a hub for the locals. Many eked out a living with black-marketing; others set up small stalls of *paan-bidi, chai* and cold drinks. Rickshaw-*wala*s started parking outside the hall, knowing that women-folk would prefer a ride home at the end of the show. With these considerations, it rapidly became a place to visit for an outing, more so because the other closest cinema was about five kilometres away. The price of admission was affordable, starting as low Rs 2.25 and going up to only Rs 3.60 for one of the 785 seats on offer. The hall would play mainstream films at the same time as they were screened at well-known halls but it was the action-packed potboilers that proved to be the favourites. Soon, the cinema's brick-lined front, like the façade of Ritz and Golcha, came to be identified in film circles.

But the decline came just as fast as the rise. A little more than a decade later, Chand's business nosedived with satellite television taking away the lion's share of viewers. The local population turned to newly procured television sets which now showed films 24 hours a day. A handful of locals who could afford to, moved on to bigger halls with better facilities.

The big banners became costlier and the admission rates had to be increased which did not go down well with the patrons. Caught in a conflict of interest, Chand lost its sheen. Out went A-grade films, in came B- and C-grade flicks but even these couldn't stop the inevitable.

Today, its walls are stripped bare, the window panes are broken and a lone caretaker waits for the hall to be turned into a multiplex. Children play *gulli-danda* and bored middle-aged men play cards on the premises.

The show has long been over.

75 RADHU PALACE, Laxmi Nagar

When the cinema was inaugurated in the early '80s, its name created a flutter: was it going to be the age-old Palace on Old Roshanara Road? Or was it likely to be similar to Radhu in Shahdara? The answer was not difficult to find as Radhu Palace, located in the busy commercial hub of Laxmi Nagar, was the brainchild of people who ran Radhu too.

Specifically targeting middle-class viewers with its neat and clean ambience and strategic location—close to upmarket Preet Vihar, Bharti Artist Colony, and more—Radhu Palace was preferred by family audiences. They ensured that its balcony section had an impressive footfall. The cinema played only Hindi films, desisting from trying out Hollywood flicks. Having opened with a tear-jerker like *Bin Maa Ke Bachche* (1980), it went on to become the best hall in east Delhi for a few years in the 1980s. Films like *Ustaad* (1989) and *Muqaddar Ka Faisla* (1987), among Vinod Khanna's early films on his comeback, attracted good crowds.

However, the multiplex boom weaned away its prospective viewers and the hall shut down a few years ago. It is now set to be turned into a multiplex.

76 KISAN, KALYAN, LAXMI, Mandawali, Seelampur and Gandhi Nagar

They were all cinemas which existed in anonymity and faded away unsung. Hardly anybody beyond their immediate neighbourhood took notice of these halls. Not many cinema lists bothered to mention them. And even newspaper insertions thought it necessary to mention the location of Kisan, Kalyan and Laxmi alongside their name.

They were simple brick-and-mortar structures with slanting temporary roofs and cement or red sandstone flooring. Sparse film hoardings and three or four posters constituted a collage on the front wall, while set-ups were rarely displayed by distributors. Inside, simple wooden chairs with little padding and a few fans, placed higher on the walls than is the standard practice, meant they rated quite low in terms of comfort and amenities. The fans on the walls of the hall were at a greater distance than was the norm elsewhere. That was done to cut down on electricity bills but the fans emitted more noise than air, often resulting in aggrieved viewers complaining in the middle of movies, *'Yeh pankha to bandh hi kar de'* (It is better if this fan is switched off). As viewers could never come to a unanimous decision, it resulted in frequent exchanges about the merits and demerits of the fans! When that din died, in came the vendors, selling *masala papad*, *chai* and bread *pakoda*. It was then that a common scene from Indian trains was replicated inside these halls: the viewers who till a few minutes ago were seen arguing about fans, suddenly become friends as they shared their *papad*, their *pakoda* and without a fuss, asked each other for a *bidi*! At times one *bidi* did the rounds of four-five seats before coming back to the actual owner.

The cinema halls usually played Hindi films. The films arrived here without any fanfare, mostly after doing long runs at most prominent halls across the city. Yet, in their own ways, Kisan in Mandawali, Kalyan in Seelampur and Laxmi in Gandhi Nagar played an important role in fulfilling the demands of the locals. Their audience comprised inhabitants of isolated villages in Delhi and elderly landowners who stayed away from traditional dwellings in Old Delhi; they derived their livelihood from agriculture and had limited contact with other Delhiites. Giving them company in the region were new immigrants from Punjab, Himachal Pradesh and pockets of western Uttar Pradesh. By the mid-'70s, Old Delhi was full to the brim and the Old Sabzi Mandi area was congested as well—only in pockets around Shahdara, Mandawali and Laxmi Nagar could newcomers find living space. These three halls fulfilled the need for affordable entertainment for all these people.

Two categories of films played here—big budget multi-starrers which showed here long after doing the rounds of cinema houses elsewhere. It did not affect their box-office prospects because there was little interaction between the residents of these areas with their counterparts in south Delhi, Connaught Place or the Walled City; films which habitually did the rounds of low-profile theatres and did not show at any prominent hall at the same time—there were honourable exceptions, though, when a cinema like Kisan, Laxmi or Kalyan showed the same film as Rivoli, Moti or Chanakya. Films like *Haath ki Safai* (1974), *Safed Haathi* (1977), *Ram Kasam* (1978), *Ganga Sagar* (1978), *Dosti* (1964), *Azaad* (1978) and even *Yaadon Ki Baraat* (1973), *Caravan* (1971) and *Dhool ka Phool* (1959) played by turn at these theatres. If a film played at Kisan, it was likely to find a screening at Kalyan too, then go on to Seble, Sudershan, Raj, Laxmi, Vijay, Robin or even

Swarn, Radhu and Gianand. In the 1980s, cinema halls like Kalamandir and Kushal joined the fray. At times, these films went to Manohar, Aradhana, Apsara and Mohanchitralok in the immediate neighbourhood of Delhi—Ghaziabad.

Laxmi, with a more impressive square, had a more commendable run than the others in east Delhi. It was also among the oldest: back in the 1960s, it enjoyed a better run when a film like *Nai Umar Ki Nai Fasal* (1965) opened here at the same time as at the illustrious Delite, Jubilee and West End. Laxmi occasionally played a film for more than a week. By the 1970s, it was known for playing devotionals: like most others, it showed *Jai Santoshi Maa* (1975) to housefull shows. It also played *Vishnu Puran* (1973), *Har Har Mahadev* (1974) and *Ganga Sagar* (1978); its screening of *Har Har Mahadev* in 1974 was made memorable by a giant cutout of Shiva placed at the entrance to the hall.

Till the early '80s, business was brisk and Laxmi was a fine model of a cinema whose audience did not go beyond the neighbourhood. However, in the early '80s, the means of communication improved and as more and more people started settling in east Delhi and the area transformed into a middle-class abode, better cinema houses like Radhu Palace came into business. Laxmi ceased to get a good slice of the film trade.

Such was also the fate of Kalyan and Kisan. The former played neat and clean family films, its audience being conservative Muslims from townships in Uttar Pradesh like Bareilly, Moradabad, Rampur and Bijnore. *Mere Huzoor* (released in 1968) garnered great applause, as did *Dosti* (1964) and *Dharam-Veer* (1977). Interestingly, by the late '70s, there was constant flow of human traffic from Old Delhi to Seelampur and colonies around it. Some fans preferred to watch a film like *Dharam-Veer* here rather than at any of the halls in Chandni Chowk because Kalyan's admission rates were more affordable. However, from the '80s, because of a combination of questionable film choices and poor safety records, business nosedived. Kalyan closed down more than a decade ago.

Kisan said goodbye a little before that. However, for years before its closure, the Mandawali theatre had a reputation for showing films which appealed to family audiences. Movies like *Dhool Ka Phool* (1959), *Caravan* (1971) and *Yaadon Ki Baraat* (1973)—perfect family fare—found a ready audience. In fact, for long, both Kisan and Laxmi had no competition in the arc from Gandhi Nagar to Mandawali. That was before all the apartments came up in the Patparganj area and private constructions sprouted in Ramesh Park, Shakarpur, and more. No wonder Laxmi was able to show films like *Sunehra Sansar* (1975) and *Chale Hain Sasural* (1966) while Kisan played *Humraaz* (1967), *Himmatwali* (not to be confused with the Jeetendra-Sridevi's *Himmatwala,* 1983) and *Main Tulsi Tere Aangan Ki* (1978).

The 1980s, though, came with fresh challenges for both Laxmi and Kisan: in came Radhu Palace and Chand with better amenities and new releases. It sounded their death knell. One by one, the neighbourhood cinemas—Kisan, Kalyan, Laxmi—bowed out of the competition.

VIII

Ghaziabad, Noida and Faridabad Go Housefull

For years, film distributors and exhibitors advertised in English and Hindi dailies, giving out the names of the cinemas playing their movies. Right at the end of any cinema listing used to be the name of the single screen hall in Ghaziabad showing the movie, often with the appendage 'G'bad'. Seldom, if ever, was such a favour extended to cinemas in Faridabad, which too was at the doorstep of the capital, and one hardly ever came across any mention of cinemas in Gurgaon till as late as the 1990s. This constant mention of Ghaziabad along with Delhi was at least partially due to the fact that films had the same distributor for Delhi and Uttar Pradesh. That was not the case with Haryana which, for long, came under the Punjab belt for film distribution.

Noida, which initially fell under district Ghaziabad, did slightly better. However, much before it came up in the late '70s and early '80s, there was a proper Ghaziabad township on the eastern border of Delhi where films were shown with aplomb. The biggest films, the sleaziest ones, all found a ready screening here. Chaudhary, Navrang, Vasant, Urvashi and Pawan were familiar names. Even closer to the Delhi border were Aradhana, Apsara, Kamla and Jyoti.

Many of the Ghaziabad halls came into limelight by releasing films at the same time as Delhi, unlike most other towns of Uttar Pradesh where films released a week or two later. Also, unlike many towns of Uttar Pradesh which changed films every Thursday, Ghaziabad halls were in sync with their counterparts from Delhi, sticking to the Friday-change schedule. Their modus operandi was similar too. Big hoardings across the city, posters at vantage points and insertions in local language newspapers, all combined to make films a successful business model for these cinemas. Where they differed from their Delhi counterparts was in the duration of the films' stay at the cinema; a film mostly ran for a maximum of three or four weeks here, unlike in Delhi where they often stayed on to complete a silver or golden jubilee. For instance, while *Sholay* (1975) completed a golden jubilee run in Delhi, it lasted only for eight weeks at Chaudhary. Of course, many films came back to have a repeat run, usually close to their silver or golden jubilee week in Delhi. The controversial *Aandhi* (1975) graced the screen at Urvashi around the time of its silver jubilee run at Rivoli and Ritz in Delhi. *Satyam Shivam Sundaram* (1978) completed a 25-week run at Regal and only in the silver jubilee week did it come to Apsara and Chaudhary. Usually, a film played at only one hall in Ghaziabad. This way the halls avoided eating into each other's business. Like in Delhi, cinemas in Ghaziabad too came to be identified with certain banners and distributors.

Among the Ghaziabad halls, most of which appeared in the 1970s, some like Chaudhary and Urvashi used to run a film for a relatively longer duration than Navrang and Pawan, which changed shows every Friday. Both those halls were keener to cater to the masses than to family audiences, which invariably found their way through to Urvashi. For instance, Urvashi showed *Mehboob Ki Mehndi* (1971) even as other halls around played films like *Mela* (1971) and *Johnny Mera Naam* (1970).

Apsara and Aradhana seldom got to show films in the week of their release. As part of the second rung, their wait lasted at least three weeks if the film was not going to be a super hit, otherwise it could extend even up to two months. Incidentally, both Apsara and Aradhana entered the fray with the aim of appealing to family audiences by concentrating more on women-centric and family-oriented films. It did not quite turn out that way. That never came in the way of Apsara in particular—it entered the scene before most others—from showing films like *Naya Zamana* (1971), *Paras* (1971), *Dharma* (1973), *Samadhi* (1972) and *Bobby* (1973). Aradhana, likewise, was happy to woo cinegoers with films like *Seeta Aur Geeta* (1972), *Chor Ke Ghar Chor* (1978), *Naya Daur* (1957) and *Jugnu* (1973).

However, even before these cinemas entered the scene, Ghaziabad had the timeless Manohar, Jai Hind and Mohan Chitralok to fall back on. For more than a decade, ending towards the end of the '60s, Manohar used to be the prime choice of exhibitors in Ghaziabad. In the mid-'60s, Jai Hind showed *Jahan Sati Wahan Bhagwan* (1965) even as Mohan Chitralok went for *Nai Umar Ki Nai Fasal* (1965). Films like *Mera Saaya* (1966) and *Daadi Maa* (1966) showed here at the same time as they did in prime halls of Delhi like Shiela, Palace and Uphaar.

Some time in the 1990s and later, more halls started appearing in the area. They also spread to newer parts of Sahibabad, Loni, Bhopura and others. Gradually, halls like Kavita, Dev Chitralok, Jindal Palace, Subhash Palace, Laxmi Palace, Sangam, Amrit, Meenaxi and Prince appeared. Most were situated in working-class localities and catered to the local population of largely blue-collar workers. When they showed new films, they invariably featured action flicks with mid-stream stars. In recent years, they have been content showing Bhojpuri films to their viewers, chiefly immigrants from eastern Uttar Pradesh and Bihar. Incidentally, these cinemas have seldom followed the advance booking norm, neither have they always put a number to every seat. They follow the first come-first served formula. Hence, there is usually a mad scramble for seats as soon as the ushers open the doors for entry.

However, while cinemas in Ghaziabad have constantly grown for over half a century, the same has not been the case with neighbouring Noida which got its first tin-shed hall in the early 1980s with Alka. The first proper big-screen hall was also established in the same period, when Dharam Palace was unveiled, followed by New Kavita in Khora more than a decade later. However, unlike the Ghaziabad halls, Dharam Palace usually showed films after two or three weeks of their release in the capital. It did play films like *Shahenshah* (1988), *Ganga Jamuna Saraswati* (1988), *Toofan* (1989), *Jaadugar* (1989), *Akayla* (1991), *Main Azaad Hoon* (1989) and *Aaj Ka Arjun* (1990), all Amitabh Bachchan-starrers, and also family fare like *Kaash* (1987), *Ghar Ghar Ki Kahani* (1988), *Maa* (1992) and *Hum Aapke Hain Koun...!* (1994). For years, it tried to woo the middle class while keeping its base of frontbenchers happy with films like *Waqt Ki Awaz* (1988), *Zakhmi Zameen* (1990) and *Naakabandi* (1990). It was followed on this track by Alka which attracted decent footfall with films like *Ek Jaan Hain Hum* (1983), *Trinetra* (1991) and *Ustad* (1989). Like Satyam and Meenaxi, Alka also had a good run with Bhojpuri cinema, fuelling hopes of a revival in fortune. It proved a false dawn, though.

New Kavita carries on with its mix of action movies in daily four shows and re-runs of old movies in the morning shows. The films are neither too new to command instant attention, nor too old to evoke nostalgia but in this way, the show continues at least at one single-screen hall. All other spaces for cinema have been taken by multiplex biggies like Wave, followed by Spice and Big.

While the cinemas in Ghaziabad almost always stayed within eye-catching distance of Delhiites, thing were slightly different in Faridabad. In the 1960s and '70s, because of wholly separate distributors, cinemas occasionally showed films here before they were screened in Delhi. Halls like Neelam, Gagan and New Metro told viewers to 'watch before Delhi'. In the mid-'70s, Neelam played *Chupke Chupke* (1975) before it was shown in Delhi, just as it showed *Warrant* (1975). Amitabh Bachchan's films were a rage here too.

Like Neelam, Gagan catered to front-benchers with a relish. A hugely successful hall till about 20 years ago, it often witnessed *lathi*-charges to control over-enthusiastic crowds. Between them, these halls, like Faridabad's version of Delhi's low-key halls of Paharganj of the 1990s, kept the cinegoers interested and satisfied.

The halls were relatively low profile and the facilities elementary. The viewers demanded nothing more than a film on a 35 mm screen, preferably in an air-cooled ambience. They usually got that and remained loyal patrons. It all changed with the coming of multiplexes.

Delhi's Cinema Culture: An Essay

When Ranjit Singh Seble speaks, you listen. He has no airs or pretensions and possesses an easy laugh. At 74, he is blessed with a fairly sharp memory too. Here is a man who loves nostalgia and speaks of the days gone by with the same passion as he plans for the days ahead. During Partition, his family had to leave home and hearth and start afresh. From being front-runners in the cinema business in Peshawar and Rawalpindi, his father and uncles—Balwant Singh Seble, Sant Singh Seble and Rawail Singh Seble—had to scrounge around for crumbs in Delhi. For a while, they lived the cinematic equivalent of a nomadic life. But as soon as they saw fresh opportunity, the Sebles capitalised on it.

In the days of yore, they had cinemas in places like Campbellpur, Cheekagali, Naushera, Khanaspur, Abbottabad and Bardia Kakul. Another was underway in Lahore before the family shifted to Delhi and settled near Kashmere Gate. In Delhi, the Sebles continued with their once-flourishing business but gave it a new twist. Instead of establishing movie halls in prime parts of Delhi, they set them up in unexplored corners and places which had not yet experienced cinema. Among the places they settled upon were Zakhira, Subhash Nagar, Model Town, Rana Pratap Bagh, Gur Mandi, Shakur

Basti, Vishwas Nagar, Rajouri Garden, Moti Nagar, Shahdara, Ramesh Nagar and Jail Road. To a city familiar with cinemas like Moti, Jubilee, Novelty, Plaza, Regal and Odeon, names like Raj Kamal, Ganesh, Ranjit Talkies, Ramesh Talkies, Chhaya Chitra, Metro and Mohan Talkies were added. There was a catch though—the cinemas were all temporary structures of tarpaulin and cotton and did not last more than a few months before the caravan moved on in search of greener pastures. The routine was repeated at the new place, with tents, chairs, make-shift screens and mobile toilets in tow.

The films screened at these cinemas were top notch and the audience was almost always eager to visit. The admission rates were pocket-friendly for the three daily shows. This was cinema that brought with it a whiff of small-town India to the capital, giving Hindustani films their much-lauded mass image, away from the rarefied confines of classical arts. In a newly independent country taking its early steps as a democracy, cinema proved a great equaliser—the have-nots watched the same film as the more privileged ones at the same time and place.

With the passage of time, this ritual of setting up and dismantling cinemas gave way to what came to be called temporary theatres, which in turn led to the setting up of cinemas beyond the once preferred locations of Old Delhi and Connaught Place. In this way, cinemas like Raaj and, predictably, Seble came to be.

If, after 1947, the Sebles had to call upon all reservoirs of energy and resources to get the business back on track in Delhi, a similar challenge raised its head following the anti-Sikh riots in 1984. At that time, Seble cinema was reduced to cinders and once again, the family's fighting spirit was called upon. The hall bounced back, bigger and better. Over a period of time, it progressed from being a temporary tin-shed structure to a permanent one. Now, Raaj is due to get a facelift shortly, completing a tale of triumph for the Seble family.

The Sebles' set up cinemas beyond Delhi in places like Bulandshahr, Moradabad and Nageena in Uttar Pradesh and distributed films like *Bin Maa Ke Bachche* (1980), *Mujhe Vachan Do* (1983), *Yaadon Ki Kasam* (1985) and *Lekin* (1990), the last one in partnership with Lata Mangeshkar.

Like them, there are other families which contributed to the cinema culture of Delhi. These include the Dayals (Regal), the Seths (Jagat, Novelty and Ritz), the Chitnis family (Excelsior and West End) and the Sahnis (Odeon and Rivoli). Adding to the list are the Kaushishs (Shiela), the Raizadas (Delite), the Soods (Eros and Vishal), the Kukrejas (Sapna) and the Guptas (Liberty). Then there have been others, notably, the Malhotras (Paras), the Agarwals and Paliwals (Alpna) and Bhawani Shanker (Amba).

Most of the early families in film business in Delhi trace their origins to Punjab in undivided India, often Peshawar and Rawalpindi. Interestingly, the cinemas they established there continue to do business with different owners. The Kapoors, the Sahnis and the Sebles had been in the cinema business for years before Independence. In fact, the Sahnis and the Sebles were competitors in Peshawar and Rawalpindi. If the Sebles ran around a dozen permanent theatres in undivided India, the Sahnis had 21 cinemas in places like Abbotabad, Murree, Cambellpur, Cheekagali, Naushera and Khanaspur—Shyam Sahni himself was born in Rawalpindi.

After Partition, Pakistan's loss was India's gain. The families which ran cinema halls shifted to Delhi, the Sahnis among them. They too came to Delhi and began their India chapter from Odeon, which they got on lease initially, followed by Rivoli. Once the Sahnis found their feet, there was no stopping them. Four cinema halls came up in Lucknow, another in Mussourie and two in Agra. In the 1960s, Shyam Sahni ventured south and a cinema came up in Chennai.

Meanwhile, back in New Delhi, within a few years of Partition, Odeon and Rivoli established themselves as names to be reckoned with. Regal had few peers while Plaza became the cynosure of all eyes. And virtually the who's who of Indian politics would visit Connaught Place to watch films, arriving in fancy cars and horse-drawn carriages. Others came on cycles and cycle-rickshaws. In the early years after Independence, there used to be more tongas than cars at the traffic intersections near Odeon and Regal. Much later came the *phut-phut*s, a kind of shared autos that connected the two most important hubs of cinema in the city—Chandni Chowk and Connaught Place.

The Dayals, with Rajeshwar at the helm, gave Regal a touch befitting its name. Tall trees lined the porch, a bar kept the guests engaged beyond the film and many live performances took place in a fine intermingling of the arts. This was a cinema for the elite, unabashedly so. While the Sahnis, the Dayals and many others concentrated their energies on cinemas in the heart of the city, Kirit Desai gave Moti the magic touch in Chandni Chowk, aligning the family business of film distribution with the daily exhibition of films at the cinema. Keeping them company were the Seths, the family of Jagat Narain Seth, who lived life king-size. The bigwigs of Hindi cinema would come to him, putting him in the enviable position of dictating terms to the market as he owned three cinemas in the most densely populated part of the city, Old Delhi. Between Jagat, Novelty and Ritz, he made sure that no big banner escaped his attention; hardly any film worthy of attention failed to get a screening at his halls. It is said not just big banners but even big stars like Dilip Kumar and Raj Kapoor would visit him to ensure availability of a cinema of their choice for their upcoming films. The family's business expanded to other parts of north India.

Between them, these early birds made sure that there was never a dull moment in the life of a movie watcher in the capital and that the latest films kept their appointments with the city. Together, they shaped the way Delhiites watched films, starting with daily three shows and moving up to four shows.

In the mid-'50s, a morning show was added. They combated many odds, among them the admission rates that were regulated by the government for many decades.

Air-conditioning was unheard of in the 1940s and much of the '50s. Even air-cooled cinemas were regarded as a luxury. Yet, cinegoers stayed loyal and thanks to the early sellers of dreams, the city came to have a lifelong relationship with cinema.

Cinema grew in layers: if Connaught Place was for the elite, Old Delhi was for the traditionalists, south, north and west Delhi appealed to middle class viewers. In these regions there was further stratification: some halls catered to families, others to a working-class audience comprising largely of men. Proprietors like the Sahnis, the Desais and the Seths catered to an upmarket audience; others like Seble catered to an audience made up largely of blue-collar workers.

At some point in the 1960s and early '70s, a new dimension was added. Families that were not traditionally in the film business were drawn to cinemas. Many were real estate magnates like the Ansals and the Soods who ran Uphaar and Anupam, Eros and Vishal, respectively. They were like the Raizadas earlier, for whom Delite was a departure from their vocation as was the case with their contemporaries, the Paliwals and Agarwals of Alpna, DC Kaushish of Sheila, a *khadhardari* and a member of the Constituent Assembly in 1940s, who came into the film business after successfully running a printing press. The new families took well-defined and well-maintained halls to newer places, marking out more places on Delhi's cine map. Incidentally, Kaushish's Shiela had been conceptualised about 25 years before it was established as a cinema hall of choice. In the late 1930s, plans were afoot to establish the hall but first World War-II, then the shortage of building material ensured that the plans did not fructify. Then came Independence, and it was only in 1955, when a new technical breakthrough emerged from the US, that the idea to establish Shiela was revived.

The first commercial trials of the 70 mm screen were successful in the US and it seemed an appropriate time to go ahead full steam with a cinema that used only a 70 mm screen and no multi-projector system. This was possible because Kaushish had watched the successful trials in the US. He decided to bring the technology to India though it meant that the initial plans of construction had to be revised. In the absence of competent professionals here, he secured the expertise of Ben Schlanger, an authority on motion pictures. Schlanger, incidentally had been involved with key international projects such as the United Nations General Assembly Hall, and Colonial Williamsburg Twin Theatres. Then came S Ajit Singh who took charge of the construction of the building, and BA Mistry, who handled the equipment installation. A six-track sound system was chosen, the first ever in the country. Some 10 years after its inception, Shiela added a new feature—Shielarama, a unique movie projection requiring absolute accuracy. It used a larger screen with a

20-feet curve and seating arrangements were yet again re-organised to enhance the film-viewing experience. It also led to the famous cinemascope logo on the hall's front, giving it a kind of smiling hall appearance.

Halls like Shiela, Odeon and Liberty worked with the latest technology, while others like Jagat, Moti and Majestic stuck to traditional equipment. Yet others like Paras, Chanakya and Vishal added newer amenities for the comfort of the audience.

For 50 years, the system ran fine. Every Friday, new films were released; a few old ones completed a jubilee run while the others moved out. People would look forward to Fridays, particularly the black-marketeers, more so on the occasions when stars would visit the cinemas. Once in a while, proprietors turned fiercely patriotic, as in the case of Kaushish and others who lent their generators to the nation at the time of the Indo-China War, or those at Delite who kept their patrons informed of the latest on the war front during film screenings. Amba's manager GK Sharma kept the premises open for any victim of violence in the 1984 riots. Excelsior cancelled some shows post-Babri Masjid demolition in 1992, as did New Amar during the late '70s when sectarian violence struck pockets of the Walled City. It was done as much for the security of the cinegoers as also to send out a message—cinemas and cinegoers existed in harmony.

This well-oiled machinery came unstuck towards the end of the 1990s, when movie-viewing changed forever. In 1997, Anupam cinema in Saket made way for the country's first multiplex, pushing the single screen into the margins. The Bijlis brought in this technique from Australia. A new partnership was forged with Village Roadshow, the Australian concern. Thus was born PVR—Priya Village Roadshow. Initially, the Bijlis planned to do convert Priya but later opted to take Anupam on lease from the Ansals.

This small step led to a giant leap in half a decade. Multiplexes sprang up across the city, with liquor barons, real estate magnates and others joining the fray. Many single-screen theatres downed their shutters, taking with them stories of the early days of cinema in the city. Like the bioscope-*wala*, they were reduced to their own shadows.

Many have bravely stayed the course but just about. Others have proved smarter, reinvented themselves, and taken on the competition in the right spirit. The old order has changed and yielded a lot of space to the new. It has not necessarily died, merely changed with the times. Just as it did when it said goodbye to naturally cooled cinemas and brought in fully air-conditioned halls; when it ushered in Asia's second 70 mm hall at Sheila; by allotting special shows to regional cinemas at halls playing Hindi films in daily four shows (like at Paras, Naaz, Sangam and Sapna); when it set up halls especially for the armed forces and reserved boxes for families and women.

The tunes have changed. The notes remain the same.

Glossary

aath	eight
adda	meeting place of a group
aftab	sun; sunlight
agarbatti	incense
akhada	wrestling pit
anna	currency unit formerly used in India, equal to 1/16th of a rupee
apna	one's own
bajra	millet
beta	son
bhajan	Hindu devotional song
bhangra	Punjabi folk dance
bidi	small and thin Indian cigarette
bindi	decorative dot worn on the forehead
billa	badge
biscut	biscuit, pronounced biscut or biscoot by Hindi-speaking people
chai	tea
chaiwala	tea vendor
chaat	savoury snacks, usually sold by the roadside
chhajja	gallery
chhatri	marquee
churidar	slim-fit pyjamas

dabba	box; also used for rundown cinemas
dafli	drum
darshan	opportunity to see a deity
deen	faith; religion
deendar	pious
diya	lamp
dupatta	scarf; stole
ek	one
ekka	horse-drawn cart
fauji	army man
garam	hot
gharara	wide-legged pants, flaring towards the ankles
ghazal	poetic form with rhyming couplets, usually romantic
gulli-danda	indigenous game played with a long stick, and a smaller one sharpened on both ends
gutka	crushed betel nut and tobacco preparation
havan	fire ritual
haveli	mansion
imam	person who leads prayers in a mosque
jaali	latticed screen
jagran	Hindu ritual, consisting of an all-night vigil, songs and dance in honour of a deity
jalebi	Indian sweet, shaped like a funnel cake
jawan	foot soldier
jharokha	balcony
jhuggie	shanty town
kadhardhari	wearer of *khadi* or home-spun cotton; Gandhian
karchi	ladle
katra	bylane
kucha	lane
kurta	long shirt

lathi	cane; baton
mahal	mansion, bigger than a *haveli*
mandva	colloquial term for theatre
mansabdar	Mughal noble or aristocrat
mard	man
masala	pure entertainer; spicy
mashq	leather pouch for holding water
matka	earthen pitcher; hip swing
maulana	honorific title used for Muslim clerics
mehtab	moon; moonlight
moulvi	doctor of law in Islam
mohalla	locality
moongfali	groundnut
mushaira	poetic symposium
namaskar	traditional Indian greeting
nawab	aristocrat; often used for the rich hailing from Awadh
nawabi	aristocratic
paan	betel leaf
paar	across
paanwala	betel leaf seller
pachisi	game played with cowries
papad	papadum
pehelwan	wrestler
paisa-vasool	money's worth
phut-phut	improvised auto-rickshaw meant for public transport
pakoda	fritter; snack
prasad	blessed food
purdanasheen	veiled woman
puja	prayer
raja	king; also used loosely for prince
rupaiya	rupee

samosa	triangular savoury
sarai	resthouse
sharaabi	drunkard
shikanji	Indian lemonade
talaffuz	sound with correct organ movement; pronunciation
taleem	education
tarannum	melody
thakur	Indian title, originally used by Rajputs
thali	metal plate or tray
vishal	huge